Asian
Supernatural

Asian
Supernatural
Including Hawai'i and
the Pacific

Alex G. Paman

Mutual Publishing

This book is lovingly dedicated to
my parents, José and Gabrielita,
who passed on to me their sense of wonder.

ISBN-10: 1-56647-924-X
ISBN-13: 978-1-56647-924-0

Library of Congress Cataloging-in-Publication Data

Paman, Alex.
Asōan supernatural : including Hawai'i and the Pacific / Alex Paman.
p. cm.
Includes index.
ISBN 1-56647-924-X (softcover : alk. paper)
1. Occultism--Asia--Dictionaries. 2. Occultism--Pacific area--Dictionaries. 3. Supernatural--Dictionaries. I. Title. II. Title: Asian supernatural.
BF1411.P35 2010
398'.4095--dc22
2010019556

Design by Jane Gillespie
First Printing, August 2010

Mutual Publishing, LLC
1215 Center Street, Suite 210
Honolulu, Hawaii 96816
Ph: (808) 732-1709
Fax: (808) 734-4094
e-mail: info@mutualpublishing.com
www.mutualpublishing.com

Printed in Korea

Contents

Preface

rowing up in the Philippines during the 1970s, ghost stories, for me, were both a highlight and a guilty pleasure. I remember many candlelight sessions with my brothers and sisters, listening to them spin frightening yarns of horror while sitting out in the fresh air and waiting for the lights to come back on. Rolling black outs (or brown outs, if occurring in the daytime) were commonplace in Quezon City back then, so we passed the time and endured the tropical heat by huddling around candles and recounting tales of the supernatural. My elder siblings never seemed to run out of them, and the stories always had a ring of truth or familiarity.

Looking back, now 30 years later, it seems that the supernatural had always been a part of our cultural upbringing. From the ghostly sightings that my relatives had of newly departed loved ones, to our supposedly haunted house in the deep province, supernatural occurrences were common and even expected. These events, along with our native pantheon of ghosts, demons, and witches who appeared regularly at the movie theaters, created a curiosity within me that continued to resonate even as my family and I immigrated to the United States.

Vampires, zombies, and serial killers had always been the norm when it came to American pop horror, but I often wondered what would happen if Asian demons came to the United States and began wreaking havoc. Since very few books were written about Asian ghostlore when I was growing up, I began collecting anthropology books while in college and literally else anything else that contained sections on Asian spirit beliefs. I had never seen a book that listed all of our native demons, so this was my small way of compiling a library that would someday help me piece together an even larger picture. I immediately noticed parallels between seemingly disparate Eastern and Western traditions: vampires, zombies, choking ghosts, vanishing hitchhikers, and mysterious balls of light apparently spanned our cultures as well.

Years later, when I still couldn't find a book that listed all the ghosts and demons from my region of the world, I decided to utilize my collection and write one myself. The result is the humble little book that you hold in your hands.

Its Scope

This book is an attempt, for the very first time, to truly catalog ghosts and monsters from all the Asian and Pacific cultures in a single volume. Its contents come from oral tales, old anthropology books, travel narratives, and other native resources that were written before the advent of the Internet. I made it a point to make this work a truly Pan-Asian effort, not using solely Chinese and Japanese entries that other writers have mistakenly referred to as the sole representatives of "Asian Horror." Contrary to popular belief, language wasn't that big an obstacle in compiling this list. The entries were all pulled from English-written sources; it was just a matter of researching beyond popular media, exploring bibliographies, and actually spending time in a library. As expected when dealing with names that span different countries, there are countless spelling variations to the characters listed. I've used the most common designations and offer alternate names when available.

There is very little reference to cinematic ghosts since many of the themes and details presented in Asian horror movies also come from the same resources I've utilized. I intentionally restricted the entries to include only ghosts, goblins, witches, fairies, and other supernatural entities. Gods, godlings and their aspects are listed only if relevant to the characters, themes, or countries being described. A few fabulous beasts have been added where appropriate, creatures with which every Asian culture aficionado should be familiar.

The individual entries are presented in alphabetical order within their respective countries, beginning with the character's name, followed by their region of origin, if available, and then a general description.

If successful, this book will fill a much-needed gap between Eastern and Western traditions of myth, fantasy, and the supernatural. A person from any Asian or Pacific nation should be able to read an entry from their own country and instantly recognize the reference. It may provide writers and artists a new palette of horror to work with, or even give them a new grove of darkness to explore. At the very least, I'm hoping its entries would prompt Western readers to look into these wondrous countries and learn more about our traditions, supernatural or otherwise.

These creatures will be waiting, gleefully dancing in the dimming twilight, before feeding upon your imagination.

Introduction

The recent popularity of Japanese, Korean and Thai horror movies in American theaters has led to a blossoming of sorts for Eastern ghost stories. Unlike their Western counterparts of emotional vampires, bloodthirsty zombies and blade-wielding serial killers, Asian spirits represent a dualism rarely seen in cinema, appearing as grotesque as they are beautiful to behold, as subtle as they are overwhelming. Though seemingly innovative, this genre of filmmaking has actually been around for many years and is just the latest incarnation of the ages-old tradition of supernatural storytelling.

Through its history, geography, and natural resources, the Asian/Pacific continent is perhaps the most culturally diverse region in the world. With the three grand religions of Hinduism, Buddhism, and Islam resonating throughout indigenous animist beliefs, this vast area is a living narrative of evolution, a melting pot of traditions and ornamentation that has long been adapted by individual cultures to suit their own needs. The recent addition of Christianity has only helped enrich the region even more. This exchange of ideas, along with responses to the physical environment, has created a wondrous supernatural setting where religion, history and mythology coexist harmoniously as one.

In contrast to the Western convention of linear thinking and definition, the Eastern approach embraces a more intuitive and cyclical approach to life. The harmony of opposites, reincarnation, ancestor worship, karma and animism (the belief that trees, rocks and locations have inherent spirits) are overlapping principles that most people are governed by, and it is this universal perception of existence that has made the supernatural an integral and accepted part of everyday life.

The Asian supernatural is a collection of gods, spirits, demons, witches and fabulous beasts that span virtually all facets of culture. From the architecture of sacred shrines and temples, the masks, props and music of traditional dance and theater, to religious doctrines and epic oral narratives, these entities are part of a larger cosmology that explain and give meaning to the natural world. They permeate festivals, are referenced in everyday expressions, and appear in both hallowed and secular rituals. But despite the diversity and differences of Asian cultures, they also share consistent supernatural themes that make them curiously similar. And, much like everything else in this region, these entities can easily be classified in several categories all at once.

Types

In all parts of Asia, spirits truly abound. Human spirits include protective guardians of a particular area or household, ancestral souls of the living and even deified historical figures. But the most notorious spirits among the human deceased are ghosts, those who have returned to the living for several reasons: improper burial, having died a violent death (particularly suicide and drowning), unfinished life and obligations and even improper worship from descendants. Ghosts have been known to impersonate the living, cause illness (especially among children and pregnant women), possess the weak, seek replacements if bound to a certain place or action and even bear children with other spirits. They roam places where great death has occurred, either trapped in a cycle of fate or actively looking for victims. They can be exorcised ritually or placated with offerings by monks, shamans and other mystical specialists.

Nonhuman spirits are equally as prevalent as their human counterparts. Unusually shaped trees, boulders and natural structures are believed to be the home of invisible beings whose permission is always required for safe passage or building. Elementals or nature spirits figure prominently in the living landscape, as playful as they are dangerous. Animal spirits are also common, with some appearing as phantoms while others shape-shifting into people. Some Asian cultures even attribute souls to inanimate objects coming to life after reaching a certain chronological age. The spirits of diseases have been blamed for a variety of ailments, particularly smallpox.

Demons are particularly feared as malevolent as they are grotesque. Trolls, goblins and ogres appear regularly in many traditions, gigantic in stature but often gullible in character. Feral demons such as ghouls, vampires, were-animals and other horrific creatures haunt the night, lurking in the darkness and preying on unsuspecting passers-by.

Divine beings such as angels, djinns (genies), and devas bridge the gap between the celestial and the mortal, while dwarves, fairies, giants and mermaids familiar to Western folklore stake their place within the mythical landscape.

Dragons, unicorns, phoenixes, mysterious ape-men, and other fabulous animals form yet another important class within the supernatural. Possessing mysterious and magical qualities, these creatures have long been attributed to the forces of nature, the source of superstitions, the inspiration of fighting methods and even the cosmological order of the universe. They comprise a bestiary of real and imagined animals, as much zoological as it is mythological.

As mystics, sages, physicians and diviners, shamans have always held an important role in traditional Asian societies. They act as intermediaries between the ordinary and the supernatural, ritually cleansing sites, banishing ghosts, predicting the future, and are often the sole bearer of sacred knowledge and tradition. Witches, on the other hand, are considered dangerous, outcasts who are able to cast spells upon victims for their own evil purposes.

Talismans, amulets and charms have long been used for a variety of purposes: protecting against harm, warding off evil spirits, bringing about fortune, inducing love and affection, even gaining superhuman abilities. In the form of statuettes, prayer beads, precious stones, inscribed paper, human and animal parts and even tattoos, they are physical extensions in the manipulation of magic over the bearer and his environment.

Due to its scope and subject matter, this book is far from comprehensive. It is, however, a good beginning for readers to do their own research in finding answers. Additions, revisions and corrections from readers are always welcome and should be sent to either myself or the publishers.

Which is Scarier, the West or the East?

And lastly, there is the inevitable comparison and debate as to which horror traditions are more frightening, Eastern or Western. No doubt, both sides are probably divided between cultural lines and have valid arguments for their point of view. Coming from the Philippines, my initial answer was, of course, *ours*! But upon reflection, the more logical answer is actually *both*. If you're alone in a cemetery and you hear disembodied screams while seeing a headless ghost materialize from a crumbled headstone, it doesn't really matter what tradition it comes from. They're *all* frightening, East and West, especially when you're alone in the dark.

Asura

India

Acheri. Playful fairies said to descend from their mountaintop homes at dusk and frolic about. Crossing their path accidentally may incur illness.

Airavata. Hindu. Three-headed elephant that is the vehicle of the god Indra. Symbolizing the clouds, it was created when the gods churned the ocean of milk. Known as erawan in Thai.

Amrita. Hindu. Sanskrit for the elixir of immortality and the ambrosia of the gods, recovered from the churning of the cosmic ocean by both the gods and the demons. Also known as soma.

Arhat (Arahat). Buddhist. "Worthy one." An ascetic who has attained enlightenment; one who has liberated himself from the Wheel of Life, free of delusions and hatred and exempt from having to be born again.

Asura. Powerful enemies of the gods, often described as demons, demigods, or titans that live on the lower slopes of Mount Meru. While the term itself originally referred to a deity, in general, its meaning had changed over time to represent the forces of evil and darkness, particularly in their opposition to the devas. They live in their own realm within the six regions outlined in the Wheel of Life, which is characterized by envy and hostility.

Atman. Sanskrit term for "self" or "soul," encompassing not only the individual spirit, but the universal one as well.

Avatar. The incarnation (or incarnations) of a given deity. In Hinduism, this most often refers to the god Vishnu, whose avatars include Krishna and Rama.

Baki. Term for shaman.

Bhagavad Gita. "Song of the Lord." Book Six of the Mahabharata; epic poem arranged in 18 cantos and comprised of 606 verses. It centers around the philosophical conversation between Prince Arjuna and Krishna, an avatar of Vishnu.

Bhakti. Sanskrit for "reverent devotion." Devotion between a worshipper and his or her personal god.

Bhopa. Term to describe an exorcist.

Bhut grasth. To be possessed by a ghost.

Bhut lag gea. "Ghost had adhered." Term to describe a type of spirit-possession.

Bhut lagna. To be attacked by a ghost.

Bhutonmada. Type of mental illness attributed to ghost possession.

Bindu. Term to describe an energy center.

Bodhi Tree. Ficus religiosa. Tree under which the Indian prince Shakyamuni Buddha first attained enlightenment, believed to still exist near Gaya in Bengal.

Buddha. "Enlightened One." Siddartha Gautama. Historical figure said to have been born from his mother Maya's side after she had a dream about a white elephant entering the same area. Growing up as a prince within a warrior caste in the city of Kapilavastu, located along the southern border of present-day Nepal, he lived a life of extravagant luxury until he saw three men (one old, one sick, and one dead). It was then that he realized the limits of his own excess and mortality and decided to leave his luxurious life for one of meditation and solitude.

He spent six years in the wilderness in meditation and, after overcoming the temptations of the god Mara and his voluptuous daughters, attained enlightenment under the famous fig tree located in the village of Bodh Gaya in northern India. He realized that desire was the root of all evil, but instead of passing into nirvana, he instead chose to go back to the real world and preach to those in need of deliverance from suffering.

Chakra. So-called "energy centers" in the human body, seven points referred to as lotuses that ascend the human body from the base of the pelvis to the head.

Chordewa. Type of witch said to have the ability to transform its soul separately into a black cat. In this form, the witch is able to harmlessly enter homes and even feed upon the host's food. One peculiar, if ingratiating, habit is its licking of the host's lips, which actually marks him for death. The cat entity will then begin to absorb the victim's life-force, strengthening the witch in exchange. One belief says that the mere licking by the cat of a person's shadow dooms him to death as well. This witch comes from the Oraon hill tribe of Bengal.

Churail. The ghost of a low-caste woman who died prematurely.

Churel. The spirit of a woman who died while she was pregnant.

Dag. General term for witchcraft, often practiced by women.

Daityas. Hindu. Giant asuras, offspring of the goddess Diti. They fought the gods to possess the amrita, the elixir of immortality.

Daka. Hindu, Buddhist. "Heroes." Male counterpart of the dakini.

Dakini. Hindu, Buddhist. "Sky walker." Type of low-ranking goddess that comes in both benevolent and malevolent forms. In Hinduism, she serves the goddess Kali. Often depicted flying or dancing through the air, they are described as nude young women but with the heads of lions or other animals. Dakinis are fond of drinking blood and devouring human flesh. They are differentiated from apsaras by having a third eye on their forehead.

Danavas. Hindu. Giant asuras who, like the Daityas, battled the gods. They were ultimately banished by the god Indra to the ocean. Although described as demonic, they weren't completely evil.

Darba. Hindu. A type of harmful demon, or rakshasa, in native mythology.

Devaputtas. Pan-Hindu, Buddhist Asia. Term to describe a male celestial being with the ability to fly.

Dharma. Sanskrit for law, duty, or truth, referring to the ultimate reality that governs the universe and the moral law that inspires humanity within it.

Dur lakshini. Term to describe a dangerous person who verbally makes predictions or curses that consistently come true.

Fakir. Arabic term for "a poor man." Ascetics who have taken a vow of poverty and undergo painful self-torture to acquire merit from the gods. They are most often depicted in movies as having the ability to levitate and even climb a rope hanging magically in the air.

Gajasimha. "Elephant lion." Mythical guardian animal placed in front of shrines; described as having the head of an elephant and the body of a lion.

Gana. Hindu. Dwarf-like obese lesser deities seen as attendants to the god Shiva.

Ganges River. Sacred river that flows from the Himalayas, down across northeast India. According to Hindu belief, bathing in its waters enabled one to reach heaven on Mount Meru.

Garuda. Pan-Hindu, Buddhist Asia. Famed king of the birds and the mount of the god Vishnu. Representing fire and the sun, he is often depicted as half-man and half-bird and is the sworn enemy of the nagas. This demigod is the son of Kisyapa and Vinata.

Ghal. Term to describe destructive or ruinous properties, as pertaining to ghosts or ghost possession.

Ghar ka devata. Term for household gods.

Guru. "Spiritual teacher." Sanskrit term to describe a saint or a teacher.

Hanthia. The spirit of a deceased woman who comes back from the afterlife to pester her previous household.

Jaddu. The ability to cast debilitating spells to inflict harm or death upon victims.

Jatakas. "Birth stories." Collection of 547 stories chronicling the Buddha's previous lives before his final birth. These stories, containing lessons in compassion, wisdom and kindness, have often been compared to Aesop's Fables. Over 2,500 years old, Jataka tales use both human and animal characters to convey their message, predating many European fairy tales.

Jigarkhwar. Sind Region. Type of witch known for extracting her victim's liver by rendering him unconscious through the use of incantations and a penetrating stare. Once removed, the organ then takes the form of a pomegranate seed, which is kept in the sorceress' calf for a time. The seed is later thrown into a fire, reverting back to a liver, and is eaten, causing the original victim to die. The victim may be saved if the seed is recovered from the calf and eaten by its owner.

Kali. "The Black One," said to have originated from the forehead of the goddess Durga as one of her aspects when she became angry. Described as

Garuda

having blood-red eyes with a third one on her forehead, she is considered the personification of death and destruction. Along with four arms (with two wielding a weapon and a severed head, respectively) and a dangling tongue, she is naked except for a necklace of skulls and a girdle of severed heads.

Karma. Buddhist and Hindu belief that the sum of one's actions in the past, both good and bad, determines one's destiny or status in future incarnations.

Kul devata. Term for family gods.

Kumari. Term to describe a reincarnated goddess, usually a prepubescent girl. In Nepal, it usually refers to an incarnation of the goddess Durga.

Kuvera. The god of wealth in Mahayana Buddhism and Hinduism. The ruler over yakshas and kinnarees, he is often depicted as obese and accompanied by seven treasures.

Lautana. Counter to the jaddu; the ability to reverse an inflicted spell and harm its original sender.

Mahabharata. Epic Hindu poem, comprised of 220,000 lines chronicling the great war between the Pandavas and the Kauravas. The work is attributed to Krishna Dvaipayana (or Vyasa for short).

Mahishasura. Hindu. Mythological buffalo demon of darkness slain by the goddess Durga.

Mandala. Sanskrit for "sacred circle that protects the mind." Circular representation or model of the universe, a diagram used by Hindus and Buddhists for visual meditation to achieve different states of mind.

Mande Burung. One of several unclassified hominids seen throughout the forests of Asia. Said to inhabit the Garo Hills of Meghalaya in northeastern India, it is described as a pungent, bipedal ape about 8 feet tall. With a blackish-brown long coat of fur, this creature is said to have an elongated head, giving it the appearance of wearing a cap.

Mandir. Term for a village temple.

Manibhadra. Hindu. Leader of the yakshas and the guardian of travelers.

Mantra. "Protection of the mind." Sanskrit term to describe the sacred sounds, syllables, chants, or incantations that carry significant cosmic or spiritual properties.

Mara. Evil Buddhist god who tried to tempt the Buddha to prevent him from reaching enlightenment. Even after this demonic spirit sent his three voluptuous daughters to distract him, the Buddha remained steadfast beneath the Bodhi tree and continued to meditate. Mara was ultimately vanquished in the process.

Mathwa devata. Term for a family deity that travels with a bride to her new home to protect her.

Matriya. Capricious sprites said to represent the ghost of young girls. Most associated with the goddess Matri and her shrine, they are a swarm of playful fairies that flutter about the countryside. Unfortunate victims who are caught in their path are suddenly struck down by a variety of serious and debilitating illnesses. Although they are considered dangerous if encountered, the affliction they impart is only by accident and not with the intent of malice.

Maya. Sanskrit for illusion. In Hindu thought, while the world is real (as dreamt by the god Brahma), a person's perception of it is an illusion. The universe and everything within it is as one and cannot be defined by categories or classifications fabricated by a person's rationalization.

Meru. Abode of the gods; cosmic mountain located at the center of the universe in both Hindu and Buddhist cosmologies, surrounded by the rings of seven oceans and seven continents.

Moksha. Sanskrit. The release or liberation of one's self from the endless cycle of death and rebirth.

Naga. Pan-Hindu, Buddhist Asia. Mythological, semi-divine serpents often associated with fertility and abundance. Residing deep within the earth, particularly in springs and lakes, they are considered very powerful and dangerous unless propitiated properly. Often depicted as cobras, nagas are the sworn enemy of garuda and figure prominently in Hindu and

Buddhist stories and traditions. They are also the protectors of the Buddha in meditation. Female nagas are called naginis.

Nagini. Hindu, Buddhist, Pan-Asia. Female naga.

Nandi. Hinduism. Fierce white bull; mount of the god Shiva that he rides into battle to fight demons.

Nazar lagna. "To look covetously." More popularly known as the evil eye, in which a person's particular stare can inflict harm upon its subject. The person is generally believed to be oblivious to having this ability, and it cannot be controlled. Special ceremonies and amulets are thought to remedy its effects.

Nirvana. "Beyond sorrow." Enlightenment in Buddhism, an end to suffering and desire and freedom from the never-ending cycle of rebirth.

Nittaewo. Sri Lanka. Term to describe unclassified bipedal hominids sighted historically on the island. They are described by the aboriginal Veddha tribe as being 3 to 5 feet tall, herbivorous, and covered with reddish fur. They are also said to live within small packs inside caves or trees and use their long nails to disembowel their victims. Despite sightings, oral folklore, and recent expeditions, proof of their existence has yet to be found.

Om. According to Indian philosophy, it is the most sacred sound of all, preceding even the creation of the universe itself. Comprised of four components (three phonetic sounds, a-u-m, with the last tone silent), it is commonly depicted as a pictograph that represents the Hindu trinity.

Oopra. Female ghost; generally applied to wives (or daughters-in-law) who died. This spirit is known to possess her own children, as well as the infants of the second wives. She can also haunt the succeeding wives of her husband.

Opra. Generic term for an evil spirit.

Pishacha. Flesh-eating demon who, like vetalas and bhuts, inhabits cremation grounds. They are said to have the ability to assume different forms and even possess their victims. It has also been considered a vampire, rising from the grave to feed upon victims slowly over time.

Naga

Pitri. Term to describe a male ancestral spirit.

Prana. Sanskrit for "breathing forth." The so-called life-force or energy that permeates all living beings.

Prayaga (Allahabad). Holy city in India; a place that is so sacred that just a small portion of its soil is said to be enough to wipe away sin. It is located where the Yamuna and the Sarasvati tributaries join the Ganges River.

Rajas. One of three universal forces in nature that the geomantic Indian art of Vastu Shastra tries to balance in a home. This is the restless principle that lies between sattva and tamas.

Rakshasa. Generic term to describe a diverse class of malevolent demons and evil spirits. They range from cremation ground-haunting ghosts, to colossal giants and ogres that threaten the gods themselves, and even genies and nature spirits. These shape-shifting entities can also appear in a multitude of animal combinations. Their realm is called Avatarana. Ravana is the king of the Rakshasas in the Indian epic, Ramayana. Female rakshasas are called rakshasi.

Rakshasi. Female form of a rakshasa.

Ramayana. Epic poem consisting of 50,000 lines chronicling the adventures of Rama, the seventh incarnation of the god Vishnu. The work is attributed to Valmiki.

Rati. The spirit of a deceased man who comes back from the afterlife to pester his previous household.

Rishi. Hindu. Term to describe a sage, hermit, or ascetic.

Saddhu. A yogi that has renounced worldly attachments and lives a life of simplicity and penance.

Samsara. Sanskrit term for the never-ending cycle of death and rebirth.

Sanskrit. "Pure." The language of ancient India, used in sacred Buddhist and Hindu texts.

Sati. Sanskrit. The self-immolation of widows upon the graves or funeral pyres of their deceased husbands.

Sattva. One of three universal forces in nature that the geomantic Indian art of Vastu Shastra tries to balance in a home. This is the positive principle of attraction, considered the highest and most spiritual of the three.

Shadow planets. Hindu. Two dragons in native astrology that represent the two points or nodes at which the celestial path of the moon crosses that of the sun. Known as Rahu ("the dragon's head") and Ketu ("the dragon's tail"), they represent the destiny and karma of the soul as it passes from life to life. Within Hindu astrology, these two complete the so-called "cosmic square" by bringing up the planetary count to nine.

Shaiad. The ghost of a Muslim.

Shakini. Type of female demon that serves the goddess Durga.

Shakti. Divine or cosmic power.

Shambhala. Mythical kingdom in Tibetan Buddhist mythology, said to be located in northeast India. Legend holds that when destruction and war threaten the world, the savior will appear from this city.

Shitala. The goddess of smallpox. As much as she is the cause of the disease, she is also invoked as protection against it. She is sometimes associated with the goddess Durga.

Siddha. A yogic master.

Simha. Sanskrit term for the lion, which is used extensively in Hindu, Buddhist imagery and symbolism.

Simhamukha. Ornate lion mask or face used as an architectural motif throughout South and Southeast Asia.

Sirkata. A type of headless ghost.

Soma. Hindu. The sacred drink of immortality.

Swami. Sanskrit term for "owner of one's self." Title given to an adept or master of a particular skill or spiritual devotion.

Tamas. One of three universal forces in nature that the geomantic Indian art of Vastu Shastra tries to balance in a home. This is the negative principle of repulsion.

Tantra. Hinduism, Tibetan Buddhism. Sanskrit for "extension" of the mind; term to describe a more mystical or esoteric form of yoga. Emphasizing action over contemplation, pleasure over abstinence, its practitioners viewed women as the wielders of divine power (shakti), and associated sexual energy with the union of opposites. Sexual intercourse between men and women played a significant role in tantric rituals, as expressed in carvings and statues adorning numerous temples. The movement peaked in the 10th century A.D.

Tantrika. A practitioner of the art of tantra.

Than. Term for an ancestral shrine.

Triguna. Collective name for the three universal forces of nature (sattva, tamas and rajas) that the geomantic Indian art of Vastu Shastra tries to balance in a home.

Upri hawa. Term to describe the spirit of a deceased married woman who is seen by the living. However, she is described as being only air (hawa). This ghost is quite benevolent and can only be seen by specific people. She is often depicted as a loving mother and wife who returns to her family to live with them. She is only feared if her husband remarries, becoming a threat to the new wife and her children.

Vanamaushas. Chamoli district. Term to describe supposedly "wicked wild men" who came from the surrounding hills and forests and raided the village of Talah Malkoti in 1965. These beings are said to be extremely hairy, their arms extending down to their knees when standing.

Vastu purusha. So-called "home demon," a mythological demon (Purusha) said to metaphorically reside in each home, lying face-down along the northeast-southwest line. Its body's placement is considered when applying the principles of Vastu Shastra, appeasing its presence while achieving structural harmony and balance.

Vastu Shastra. Native form of geomancy, similar to the Chinese Feng Shui. It is a formal system of principles designed to benefit its occupants, harmonizing a structure with the placement of objects inside it in accordance with the flow of prana (pure energy, or chi in Chinese). It uses the square (sakala) as its base-grid of alignment, dividing it into quadrants that represent numerological and even Vedic principles. Vastu Shastra also seeks to harmonize the three forces (triguna) that permeate nature: sattva, tamas and rajas.

Vetala. A malevolent spirit that enters dead bodies and reanimates them as if they were still alive.

Yali. Mythical lion-like creature used as an architectural motif in native temples, often depicted in a rearing-up position.

Yantra. Sanskrit for "instrument." Term to describe linear symbolic diagrams that tantrikas (practitioners of the art of Tantra) use as a tool for meditation. Coming in the form of various geometric combinations (squares, circles, triangles and pentagons), the diagram has a center called a bindu that represents the center of the universe. Different forms of energy can be manifested from the bindu, depending on the geometric combination surrounding it. The tantrika can attain different levels of consciousness by staring at the yantra and internalizing the energy produced from the visual composition.

Yogi. A practitioner of the art of yoga; physical and spiritual cleansing that would lead to enlightenment.

Yuga. Hindu. Term to describe an epoch or a cycle of time. A yuga can last for thousands and even millions of years.

Tibet

Akshamala. Hindu, Buddhist. Prayer beads.

Ani. Tibetan Buddhism. Native term for a nun.

Avalokiteshvara. Tibetan Buddhism. "Glorious gentle one." He is the Bodhisattva of compassion and the patron saint of Tibet. He is often depicted as having 11 heads and several pairs of arms. The Dalai Lamas are said to be manifestations of this deity. His mantra, "Om mani padme hum," is inscribed on rocks and stone tablets throughout the country.

Bag of Diseases. Hindu, Buddhist. One of the five magical weapons of the goddess Shri Devi, the only female among the eight wrathful Dharmapalas. It is traditionally described as a bag made of a boneless human corpse, filled with the organs of those who have died from the most lethal of contagious diseases. It is meant to be used against the enemies of Buddhist teachings and hangs from small venomous serpents that decorate the saddle of her mule.

Ball of thread. Hindu, Buddhist. One of the five magical weapons of the goddess Shri Devi, the only female of the eight wrathful Dharmapalas. It is described as a ball of colored thread that the goddess uses to bind her enemies using invoked curses for annihilation or subjugation. This weapon hangs from small venomous serpents that decorate the saddle of her mule.

Bardo. Tibetan Buddhism. Term to describe the transitional state between lives, as inbetween death and rebirth. There are three so-called "intermediate" states within the process of death, in a sequence: Chikhai bardo (bardo at the moment of death), Chonyid bardo (bardo of reality), and Sidpa bardo (bardo of mundane existence).

In the first state, Chikhai bardo (bardo at the moment of death), if one is able to recognize the profound "clear light" consciousness that emerges as reality itself, then one is liberated from the cycle of rebirth and becomes an enlightened being, or even a Buddha. If not, then one transitions to the second state, or Chonyid bardo (bardo of reality). One's body, perceptions, and sensations disintegrate, allowing reality to be revealed. Forty-two peaceful and 58 wrathful deities even appear in the consciousness over a period of several days. If one is able to distinguish reality in the state, then one escapes the process of rebirth. If not, then the deceased enters the third state, or Sidpa bardo (bardo of mundane existence), and is obliged to be reborn again.

These phases are discussed at length in the funerary text, "Bardo Thodol," ("Liberation Through Hearing in the Bardo"), also known as the "Tibetan Book of the Dead."

Bardo Thodol. Tibetan Buddhism. The famed "Tibetan Book of the Dead," or more accurately, "Liberation Through Hearing in the Bardo." Eighth-century funerary text attributed to Padmasambhava (or Guru Rinpoche), founder of Tibetan Buddhism. Traditionally read out loud during funerary rites, this manual is meant as a guide for the deceased to navigate through the three transitional states between death and rebirth (known as bardos). Centering around the fundamental Buddhist principles of karma and samsara, it emphasizes the notion that the hallucinatory visions the deceased encounters in the 49 day period, both quiet and horrific, are nothing more than products of the mind. It is this realization that will ultimately vanquish fear and lead to liberation.

Bhutadamara-mudra. Hindu, Buddhist. Spirit-subduing Gesture. Hand gesture or mudra specific to the Bodhisattva Vajrapani, who represents the power of all the Buddhas. Depicted in his four-armed wrathful form, this mudra is created by crossing the right forearm over the left and linking the little fingers together at the level of the heart. With the second and third fingers curled in and the index finger pointing out, this shape resembles the outstretched wings of the mythical garuda. It is believed that this gesture frightens and subdues malignant spirits.

Bodhisattva. Indian. Buddhist. "One Whose Essence is Supreme Knowledge." Compassionate divine figure on the verge of enlightenment, but delays it in order to help others achieve salvation.

Bon. Tibetan. Indigenous folk religion of Tibet prior to the coming of Buddhism. This shamanistic faith encompasses ritual exorcisms as well as dealings with native gods, spirits, and demons. It is said to have greatly influenced the direction of Buddhism in Tibet, existing today as its own school within that religion (Bonpo).

Bundle of Red Curses. Hindu, Buddhist. One of the five magical weapons of the goddess Shri Devi, the only female among the eight wrathful Dharmapalas. It is described as a rectangular text held between a pair of book covers. Shri Devi uses this text to cast spells and curses upon the enemies of Buddhist teachings. This weapon hangs from small venomous serpents that decorate the saddle of her mule.

Cham. Tibetan Buddhism. Masked ritual dance performed at the New Year festival (Losar) by lamas and monks. To the accompaniment of trumpets, drums and cymbals, cham is a performance exorcism meant to suppress evil spirits.

Chintamani. Indian. Hindu, Buddhist. Sanskrit term for the wish-granting gem, jewel said to have the power to grant all the benevolent wishes of its owner. It is depicted in art as pearl-shaped, coming in green, red, orange or blue colors, and sitting in a lotus crowned with ornate flames or light.

Chod. Tibetan. Type of "exorcism of the soul." The Tantric practice of directing compassion at the spirits or demons possessing laypersons. Ritual objects used include a drum made from a human skull as well as a human thigh bone.

Chorten. Tibetan Buddhism. Native term for stupa, used primarily as a repository for the remains of cremated lamas.

Citipati. Tibetan Buddhism. "Lords of the Funeral Pyre." Frightening male and female skeletal beings commonly found in Tibetan art. Shown dancing and holding thunderbolts, they are attendants of Yama, the god of death, and are meant to remind us that all life is transitory and that death may come at any time.

Dalai Lama. Tibetan Buddhism. The 14th (and latest) manifestation of the Bodhisattva Avalokiteshvara, the patron saint of Tibet and the embodiment of compassion. This title comes from the Gelug-pa Buddhist order.

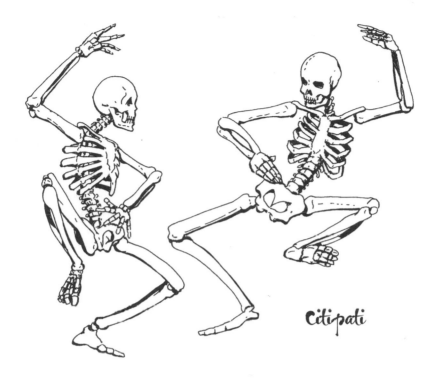

Citipati

Demon Cross-Stick. Tibetan Buddhism. One of the five magical weapons of the goddess Shri Devi, the only female of the eight wrathful Dharmapalas. It is described as an intricately engraved baton used by the goddess to tally and implement the punishments of the enemies of Buddhist teachings. This weapon is tucked in a girdle around her waist.

Dharmapalas. Tibetan Buddhism. "Protectors of the Dharma." Ferocious guardians of the Buddhist faith, some of whom were originally pre-Buddhist gods who were subdued by the saint Padmasambhava and absorbed into the religion. They also protect the faithful from evil influences that may thwart their spiritual progress. There are two major types: Mahakalas (male) and Mahakalis (females). Grouped in Tibet as the "Eight Terrible Ones," they are Yamantaka, Hayagriva, Mahakala, Brahma, Yama, Kuvera, Beg-Tse and Shri Devi. These wrathful deities are most often depicted as dark blue or black with many arms, legs, and heads. They also have a third eye, along with flaming red hair. The Lokapalas, who can be both wrathful and peaceful, also belong in this category.

Dorje. Tibetan Buddhism. Native term to describe the vajra, a small scepter in Tantric Buddhism said to be as powerful as a thunderbolt and as hard as a diamond.

Drolma. Tibetan Buddhism. Native term for the goddess Tara.

Five Magical Weapons of Shri Devi. See Bag of Diseases, Ball of thread, White and Black Spotted Dice, Bundle of Red Curses, and Demon Cross-Stick.

Four maras. Hindu, Buddhist. Four manifestations of Mara, the demonic Buddhist spirit that tried to tempt the Buddha to prevent him from reaching enlightenment. They are Devaputra Mara (demon of lust and pride), Klesha Mara (demon of emotional defilements), Mrityu Mara (demon of death), and Skandha Mara (demon of the so-called five aggregrates).

Four Supernatural Creatures of the Four Directions. Tibetan. Native interpretation of the Chinese model, which ascribes creatures that represent various geomantic and astrological properties for each direction. Unlike the traditional Chinese creatures of the dragon, phoenix, tiger and tortoise, the Tibetan model uses the dragon, garuda bird, tiger, and snow-lion, respectively. They surround the mythical wind-horse on the Tibetan prayer flag.

Guzan

Garland of severed heads and skulls. Hindu, Buddhist. Sanskrit term to describe the horrific necklaces worn around the neck of wrathful deities.

Gau. Tibetan Buddhism. Amulet containing the image of important spiritual figures. Also referred to as a "portable shrine," it most often holds a picture of the Dalai Lama.

Gesar of Ling. Tibetan. Legendary warrior-king from the seventh century whose life and epic adventures are recounted in numerous poems and songs. He is a national hero and has been compared to the Western St. George and even King Arthur. As the defender of the Buddha's teachings and the conqueror of evil, he set out on a quest to purge the country of evil kings, spirits, and demons.

Gnyan. Tibetan Buddhism. Snow-lion. Mythological creature that is Tibet's local deity of the snowy mountain ranges. It is also one of the country's most frequently used emblems, appearing on stamps, seals, paper, and coin currency, and even on the national flag. Described as white with a turquoise mane, they are often depicted in pairs and sometimes playing with a ball. Based on the Chinese model of astrology, it is one of the supernatural creatures of the four directions.

Gon-khang. Tibetan Buddhism. Special chamber found in many Buddhist temples, reserved for ancient deities who were forced out with the arrival of Buddhism. They are now considered the protectors of the very sacred sites that once belonged to them.

Gzi stone. Tibetan Buddhism. Protective amulet worn to ward off evil or malevolent influences. They are etched or banded agate stones, classified as male or female, circular as well as cylindrical, and vary in design, shape, and color.

Heruka. Tibetan Buddhism. Term to describe blood-drinking deities that appear in thangkas.

Impaled corpse club. Hindu, Tibetan Buddhist. Variation of the shava-danda, or corpse club; described as an elongated wooden stake capped with a human corpse impaled through its anus. The corpse itself is identified as a criminal, and the club symbolizes that all phenomena are without substance.

Heruka

Jokhang (Tsuglagkhang). Tibetan. The most sacred of all the temples in Tibet, as well as one of the most ancient. Legend holds that it was built on a lake in Lhasa that was thought to be the heart of a great female demon. The lake was filled in, effectively exorcising the creature. Containing many statues and chapels dedicated to several Buddhist deities, the temple underwent many structural renovations during its turbulent history.

Kangling. Hindu, Buddhist. Ritual trumpet used to drive away evil spirits. It is made of a human femur.

Kapala. Hindu, Buddhist. Bowl used in Tantric rituals; made of half of a human skull. It is often depicted being held by various wrathful deities in artwork. When it is filled with blood, it is called Asrkkpala, and when filled with flesh, is known as Mamsa Kapala.

Kapala-danda. Hindu, Buddhist. Sanskrit term for a skull club, described as a slender rod capped with a white human skull. It is a weapon held by deities in their right hand and used against demons to terrify and subjugate them.

Kar tsi. Tibetan. Native term for astrology.

Kinkara-danda. Hindu, Tibetan Buddhist. Sanskrit term for a skeleton club, described as a handle fashioned from human vertebrae and capped with a skull, rib cage, and pelvis. A shawl of flayed corpse skin is sometimes draped around its neck. It is a weapon held by Tibetan wrathful deities in their right hand and is a variation of the skull club.

Kirtimukha. Indian. "Face of majesty." Popular decorative and architectural motif found in archways, lintels, door handles, and even as heraldic devices on various armor and weapons. It is often depicted as a demonic, horned face without a lower jaw, flanked by a pair of hands that grip a bar curving out of its mouth. A net of jewels radiates out from below its upper jaw. It is used to protect the devout and drive away evil spirits. Popular in Nepalese and Tibetan art, its variations include kalamukha (Rahu, the devourer of time), as well as other animal combinations.

Kutan. Tibetan. Term for a native spirit medium.

Lama. Tibetan Buddhism. "Unsurpassed." Native term equivalent to a "guru." It is a title ascribed to monks who have achieved high spiritual attainment.

Lha. Tibetan Buddhism. "Life spirit." Term to describe a life force that may also be present in inanimate objects and places in nature (trees, lakes, and mountains).

Lha khang. Tibetan. "Deity house." Village shrine presided over by a monk.

Lungta. Tibetan Buddhism. "Wind horse." Term to describe a prayer flag or banner inscribed with prayers, symbols, and mantras and positioned on monastery rooftops so the winds will distribute the prayers across the land. A popular motif is a galloping horse that carries the chintamani (wish-granting gem), which spreads peace and prosperity. Culturally, horses and the wind are closely associated, complementary components of speed and movement.

Mala. Tibetan Buddhism. Sanskrit term meaning "rosary" or "garland," it is a string of 108 beads made from various materials such as bone, crystal, or sandalwood. It is used for counting mantra recitations and other devotional rituals.

Mamo. Hindu, Tibetan Buddhist. Term for disease or plague-causing demons.

Mani 'khor-lo. Tibetan Buddhism. Hand-held prayer wheel; described as a small metal drum that rotates on a pin by way of a weighted chain. Used by both monks and laypersons, it contains prayers on rolled-up slips of paper, usually with the inscription, "Om mani padme hum." Spinning the prayer wheel with one's wrists is thought to be a form or prayer and of reciting mantras, and the act itself brings about divine blessings and religious merit.

Mo Sho. Tibetan. Native dice divination based on books and rituals associated with a protective deity. Performed by monks for laypersons, this method allows them to see the obvious and the background influences of spiritual energies, karma, and even deities as they pertain to various events in their future.

Monlam Chenmo. Tibetan Buddhism. Great Prayer Festival. Massive ceremonial exorcism held during New Year's (Losar); meant to drive out evil forces and malevolent spirits of the old year.

Mudra. Indian. Hindu, Buddhist. Term to describe various hand gestures found in traditional statues and sculptures. These gestures symbolically represent specific acts of saluting, offering, or understanding.

Mundamala. Hindu, Buddhist. Garland of severed heads and skulls. Sanskrit term to describe two types of horrific necklaces worn around the throat of wrathful deities. The garland of 50 heads is usually attributed to male deities, while the garland of 50 skulls is attributed to female deities. They both represent purification of speech, symbolizing the vowels and consonants of the Sanskrit alphabet.

Na tsi. Tibetan. Native term for the casting of horoscopes.

Nechung State Oracle. Tibetan. Monk oracle that is the living incarnate of the pre-Buddhist demon Dorje Drakden, an entity considered to be an advisor to the Dalai Lama himself and the protector of the Tibetan people. Consulted for important events and decisions about the future, this position and its prophecies have played a significant role in Tibetan politics and history.

Nirvana. Indian. "Without desire." Complete detachment from the material world; state of enlightenment sought by all Buddhists.

Om Mani Padme Hum. Tibetan Buddhism. "A-compassion-jewel in wisdom-lotus-amen." A mantra associated with Avalokiteshvara, the patron saint of Tibet, uttered by all Tibetans as an affirmation of their faith.

Parijata. Hindu, Buddhist. Sanskrit term for the wish-granting tree. One of five wish-granting trees that blossoms in the paradise gardens of the god Indra; located on the summit of Mount Meru. The other four trees are kalpa, mandara, santana, and harichandana. Originally emerging from the primal waters when the cosmic ocean was churned, access to these magical trees were said to be the primary cause for the war between the devas and the asuras.

Pho lha. Tibetan. Male household deity invoked in everyday rituals to protect the home from evil or malevolent forces.

Phuk lha. Tibetan. Female household deity invoked in everyday rituals to protect the home from evil or malevolent forces.

Phurba (purbu). Tibetan Buddhism. Ritual triple-bladed dagger used in Buddhist rites to subdue evil influences. When used by a shaman, these iron daggers are said to have magical powers, such as controlling the weather, flying through the air, and even pinning down evil spirits.

Prayer drum. Tibetan Buddhism. Large vertical drums painted with colorful mantras; found in most Tibetan temples. Arranged in rows in a cloister, devotees would spin these drums as they walked by. The rotations are believed to distribute the inscribed invocations to the world.

Ransom sticks. Tibetan Buddhism. Small wooden implements used to avert or remove afflictions brought on by spirits.

Rinpoche. Tibetan Buddhism. "High in esteem." Designation given to highly revered lamas.

Rolang. Tibetan. Bonpo. "The corpse that stands up." Class of pre-Buddhist rituals performed by shamans during funeral ceremonies. One such ritual involves an adept procuring a magical talisman. Staying inside a dark room with a corpse, the practitioner proceeds to reanimate the body by embracing it, laying his mouth over the mouth of the deceased, and mentally repeating magical words in its head. He then must physically restrain the body as it awakes. Eventually, the corpse's tongue will protrude the practitioner must bite it off at the correct moment. The tongue itself becomes a talisman with magical powers.

The corpse, if not properly subdued by biting off its tongue, will kill the adept. Resurrected rolang corpses can escape the room and roam freely among people.

Sankha. Hindu, Buddhist. Conch shell; used as a musical instrument. Its sound is used as a weapon to ward off demons and is one of the main attributes of the god Vishnu. The spiral pattern on the shell represents infinite space, which naturally expands clockwise. If a shell spirals in the opposite direction, nature is said to be reversed and the conch belongs to the god Shiva.

Shava-danda. Hindu, Tibetan Buddhist. Sanskrit term for a corpse club;described as a weapon fashioned from a dried, rigored, or mummified human corpse and wielded by Tibetan wrathful deities in their right hands to destroy enemies of Buddhist teachings.

Shen. Tibetan. Bon. Term to describe a traditional priest.

Sky burial. Tibetan. Traditional funerary practice of taking dead bodies to a designated high area, dicing them up into pieces, and then leaving them for the birds to devour.

Sorcerer's Magical Horn. Tibetan Buddhism. Thun-rwa. Hollowed-out yak horn used ritually in black magic. Filled with various magical substances (blood, hair and nails, written curses, bones, and seeds), it is then plugged and used for exorcisms against ghosts and spirits and the intended victims of killing rituals.

Tagsen Mo. Tibetan Buddhism. Cannibal ogress said to be an incarnation of the goddess Tara. Tagsen Mo and a macaque monkey incarnation of Avalokiteshvara are believed to have produced six children that became the ancestors of the six classes of beings that inhabited the universe. These six offspring then created the first Tibetans.

Tara. Tibetan Buddhism. "She who delivers." Female deity sometimes referred to as the mother of all Buddhas. Divine savior and capable of granting wishes, she was said to have emerged from the lotus flowers that sprang from the tears of the Bodhisattva Avalokiteshvara. She has 21 different aspects or manifestations, each with its own corresponding posture, color, and attribute. Two of her manifestations stand out: White Tara (Shveta Tara), goddess of daytime, and Green Tara (Utpala Tara), goddess who aids at night. While these two aspects are considered gentle and loving, her "red," "yellow," and "blue" aspects are menacing.

Thags yang. Tibetan. Term to describe a malevolent demon that takes the form of a tiger and prowls the forests and villages in search of travelers unprotected by magical prayers and gestures.

Thangka. Tibetan Buddhism. A brocade framed portable scroll painting that depicts a Buddha or other deity.

Three Victorious Creatures of Harmony. Hindu, Tibetan Buddhism. Three creatures, hybrids, or chimeras, formed from the union of two traditionally opposing animals that are found in numerous astrological diagrams, victory banners, thangkas, and prayer flags. They are the garuda lion (made of the rivals garuda bird and lion), the water monster (made of the makara creature and its prey, the water-snail), and the fish with hair (made of the otter and its prey, the fish).

Towos. Tibetan. Term for ferocious, brain-eating beings.

Trapa. Tibetan Buddhism. Native term for "monk."

Trong jug. Tibetan. Bonpo. Term to describe a ritual that allows the spirit of the deceased to enter a different corpse and reanimate it.

Trulku. Tibetan. An incarnate lama; the constant manifestation of a deity as expressed through a series of human rebirths.

Tsha-tsha. Tibetan Buddhism. Term to describe native talismans or small votive tablets. Made of clay and sometimes containing consecrated substances, they are stamped with holy text and images and are left in great numbers at pilgrimage spots and holy places.

Vajra. Indian. Hindu, Tibetan Buddhism. Sanskrit term used to describe a small scepter in Tantric Buddhism that is said to be as powerful as a thunderbolt and as hard as a diamond. It symbolizes the power of universal compassion within the enlightened universe. It was originally the weapon of the god Indra, who hurled it as a thunderbolt against his enemies. It is known as dorje in Tibetan Buddhism. In Tantric rituals, it is considered masculine, complementing the feminine bell (ghanta).

Vritra. Indian. Sanskrit term for dragon.

Wheel of Life. "Bhavachakra" in Sanskrit. Circular diagram that represents the Buddhist cosmos believed to have been traced by the Buddha himself. It depicts the cyclical nature of existence as well as the six realms in which rebirth takes place (the divine heavens of the gods and devas; the realm of the demigods, or asuras; the animal realm; the human realm; the realm of the hungry ghosts or pretas; and the hell realm.)

White and Black Spotted Dice. Hindu, Buddhist. One of the five magical weapons of the goddess Shri Devi, the only female among the eight wrathful Dharmapalas. It is described as a pair of black and white divination dice. It hangs from small venomous serpents that decorate the saddle of her mule. See also Bag of Diseases, Bundle of Red Curses, Ball of Thread, and Demon Cross-Stick.

Yab-yum. Tibetan Buddhism. Native term to describe the union of complementary principles. "Yab" means honorable father (representing wisdom), while "Yum" means honorable mother (representing compassion). Yab-yum refers to the union of the two principles, visually depicted in Tibetan Buddhism as two deities locked in a sexual embrace.

Yeti. Tibetan. "Abominable Snowman." Famous unclassified hominid believed to inhabit the Himalayan region of Tibet, Nepal, and China. Known mostly from massive footprints in the snow, eyewitness accounts describe the creature as ape-like and bipedal and covered in long, dark fur. The creature is part of the native folklore and is also referred to as migoi and meh-teh.

Reports of sightings date back to the early 19th century, but the actual term "abominable snowman" wasn't coined until 1921. So-called "proof" of the yeti's existence has always been met with skepticism. Its numerous tracks have been explained as the prints of various native bears that have degraded and expanded in the snow. The creatures themselves, seen from a distance, may also be bears, which are capable of standing erect on their hind legs.

Yidam. Tibetan Buddhism. Personal male or female Tantric guardian deity that can be summoned in times of need. Possessing both wrathful and peaceful aspects, it is also considered a "meditational" deity; selected by a lama from a particular school and assigned to a student to help the initiate attain spiritual powers.

Siberia and Mongolia

Abaahy. Northeastern Siberian. Yakut term for evil spirits that require blood sacrifices to be appeased.

Abassy. Yakut. Term to describe a type of evil spirit.

Abassy-oibono. Yakut. "Hole of the Spirits." The opening into the earth through which shamans descend into the nether regions.

Abassy ojuna. Yakut. A class of shamans that deal with so-called "evil spirits."

Ajy ojuna. Yakut. A class of shamans who make sacrifices to the gods.

Ak kam. Altaic. So-called "white shaman," capable of traveling to both the sky and the underworlds.

Allara kyrar. Yakut. Direction shamans designate in traveling to their mystical journey. This term means "to the spirits below."

A'lma. Yukagir. Term to describe a type of shaman that cures illnesses, offers sacrifices to the gods and maintains relationships with both the so-called "Kingdom of Shadows" and the supernatural world.

Almas. Mongolian. "Wild Man." Type of unclassified hominid found in the Altai Mountains in Western Mongolia and in the Tien Shan by Sinkiang in China. It is described as bipedal, about 5 feet tall in height, and covered with reddish-brown fur. They are considered shy and herbivorous and are theorized to have been an earlier form of human being. The earliest recorded sighting dates back to the 1420s.

Almas

Been. Western Tungus. One of several souls believed to reside in the body. This is the corporeal soul, which descends to the afterlife after the person's death.

Emekhet. Northeastern Siberian. Yakut term to describe one of two types of souls used by a shaman as a familiar spirit, giving the practitioner its mystical powers and abilities. The emekhet is a guardian spirit, the soul of a dead shaman, that protects and counsels him at all times.

Enenalan. Koryak. "Man inspired by spirits." Type of shaman whose vocation is actually determined by the spirits and not by the shaman's free will.

Iicheen. Northeastern Siberian. Yakut term for a wise medical or spiritual specialist.

I'rkeye. Yukagir. "The trembling one." A type of shaman.

Kara kam. Altaic. So-called "black shaman," capable of traveling to both the sky and the underworlds.

Karain bo. Buryat. A class of "black shamans" that deal with the spirits. Unlike their "white" shaman counterparts who wear white costumes (sagani bo), the Karain bo wear blue costumes.

Ke'let. Chukchee. A spirit that enters a shaman's body during a healing séance.

Kenniki oyuna. Yakut. So-called "last shamans," who are dream interpreters and diviners.

Korbuochhu. Northeastern Siberian. Yakut term for an oracle or seer of the future.

Kormos. Altaic, Teleut. Term to describe the evil spirits of the dead.

Main. Western Tungus. One of several souls believed to reside in the body. This external soul is believed to be a mystical link between the person and Seveki, a spirit in the higher world. Becoming independent from the body after the person dies, the main is believed to lead the hunter through the swamps of the higher world; his experiences are then reflected into his earthly life.

Mongolian Death Worm. Fabulous creature found in the Gobi Desert; described as a bright red worm resembling the intestines of a cow. Growing to a size between two and five feet long, locals claim it is able to spew acid and kill from a distance by creating an electric discharge. Despite several expeditions to its reported habitat, its existence has yet to be proven.

Omi. Western Tungus. One of several souls believed to reside in the body. This is the eternal life essence that eventually gets reincarnated after death to ensure and continue the clan's reproductive capability.

Orgiski. Tungus. Literally "in the direction of orgi (lower or 'western' region)." Dangerous ceremonial séance in which the shaman travels to the underworld to cure an affliction or to solve a problem affecting the living.

Mongolian Death Worm

Orto oyuna. Yakut. So-called "common" shamans who are primarily healers.

Otohut. Northeastern Siberian. Yakut term for a healer shaman.

Oyun. Northeastern Siberian. Yakut term for a so-called "black" or "white" male shaman.

Sagani bo. Buryat. Term to describe a class of "white" shamans that deal with the gods. Unlike their "black" shaman counterparts who wear blue costumes (karain bo), they wear white costumes.

Shaman. Tungus. Although this term is widely used today to describe any medicine man or witch doctor, the word historically originated from the Evenk (Tungus) language that meant a religious specialist, as defined by herders and hunters living in Siberia. Technically, it can be applied to a specialist within the Siberian and Mongolian religious systems.

Tuulleekh kihi. Northeastern Siberian. Yakut term for a dream interpreter.

Udaghan. Northeastern Siberian. Yakut term for a so-called "black" or "white" female shaman.

Uor. Yakut. Native term to describe a ghost.

Usa kyrar. Yakut. Direction shamans designate in traveling on their mystical journey. This term means "to the spirits above."

Yekyua. Northeastern Siberian. Yakut term to describe one of two types of souls used by a shaman as a familiar spirit that gives the practitioner his mystical powers and abilities. The yekyua is a malevolent spirit, owned by both the shaman and a living wild animal, that empowers him to cause harm in that harmful spirit's interests. Unfortunately, being linked to the yekyua subjugates the shaman to that spirit's misadventures and even survival.

China

Ancestor worship. Pan-Buddhist and Confucian Asia. Broadly speaking, it is the veneration of deceased family members and ancestors. This is derived from the belief that the well-being of living descendants, as well as that of their ancestors in the afterlife, is closely dependent upon the other for prosperity. Unlike the traditional model of worshipping a deity in exchange for goods, services, or spiritual salvation, ancestor veneration is performed more for familial piety, loyalty, and obligation.

Ancestral tablet. Small wooden board on which the name and rank of the deceased are inscribed. They are arranged according to familial hierarchy and are usually kept in a family shrine or in a hall in a temple. Believed to sometimes contain the soul of the deceased, these tablets are given tributes on certain days of the year and are often used for spiritual help and guidance.

Ang-thau-a. So-called "read-head" Taoist priest. Type of Taiwanese exorcist who is called upon to perform purification rites on houses, villages, and even families to protect them from misfortune and illness.

Animals of the Four Cardinal Directions. The four creatures that represent each direction; believed to comprise both the opposite and complementary forces of the universe. The White Tiger represents the West; its season is autumn and its element metal. The Green Dragon represents the East, its season spring and its element wood. The Red Bird or Phoenix represents the South, its season summer and its element fire. The Dark Warrior (a tortoise and a serpent) represents the North, its season winter and its element water.

Ba Gua. Eight Diagrams; a series of eight symbols used extensively in the I Ching. Each diagram consists of three alternating solid and broken lines of which there are eight possible combinations arranged in an octagonal formation. Each symbol and its ascribed placement correspond to specific elements, attributes, colors, animals, and even familial kinships, which, in turn, are used to divine a person's future. Hanging a Ba Gua octagonal plaque or mirror above the front door of one's home is said to bring good fortune.

Bathroom Ghost. Hong Kong urban legend in which witnesses claimed to have followed a beautiful girl to the women's bathroom inside a movie theater only to be mysteriously locked inside and confronted by the same woman who now had no facial features.

Bei guai chaak. Term used to describe the phenomena of being pressed down by a ghost, possibly linked to sleep paralysis.

Bei guai jui. Term used to describe being chased by a ghost while asleep and dreaming, only to wake up completely immobile as if being pressed down by a spirit.

Chan. Mythical giant sea clam whose breath could exhale clouds that transformed into terraces and palaces.

Chang Kuo Lau. One of the famous Eight Immortals of Taoism (Pa Hsien); often depicted as riding a donkey backwards. Believed to possess great supernatural powers, he carries a Yu Ku, an odd-shaped musical instrument. He is also invoked upon by couples for bearing children, particularly when desiring males.

Chao yao ching. "Illuminate-demon Mirror." A personal charm worn by brides.

Chiang-shi. Notorious "Hopping Ghost" commonly seen in Hong Kong cinema. More vampire or blood-thirsty corpse than ghost, these P'o-animated bodies are so limited in their movements from rigor that they have to literally hop to get from place to place. Dressed in Qing Dynasty burial clothes and wielding dangerously long blue fingernails, they attack their victims at the throat. They avoid sunlight, are placated with oil lamps and incense, and can be warded off with sticky glutinous rice, chicken blood, a Taoist mirror, and incantations. Placing a yellow death blessing piece of paper on its forehead also settles its soul. Also known as Jiang-shi or Kyonsi.

Chiang-shi

Chiao pai. A pair of wooden blocks used for divination; shaped like commas with one side flat and the other side curved.

Ch'ih-mei. Term to describe ogres, including malevolent spirits of waters and forests.

Child-stealing Devil. The soul of a young girl who died prior to getting married. She now seeks out children to kill for the purpose of taking her place. This act enables her the right to be reincarnated as a human being.

Ch'i-lin (Qi-lin). Unicorn. Mythological creature not to be confused with the single-horned horse in classical Western lore. It is more deer-like in appearance, generally white in color, and can have up to three horns that are covered with fur. This "dragon horse" has also been described as having the tail of an ox and the scales of a fish. A benevolent and extremely righteous creature with the ability to walk on grass without crushing it, it is able to determine the guilty from the innocent. Along with the tortoise, the dragon, and phoenix, it is one of the four supernatural creatures that guard the four quadrants of heaven.

Chim. Common form of personal divination in which worshippers shake a cylindrical box of bamboo slips until one falls out. This slip is then taken to a fortune-teller who interprets its meaning based on a number marked on the slip itself. It is said to be a form of communication with ancestors or the afterlife.

Ching. Term to describe demons or goblins. Sometimes used synonymously with the Kuei.

Chung Li Ch'uan. Chief of the famous Eight Immortals of Taoism (Pa Hsien). A former political official who lived as a hermit in his old age, he is most associated with inventing the pill of immortality. His symbols are the peach of immortality, and a feathered fan that he was believed to have used to revive the souls of the deceased.

Dang ki (Tang ki). "Divining youth." Type of male and female spirit mediums found in Singapore and Taiwan that communicate the voice of a deity verbally. The process of possession is as much a performance as it is a ritual, usually involving self-mortification.

Dawshyh. So-called "black-head" Taoist priest.

Fang-Shih. Magician-diviners who wandered the courts of historical China, predicting social, personal, and even cosmic events through the use of patterns, signs, and symbols.

Fangshuideng. "Release of the Water Lanterns." Custom held in various Chinese communities during Gui jie (Hungry Ghost Festival) in which water lanterns and paper boats are floated downstream to invite the souls of drowned victims to the next day's feast.

Fang-zhang. "Square Fathom." One of three islands in traditional mythology that the first emperor of China believed was the paradise home of immortals. The islands were also said to be inhabited by fairies who drank from the fountain of life and ate gems scattered on the shores.

Feng huang. Phoenix. Mythological bird not to be confused with the self-rejuvenating Egyptian phoenix in classical Western lore. Possessing the plumage of five magical colors (yellow, black, green, white, and red), this beautiful bird has been described in part as resembling a swan, with the hind parts of a unicorn and the stripes of a dragon. It also has 12 tail feathers, except in years with an extra month when it has 13.

A symbol of the Empress (the dragon symbolizing the Emperor), its presence in the land signifies peace and the governance of a just ruler. Seemingly derived from the pheasant (rather than an eagle, in the case of its Egyptian counterpart), the Feng huang is benevolent and doesn't feed on living creatures. It is also one of the four supernatural creatures that guard the four quadrants of heaven (along with the tortoise, the unicorn, and the dragon).

Feng-shui. Literally, "wind-water." A native form of geomancy that uses the dynamic principles of Yin and Yang to determine the most harmonious placement and orientation of objects, houses, and gravesites. It is used extensively in architectural planning, even in modern times, particularly to direct luck and to appease the dead.

Fomao (yu). "Buddha hair and Buddha plumes." Type of spiritual currency ritually burned and offered to spirits in the afterlife. These are thin sheets of yellow paper inscribed with prayers and incantations, used specifically to help one's ancestors enter the Western Paradise.

Fu Chi. Type of automatic writing device described as a sifting basket with an attached short stick that is held by two mediums over a bed of sand. As the mediums enter into a trance, the stick moves in circles and form characters. This method was used to inquire about the well-being of departed relatives in the afterlife as well as receiving messages from them.

Fu gei sau. "Character writer." Type of Cantonese male spirit medium who enters a trance and communicates his messages through automatic writing, using a stick to draw in the sand.

Gui jie. Hungry Ghost Festival. Traditional festival honoring the dead. Climaxing on the 15th day of the seventh month, this event is held to appease neglected and hungry spirits, ghosts devoid of worship or offerings. On this month, it is believed that souls from hell are released to wander about the earth. Various foods, spirit money, incense, and paper clothing are offered to them in turn, ritually presented on altars and in temples. On the evening before the actual festival, water lanterns and paper boats are floated downstream to invite the souls of drowned victims to the next day's feast (called fangshuideng).

Han Hsiang Tzu. One of the famous Eight Immortals of Taoism (Pa Hsien). This Immortal is considered the patron saint of musicians, his symbol being a jade flute. He represents serenity, beauty, and harmony with the universe and had the power to make flowers grow and bloom instantaneously.

Hare on the Moon. Mythical hare or rabbit that resides on the moon and is said to pound the elixir of immortality in a large vat.

Heitor Dawshyh. So-called "black-head" Taoist priest. Type of Taiwanese priest who is called upon to perform various rites, at times overlapping with the duties of the "red-head" Ang-thau-a.

Ho Hsien Ku. One of the famous Eight Immortals of Taoism (Pa Hsien). The only female immortal, her symbol is the lotus flower, which represents wisdom and openness.

Hsi Wang Mu. Famous "Queen Mother of the West." An extremely popular fairy goddess said to live in the fabled K'un Lun Mountains, residing in a beautiful palace that grew peaches of immortality. She is often depicted wearing the garb of a princess while riding a crane, being attended to by a pair of handmaidens, who hold a fan and a basket of peaches. Her five principal attendants, each wearing the color of the five directions, are called the Gemmeous Lasses.

Hu chao. "Tiger's Claw." Personal charm said to guard its bearer against sudden fright, magically imbuing him with the animal's courage.

Hu Hsin Ching. Term to describe ancient mirrors that had the power to protect their owners from evil. It was historically believed that mirrors had the ability to make spirits visible.

Huli jing. Fox spirit; creature known for shape-shifting into people in order to seduce them. They are nefarious for taking the form of a beautiful woman to seduce virtuous scholars and lead them astray. It is known as kitsune in Japan, and kumiho in Korean.

Hun. One of two souls believed to inhabit the body. The yang, or positive aspect of the two, it is considered celestial and can travel to heaven or hell upon death. Sometimes referred to as shen.

I Ching. Classic "Book of Changes." Ancient literature used extensively for divination. Attributed to Emperor Fu-Hsi (2853 B.C.), the book consists of 64 sections, each section categorized by a compound hexagram of solid and broken lines derived from the Ba Gua system of attributes.

Iauguay. Diverse class of so-called "evil fairies," which includes the ghost of animals.

Iaujing. Type of spirit in the category of Iauguay ("evil fairies"), this one being anthropomorphic inanimate objects.

Japanese-occupation ghosts. Pan-Asia. Phenomena in which witnesses claim to see the apparitions of Japanese soldiers performing various functions as if still alive, usually in sites of significant death during World War II.

Jen hsien. Class of spiritual entities described as people who have achieved immortality in heaven.

Jiama. "Armor and horses." Type of spiritual currency ritually burned and offered to spirits in the afterlife. These are sheets of white paper stamped with images of horses and armor, used specifically as offerings to soldiers and a particular deity's assistant.

Kio-a. So-called "little palanquin," or divination chair; a small wooden chair meant to literally seat a supernatural spirit for the purpose of divination. Held by two men, the chair is said to bounce and jostle about violently in place when the spirit has occupied it, much to the pain and difficulty of the two supporters. The chair eventually crashes on a prepared table and begins tracing characters upon its surface. These traces are then read and interpreted.

Kitchen God. Benevolent deity believed to reside inside the kitchen stove. Known also as Zao Jun (Lord of the Hearth), he is often depicted wearing the garb of a magistrate while seated next to his wife. He is also attended to by celestial lads and lasses. After spending the year with the host family, he returns to heaven and reports to the Jade Emperor.

Ku. Native black magic traditionally performed by female shamans. They attack by secretly inserting poisonous insects into the food of their victims. The spirits of those who die by this witchcraft are also said to become slaves of the Wu-ku witch.

Ku t'ung ching. "Old Brass Mirror." Personal charm that grants its bearer the power to heal anyone who becomes afflicted after seeing a spirit.

Kuan ti. God of war. Extremely popular divinity who was originally a highly decorated general, but who was later deified as a god. Easily identifiable by his red face and enormous halberd sword, he has countless shrines and temples in his honor and is worshipped as a god of righteousness and justice. He is also sometimes associated with wealth and money-making enterprises.

Kuan Yin. The extremely popular goddess of mercy and compassion; originally a male Buddhist saint named Avalokitesvara. Her name in Chinese translates as "someone who listens to sounds." Several theories abound as to why he was transformed from male to female, ranging from his feminine appearance in classical Indian and Tibetan art to his ability to shape-shift to elicit compassion from others. She has been called the Chinese Madonna, often depicted with a child in her arms and accompanied by a girl carrying a willow and a boy holding a bottle. She is sometimes associated with the sea-faring goddess Ma-zu.

Kuei (guei, gui, kuai). Generic term for a class of devils, ghosts, imps, and demons. In ghostly terms, they are said to be formerly human, casting no shadows, and wearing hemless clothing.

Kuei hsien. Class of supernatural spirits described as ghosts with no bodies and who are denied peace or a home.

K'un-lun Mountains. One of the longest mountain chains in Asia, it is also associated with the gods, particularly as the paradise abode of Hsi Wang Mu. With rivers of various colors flowing from its base, it was reported to also grow trees bearing precious stones, particularly jade and pearls.

Lan Ts'ai Ho. One of the famous Eight Immortals of Taoism (Pa Hsien). Very unusual immortal whose form shifts from male to female. This entity is often depicted carrying a basket of flowers and is the patron saint of florists.

Li T'ieh Kuai. One of the famous Eight Immortals of Taoism (Pa Hsien). Short-tempered immortal associated with medicine, his symbol being an iron crutch. His other symbol is a magical gourd, favored by exorcists for it represented his soul's ability to leave his body. He appears as a beggar and fights on behalf of the poor and needy.

Liaozhai Zhiyi. Classic collection of nearly five hundred supernatural stories written by Pu Songling. Populated with characters that include ghosts, exorcists, court officials, and scholars, this anthology has inspired many modern adaptations in movies and literature. Also known as "Strange Stories from a Chinese Studio," and "Strange Tales of Liaozhai."

Linghwen. Generic term for the human soul.

Ling-zhi. So-called "Herb of Immortality." Depicted variedly as a grass or fungus in classic literature, it is used as a potent curative, hallucinogen, or alchemistic additive.

Lohan. An immediate disciple of the Buddha; one who is on the verge of attaining enlightenment and becoming a bodhisattva.

Lo-Pan. Term to describe the geomantic compass used by fortune-tellers, diviners, and feng-shui experts.

Lu Tung Pin. One of the famous Eight Immortals of Taoism (Pa Hsien). Immortal most associated with medicine as well as the elixir of life (which he learned from Chung Li Ch'uan). The patron saint of barbers, he also possessed the Chanyao Kuai, the Demon Slayer sword, which gave him the power over evil spirits. His other symbol is a fly whisk, representing someone who could fly.

Lunar mansions. Twenty-eight lunar mansions that are actually celestial constellations, similar to the stars of the Western zodiac but ruled by a spirit. Lying along the celestial equator and clustered by season in four groups of seven, each constellation is said to be ruled by a disciple of T'ung-t'ien Chiao-chu, the Taoist who achieved immortality.

Lung (Long). Chinese dragon. Classic mythological creature; described as having the head of a camel, the eyes of a rabbit, the horn of a stag, the ears of a cow, the neck of a snake, the claws of an eagle, the soles of a tiger, the scales of a carp, and the belly of a frog. One of the guardians of the Four Celestial Directions (representing the East and the color green), it is the fifth animal in the Chinese zodiac and the enemy of the tiger.

Unlike its Western counterpart, the Chinese dragon is a magical and benevolent creature that is most associated with rain and treasure. They are generally aquatic, but are often depicted playing in storm clouds. They are also more serpentine in appearance, possessing whiskers and a beard but rarely wings. Chinese dragons generally have five fingers on each claw. They are also known to spew pearls, believed to be the distilled essence of the moon. Although many varieties exist, there are three main types of dragons: chiao, which live in swamps and mountain dens; li, a hornless species that lives in the ocean; and the heavenly lung, which lives in the sky.

The emperor and the imperial family have traditionally used the dragon motif as a symbol of their authority. Dragons are sometimes associated with the Buddhist naga.

Lung Wang. The Dragon King in classical mythology; said to live in a majestic palace under the sea.

Ma Mien. Horse face. Along with the demon Niu T'ou, a spear-wielding, horse-headed attendant and messenger to Yen-lo, king of hell.

Ma-gu. Fairy goddess popular in literature; often portrayed as having unusually long fingernails. She is said to carry a bamboo staff with a basket dangling from it while being escorted by an attendant carrying the peach of immortality.

Mani. Sanskrit. Wish-granting jewel; the Buddhist symbol of riches and donation. Also known as Ratna.

Mazu (Ma Tsu P'o). Goddess of the sea. Benevolent deity worshipped in coastal areas in southern China and Taiwan and even as far away as California. Accompanied by her vigilant attendants Qian-li yan (Thousand-mile Eyes) and Shun-feng er (Favorable-wind ear), she is the patron goddess of sailors and protects seafarers and mariners from peril. She is also known as Tian Hou, the Queen Empress of Heaven.

Offerings and sacrifices are made in her honor before every long voyage. The fishing nets are also blessed. With temples throughout China (Taiwan alone has 300 in her honor), she is an extremely popular deity.

Lung

Her statue was even brought to Thailand to placate the restless spirits of those who drowned in the 2005 tsunami.

Menshen. Door gods. Two guardian deities, Shentu and Yulu, who protect families from demons by binding them and throwing them back into the underworld. Heavily armored and brandishing weapons, these fierce figures often decorate door panels and gates during Chinese New Year.

Merlion. Singapore. Composite creature described as having the head of a lion and the body of a fish. It is used extensively in sculptures and as souvenirs by the Singapore Tourism Board to symbolize the country.

Mu-jen. Type of small, wooden effigy shaped like man and used in witchcraft. Meant to represent the intended victim, the figure itself can be subjected to various rituals and punishments to harm the victim indirectly. One type of Mu-jen (called tao-nu, or Tao Women) uses the figure as an instrument of spirit possession in which a spirit enters the object to communicate with the living.

Mun mai gong. "Ask-rice men." Rare type of Cantonese spirit medium (in this case, a male) in Hong Kong who enters a trance and verbally communicates his messages.

Mun mai poh. "Ask-rice women." Type of Cantonese spirit medium in Hong Kong who enters a trance and verbally communicates her messages.

Nian. Literally, "year." Mythological monster said to have prompted the tradition of wearing the color red in Chinese culture. According to legend, the nian creature emerged at the end of the year to attack villagers and ravage their livestock. It was later discovered that nian had three distinct weaknesses: It detested sunlight, was terrified of loud noises, and was fearful of the color red. Villagers, in turn, created a huge bonfire, painted their doors red, and ignited firecrackers when the creature emerged at the end of the year, driving it away forever. Since then, the tradition of wearing red has continued to be honored.

Niu T'ou. Ox head. Along with the demon Ma Mien, a trident-wielding, ox-headed attendant and messenger to Yen-lo, king of hell.

Pa Hsien. The Eight Immortals of Taoism. Immensely popular group of quasi-historical deities who represent the various levels of society (youth and elderly, wealth and poverty, masculine and feminine). Depicted frequently in art, architecture, and folk-tales, they are most associated with the Taoist attainment of immortality. The Eight Immortals are: Lu Tung Pin, Ti Kuai Li, Chang Kuo Lau, Ts'ao Kuo Chiu, Han Hsiang Tzu, Han Chung Li, Lan Ts'ai Ho, and Ho Hsien Ku.

Pai chia so. "Hundred Family Lock." Personal charm placed around a child's neck. The charm itself is a lock made from the money given by 100 friends to the father, who, in turn, adds his own money and symbolically binds his child to the 100 donors, ensuring him a long life.

Peng-lai. "Profusion of Weeds." One of three islands in traditional mythology which the first emperor of China believed was the paradise home of immortals. They were also said to be inhabited by fairies who drank from the fountain of life and ate gems scattered on the shores.

P'eng Niao. Mythical bird of colossal size; first referenced by the philosopher Chuang Tzu. With wings that spanned the heavenly clouds, it was said to have transformed from the oceanic leviathan Kun.

Peng-zu. Often called the Chinese Methuselah. Most associated with long life and surrounded by children in pictures. He was said to have lived 800 years.

P'o. One of two souls believed to inhabit the body. The yin, or negative aspect of the two, it is considered terrestrial and stays with the corpse upon death. If its descendants fail to placate it with a proper burial or with offerings adequate to sustain it in the afterlife, then the P'o can potentially turn into a malevolent Kuei.

Poe. Type of divination blocks consisting of two wooden pieces cut in the shape of two crescent moons that form a whole when joined together. This shape is raised to the forehead of the kneeling believer, then is dropped to the floor. The pattern formed on the floor is then read and interpreted, with both "good" and "bad" combinations.

Preta (Pret). Pan-Asian. Infamous "hungry ghosts" derived from Hinduism and Buddhism; denizens of the nether regions of afterlife who are literally starving for offerings their descendants have failed to provide. Described as having bloated bellies and extremely small mouths with drooping tongues, they are released upon the earth once a year by the King of Hell to look for offerings in an event known as the Gui Jie, the Feast of the Hungry Ghosts Festival.

In traditional belief, there are several types of deaths that can cause a spirit to become a hungry ghost: a particularly violent death, improper burial, suicide (forcing the soul to wander about the earth until its allotted time has expired, allowing it to go to the various hells), drowning (which removes the soul from the reincarnation process until a replacement is found), and dying without any living descendants.

Pu Songling. Chinese author most noted for writing the classic ghost stories anthology, "Liaozhai Zhiyi," or "Strange Stories from a Chinese Studio."

Pua pou. Beans used for divination; inscribed with markings or indents which the adept uses to determine positive or negative responses when answering inquiries.

Qian-li yan. Thousand-mile Eyes; one of two attendants (with Shun-feng er) who accompany the seafaring goddess Mazu and rescues sailors from peril.

Qingming jie. Clear Brightness Festival. Traditional spring celebration honoring the ancestral dead. In keeping with the belief that the prosperity of living descendants are closely related to the welfare of their ancestors in the afterlife, offerings of prayers, spirit money, food, incense, and candles are given to the latter to appease them. Celebrants visit family graves and clean them, with each family member given a specific function to fulfill. Later that day, it becomes an occasion for picnics and games, particularly kite-flying.

Quianchang. Term to describe a type of paper spirit money.

Ratna. Sanskrit. Wish-granting jewel; the Buddhist symbol of riches and donation. Also known as Mani.

Roc (Rukh). Mythical bird of colossal size.

San chiao fu. "Triangular spell" written on a piece of paper and then folded into a triangle. It is attached to the clothing of children to protect them against sickness and evil spirits.

Shan-kuei. Term to describe genies or celestial nymphs.

Shan-xiao. Mountain spirits that resemble one-legged monkey that dwell in trees. Living in central and southern China, they are said to be driven away by fireworks.

Shang Tu. More popularly known as "Xanadu." Popularized by Samuel Taylor Coleridge's poem, "In Xanadu did Kubla Khan/A stately pleasure-dome decree/Where Alph the sacred river ran/Through caverns measureless to man/Down to a sunless sea." Shang Tu was the summer capital of the Mongol Emperor Kublai Khan's Yuan Dynasty and was described as a paradise garden of epic delight and abundance.

Shao hui t'un fu. "Swallow-ashes Charm." Personal charm described as a piece of yellow paper inscribed with incantations meant to protect its bearer against demons. After it is burned, its ashes are mixed with water and then eaten.

Shen. Generic term for a class of benevolent spirits that includes ghosts, fairies, angels and genies. The ghosts are usually males who performed good deeds when alive, but died prior to having a son.

Shen hsien. Class of supernatural spirits described as non-human entities that were once mortal but have since regained immortality.

Shentu. One of the two door gods (Menshen) who protect families from demons.

Shenyi. "Deity clothing." Type of spiritual currency ritually burned and offered to spirits in the afterlife. These are thin sheets of yellow paper embellished with silver foil and a gold wash and adorned with images of dragons and characters of longevity. It is folded and wrapped around spirit money bundles and used specifically as offerings to the gods, particularly during festivals.

Shiehtuu. Type of cleansing exorcism performed in Taiwan on a specific family and their home for the purpose of reversing financial misfortune, disharmony within relationships, and illness. It is a highly complex ritual that involves much chanting and other ritual procedures.

Shi-zi. Lion. Popular animal not indigenous to China; most likely originating as gifts to imperial zoos from Western Asia. They equal dragons as decorative sculptures; most often depicted as guardian statues of gates, buildings, and temples. Appearing in pairs, the male lion on the right rests its left paw on a ball, while the female lion on the left rests its right paw on a cub.

Lions are more commonly seen today as human-operated puppets at Chinese New Year's composed of an enormous paper-mache head with fluttering eyes, a hinged mouth, and a streaming cloth body. These enormous costumes are used to perform the "lion dance" for special events to ward off evil and bring luck to weddings and new businesses. The lions are often accompanied by drums and gongs and escorted by masked performers called "lion lads," who tease the creature with fans for the crowd's enjoyment.

Shoujin. "Longevity gold." Type of spiritual currency ritually burned and offered to spirits in the afterlife. These are thin sheets of yellow paper embellished with a gold wash and adorned with images of the gods of longevity, happiness, and wealth.

Shou-xing. The god of longevity; depicted as an old man with an elongated forehead and carrying a peach, which is the symbol of life. Accompanied by a boy attendant, he is said to live in a palace in the South Pole that is surrounded by a garden that grows the herb of immortality.

Shui gui. Dangerous spirits of people who drowned or were hung. These ghosts cannot be reborn unless they find a proxy to replace them, someone who has to die in the same place and in the same manner as they did. Water ghosts are particularly feared in Chinese culture, lying in ambush for those who frequent the edge of the water.

Shui-kuei. Term to describe genies or celestial nymphs.

Shun-feng er. Favorable-wind ear; one of two attendants (with Qian-li yan) who accompany the seafaring goddess Mazu and rescues sailors from peril.

Sip ching guai. "Sneaky, Green Smoke Ghost." Type of poltergeist that manifests itself as green smoke.

Soul. Traditional belief holds that each person contains at least two souls: the yang, or positive Hun soul, and the yin, or negative P'o soul. The Hun (sometimes referred to as Shen) is celestial in nature and can potentially travel to paradise in the afterlife or to hell to be judged. The P'o (sometimes referred to as guai) is the more terrestrial of the two, remaining with the corpse for a time after death. If its descendants fail to placate it with a proper burial, or with offerings adequate to sustain it in the afterlife, the P'o can potentially turn into a malevolent Kuei.

Spirit Bride. The spirit of a deceased woman who died as a child and has returned in the dreams of living relatives, asking to be wedded to a living groom.

Spirit Marriage. Traditional practice of marrying the spirit of a deceased woman to a living groom. Having died as a child, this so-called "spirit bride" usually appears to living relatives in the form of a dream to express her desire to be betrothed. Family members usually find a groom by placing a "bait" in the middle of the road, normally a traditional red envelope. When a young man picks up the bait, the spirit bride's family quickly informs him that he is the chosen mate. Refusal of the role risks angering the bride, but a dowry is sometimes offered to allay his reluctance. They are then betrothed in a normal wedding, except the bride is represented only by her spirit tablet.

Spirit money. Spiritual currency ritually burned and offered to spirits in the afterlife. Types include the Fomao, Quianchang, Jiama, Shenyi, Shoujin, and Yuanbao.

Tao-nu. "Tao Woman." Type of sorceress known for curing ailments or communicating with spirits in the afterlife. They also use a Mu-jen, a small wooden effigy, as an instrument of spirit possession in which a spirit enters the object to communicate with the living.

Thao-thieh. Mythical creature described as only the horned head of a tiger or a dragon which lost its body as punishment for being a "glutton" and devouring human beings. Its face or mask is a recurring decorative motif in various ancient Chinese artifacts, including wine vessels, door handles, and bells.

Thou-tzu kuei. The spirits of women who died prior to having children and who now try to steal babies.

Three-legged Toad. Mythical three-legged amphibian said to reside on the moon and swallows it during eclipses.

Ti hsien. Class of spiritual entities described as living saints; people who have liberated themselves from the needs and bonds of human mortality.

Ti T'sang Wang. The King of the Earth's Womb and the ultimate authority of the underworld, even above Yen-lo. He is the deliverer of souls from hell.

Ti yu. Hell, literally, "earth prison." Place of punishment in the afterlife; made up of 10 levels (in some accounts 18) with 16 sub-hells within each layer. As bureaucratic as the world of the living, each level has its own tribunal, complete with a judge, a set of enforcers, and a particular form of punishment appropriate for the crime committed. The first level is said to be a type of courtroom where sentence is initially passed, and the last level is where sinners are reborn in whatever form their merits have afforded.

The concept of "hell" and punishment most likely came from India, introduced through Buddhism. Hell is ruled by Yen-lo (Yama in Hinduism) and has several attendants: Ma Mien (Horse Face) and Niu T'ou (Ox Head) and two ministers collectively called Wu Ch'ang Kuei (Yang Wu

Ch'ang and Yin Wu Ch'ang, Male and Female Impermanence Ghosts, respectively). However, they are all subordinate to the ultimate authority of the underworld, Ti T'sang Wang, the King of the Earth's Womb. It is he who delivers souls from hell.

T'ien hsien. Class of supernatural spirits described as deities who have eternal life in heaven.

Tou Shen. The dreaded Spirit of Smallpox.

Tou-shen Niang-niang. Taoist goddess who protects against smallpox. She had four sons (Sha Shen, Chen Shen, Ma Shen, and P'an Shen) who protect the afflicted at different stages of sickness and recovery.

Tsang fang. Term to describe a haunted house, usually where a violent crime or death has occurred.

Ts'ao Kuo Chiu. One of the famous Eight Immortals of Taoism (Pa Hsien); a former member of the imperial court and the patron saint of theater. His symbols are a tablet of recommendation and a pair of castanets.

Wang-liang. Term to describe ogres, including malevolent spirits of waters and forests.

Wu. Term to describe a traditional shaman or witch; the original shaman of old China. Its role has varied over the centuries, ranging from spirit-mediums to the afterlife, exorcising spirits to overseeing funeral ceremonies, and even rain-dancing. Its existence has been recorded since ancient times and it continues to exist today in rural areas and provinces.

Wu Ch'ang Kuei. Collective term for the Ghosts of Impermanence: the male Yang Wu Ch'ang and the female Yin Wu Ch'ang. Accompanied by Ma Mien and Niu T'ou, they are the messengers of Yen-Lo, the king of hell.

Wudu. The so-called "Five Poisons" of Chinese culture: the lizard, the snake, the toad, the scorpion and the centipede. Known for their potency, images of these animals are incorporated within cakes, clothing, and paper charms on the belief that its bearer is protected against the collective creatures' bites and stings.

Wu-xing. The five elements that comprise all matter in the world. Each element is associated with a specific color and direction: wood (blue, east), earth (yellow, center), metal (white, west), water (black, north), and fire (red, south).

Xian nu. Fairies. "Sacred maidens." Diverse class of magical beings often associated with goddesses and immortals. Living in lunar and earthly paradises, they are popular in legend and literature. Unlike fairy goddesses (Shen), however, the Xian nu are not worshipped.

Yao. Term to describe demons or goblins. Sometimes used synonymously with the Kuei.

Yeren. "Wild Man." One of several unclassified hominids found throughout Asia. Living in the mountainous forest regions of Hubei Province, it is described as bipedal, ranging from 6 to 10 feet tall, and covered with reddish-brown fur. Because of the discovery of fossils of the massive Gigantopithecus ape in China, some scientists have theorized that the Yeren may be a living descendant of that prehistoric species.

Yin fu. "Sealed spells." Spells written in red ink on yellow paper, stamped with a seal, and placed in front of temple idols.

Xian Nu

Yin Yang. Taoist principle of duality that permeates the entire universe; the coexistence and harmony of opposites. Yin is the feminine, negative principle, while Yang is the masculine, positive principle. Together, they comprise the Tao.

Yin Yang eyes. Term to describe the ability of some people to see ghosts clearly and regularly.

Ying-zhou. "Ocean Continent," or Fairyland. One of three islands in traditional mythology that the first emperor of China believed was the paradise home of immortals. They were also said to be inhabited by fairies who drank from the fountain of life and ate gems scattered on the shores.

Yuanbao. Term to describe a type of paper spirit money.

Yulu. One of the two door gods (Menshen) who protect families from demons.

Zhong-gui. Famous exorcist and demon queller. Originally a man who killed himself after failing to attain first class ranking in the civil service examinations, he was later honored by the emperor with an imperial burial. In gratitude, he vowed to free the world of demons and ghosts. He is often depicted in pictures brandishing a sword and chasing five creatures. Known also as Chung Kuei.

Zhong-gui

Japan

Ao Ando. Type of goblin that appears at night when the lamp runs out of oil.

Abura-sumashi. "Oil presser." Spirit believed to be originally a man who stole oil used for heating a home or lighting lamps. The spirit now surprises people along the mountain pass.

Akai-kami-aoi-kami. "Red toilet paper, blue toilet paper." Disembodied voice said to be heard in bathrooms, asking victims occupying the toilets if they require their toilet paper to be in either red or blue colors. Selecting red brings about a bloody death, while selecting blue means having their blood drained from their bodies. Selecting neither meant being whisked off to the underworld.

Akamanto. "Red Cape." Disembodied voice said to be heard in bathrooms, asking victims occupying the toilets if they desired a red cape. If they say "yes," their skin is ripped off their backs.

Akaname. Type of monster that appears in neglected bathrooms with filthy bathtubs. Described as red in complexion, it uses its long, dangling tongue to dine on the mildew and scum around the tub late at night.

Amikiri. So-called "Net Cutter." A mischievous, clawed creature that is fond of cutting nets and lives within the eaves and hidden spaces of a house.

Anoyo. Term to describe the world beyond our world, a place over yonder that usually means the realm of spirits.

Aramitama. Impure spirit; the initial status of a ghost immediately after a person's death. Offerings from the deceased's family can later turn this ghost into a sorei, or ancestral spirit, capable of helping and guiding descendants in times of need. However, spirits who do not achieve the status of sorei can become caught in the purgatory between life and death and may return to haunt the living.

Ashiarai Yashiki. "Foot-washing mansion." Unusual supernatural entity described simply as a disembodied foot and leg, enormous in size, that crashes through roofs and ceilings in the middle of the night and vocally demands to be washed. Failure to comply with its request meant continuous trampling and destruction.

Azuki Arai. "Red bean washer." Unusual supernatural entity more often heard than seen, although some accounts describe it as a short, balding, and physically disproportionate male. It is often heard washing native azuki beans in a basket, all the while singing, "Wash me beans, or catch me a human to eat…shoki-shoki!" Generally considered harmless, those who hear this creature can seldom see it.

Bakechochin. "Haunted lantern." Ghostly lamp said to be the home of spirits, particularly the ghosts of people who died with hate-filled hearts. Described as having eyes and a mouth with a protruding tongue, the residing spirits are said to attack anyone foolish enough to light the lantern.

Bake-Jizo. The statue of the Bodhisattva Jizo, the savior of children's ghosts; believed to walk around at night in various guises.

Bakemono. From "bakeru," meaning "to change." It is a generic term for a diverse class of human and non-human supernatural entities that have undergone some type of transformation or shifting of form. The term includes beings with horrific features, shape-shifting animals, and even animated objects. They are classified separately from yurei and oni.

Bakeneko. So-called "ghost cat." A feline that develops supernatural attributes through various means (developing a long tail, living past 13 years, growing to a certain weight). These cats are said to be able to speak, shape-shift, and even walk on two legs. Bakenekos have also been known to raise the dead, hence the Japanese superstition of keeping cats away from bodies of the recently deceased. They can be both good and bad.

Bakenekos with long tails that forked into two are called nekomata.

Baku. Fabulous creature said to devour bad dreams. Described as having the snout and tusks of an elephant and the curly-haired body of a Chinese lion, they are used as a talisman against nightmares.

Bancho Sarayashiki. Popular ghostly folktale about the spirit of a murdered woman named Okiku. Her origin varying with each retelling (from daughter to servant to even object of desire), the story revolves around Okiku's spirit, which appears every night by a well and counts out loud the 10 plates she is supposed to possess—only to come up one short at nine. She then weeps and must continue counting cyclically until she finds the 10th plate, but with the exact same results. In one version, she is finally put to rest when a friend, upon hearing her fate, jumps out and yells "10" before Okiku can sob for not reaching the correct count, thus, ultimately releasing her from her fate.

Benzaiten (Benten). One of the Seven Gods of Good Luck (Shichi fukujin). Female deity regarded as a patroness of art and music and associated with the accumulation of worldly possessions. She is said to be named after the Sarasvati River in India.

Bishamonten (Tamonten). One of the Seven Gods of Good Luck (Shichi fukujin). Deity of wealth; depicted as wearing armor and carrying a trident and a small pagoda. His Sanskrit name is Vaishravana and he protects the northern quadrant as one of the Guardians of the Four Directions.

Biwa-bokuboku. Term for a type of musical instrument that has gained sentience and mobility over its years of use. It is described as humanoid and wearing a kimono, but having a traditional Japanese lute for a head. It is considered a type of Tsukumo-gami.

Boroboro-ton. Term for the haunted comforter, or blanket, for a futon, described as battered in appearance and having eyes. Considered a type of tsukumo-gami, it is believed to walk about the room in search of prey.

Bosatsu. Native term for a bodhisattva.

Botandoro. Famous ghost story in which a student, Saburo, falls in love with Otsuyu, the beautiful daughter of his father's best friend. They secretly meet and decide to wed. However, Saburo falls ill and does not see Otsuyu for a long time. When he later searches for her, he is told that she and her maid have died. As Saburo is praying for her during the

Obon Festival, he is miraculously approached by Otsuyu and her maid! Opposed to their union, it is revealed that Saburo's aunt started the rumor of Otsuyu's demise and also told Otsuyu that Saburo had died.

Seemingly reunited, Saburo and Otsuyu resume their secret meetings and consummate their love while her maid, holding a lantern decorated with peony flowers, keeps watch. Saburo's servant, however, witnesses one of the unions and sees his master making love to a corpse while another corpse stands guard.

Saburo's servant seeks help from a Buddhist priest and the three finally locate the graves of Otsuyu and her maid. Convinced that the two women were actually ghosts, Saburo imprisons himself inside a house covered with amulets and charms to ward off the spirits. But upon breaking their union, he immediately falls ill without his love.

Fearing for his deteriorating health, the servant removes the protective amulet from the front door, allowing the two spirits to enter. The next morning, he finds his master in the embrace of a corpse, but his face is filled with peace.

Bura-bura. Term for a type of supernatural paper lantern described as having human facial features and lit from within by a candle. Together with the Kara-kasa, they fly through the air and scare unsuspecting passersby. Like some tsukumo-gami, they were once believed to be household objects that became mischievous spirits due to their former owner's abuse or neglect.

Buruburu. Ghost whose name is derived from the sound of shivering. It is described as a quivering elderly man or woman who attaches itself onto the back of its victim, sending a chill down the spine and causing the victim to die of fright.

Butsudan. Term for a household Buddhist shrine.

Butterfly. Insect considered by both Chinese and Japanese as souls of the living and of the dead.

Chokaro. Native term for Chang Kuo Lau, one of the Eight Immortals of Taoism (Pa Hsien).

Cho-ken-ju-jiki-netsu-gaki. Type of gaki; native term for the "Hungry Ghost," or preta, in Hinduism and Buddhism. This kind is said to devour the refuse of funeral pyres and even the clay found in graves.

Daikokuten (Daikoku). One of the Seven Gods of Good Luck (Shichi fukujin). Benign deity representing prosperity. He carries a magic mallet, a radish, a rat, and bales of rice.

Dojojin. One of Emma-sama's two assistants in hell that holds the karmic scrolls and mirror.

Domeijin. One of Emma-sama's two assistants in hell that holds the karmic scrolls and mirror.

Dorotabo. "Rice-paddy man." Folkloric creature described as being composed entirely of mud, emerging from the paddies as an upper torso with three-fingered hands and a single eye in the middle of its forehead. Several accounts detail his origins as that of a farmer who lost his land while alive, returning to haunt the living and repeatedly chanting, "Return my field."

Ebisu. One of the Seven Gods of Good Luck (Shichi fukujin). Patron deity of fishermen, depicted as being portly and carrying a sea bream and a fishing rod. He is said to be a descendant of the founding gods of Japan.

Ema. "Horse picture." Wooden wishing plaques or placards upon which worshippers write their wishes, then hang them on Shinto shrines for the kami gods to see and fulfill. They are often painted with animals and other imagery.

Emma-sama (Emma-O, Emma-ten). From the Sanskrit Yama; King of jigoku, or hell. He is sometimes shown with two assistants, Dojojin and Domeijin, holding the karmic scrolls and mirror.

Enen-ra. Atmospheric supernatural entity best described as smoke derived from fires. Although considered harmless, it has the ability to take the form of people, animals, and occasionally even monsters.

Eyeless Woman Monster. A literally eyeless woman who is used by ravenous ghosts as a lure to procure victims. She frequents graveyards and shrines, enticing men into a romantic dalliance, only to have them meet certain death.

Eyes-in-Hand Freak. Type of blind spirit that has its eyes on its palms. Haunts marshes and spies on lovers having trysts within the reeds.

Fei Tcheu. Chinese. Men with flying heads; known as Hitoban in Japan. Sometimes associated with Rokurokubi.

Fuda-hegashi. Type of ghost that will either bribe or threaten a person to remove a protective ofuda from the front door so that it can gain entry into a household.

Fujo-ko-byaku-gaki. Type of gaki; native term for the Hungry Ghost, or preta, in Hinduism and Buddhism. This type of gaki is said to devour the refuse and filth of the street.

Fukkeshi-baba. Fire extinguishing gag. A woman who is blamed for extinguishing candles on a seemingly windless night.

Fukurokuju. One of the Seven Gods of Good Luck (Shichi fukujin). Deity of wisdom and one of the Three Stars of Longevity. He is often depicted with an extremely elongated forehead and wielding a fan.

Funa yurei. "Ship ghouls." General term to describe a ghost ship (similar to the Flying Dutchman motif) and drowned crew, as well as other sea-faring phantoms. This belief is most common in coastal areas, which are always potentially dangerous. Appearing as both living sailors and as corpses, they are often encountered in twilight or in foggy weather conditions, particularly around Obon.

These phantoms have also been known to ask sailors for a ladle upon meeting and then to proceed to capsize the boat by scooping water into it. To this day, many fishermen bring a bottomless ladle with them during their voyages.

Fusui. The native term for the art of Feng Shui.

Futakuchi Onna. "Two-mouthed woman." Female monster described as a woman with two mouths: a normal one in front and another mouth on the back of her head that's hidden beneath her hair. The secondary mouth is even said to have a mind of its own. The woman is depicted in various stories: In one, she is married to a miser who rarely eats. Another story maintains that the woman was originally a step-daughter who was left to starve because her new mother favored her biological daughter. This scarcity of eating prompted the second mouth to develop, demanding food and even gaining the ability to animate the woman's own hair as tendrils to bring the food to itself.

Gaki. Native term for the Indian and Chinese hungry ghost, Preta.

Gashadokuro. "Starving skeleton." Towering skeletal ghost said to be made up of the bones of many people who died in battle or who starved to death. They appear in areas where great numbers of bodies have been left out, unburied. Reaching over a hundred feet in height, it roams the streets after midnight, emitting a ringing noise and devouring the head and flesh of victims unable to escape its approach. It then adds the new bones to its body.

Goryo. The deified spirit of an aristocratic person who died as a martyr. Considered extremely vengeful and capable of wreaking havoc against their living antagonists.

Gozu. Bull-headed demons in Buddhist hell.

Hakutaku. Fabulous beast culturally imported from China; described as a four-legged furry mammal with the head of a horned, bearded man with a singular eye on its forehead. It also has horns and a pair of three eyes on each flank. Its image is used as a charm against misfortune and calamity.

Hanadaka tengu. One of two types of shape-shifting mountain goblins notorious for preying on the secret desires of pious monks and leading them astray.

Hannya. Horned female demon that frequently appears in Noh and Kabuki plays. Once a beautiful woman, she went mad and became demonically possessed. She is infamous for devouring children.

Hashi Hime. "Bridge princess." Supernatural entity that attacks travelers and couples who cross bridges. Often described as the embodiment of revenge and jealousy, it was said to have orginally been a human being, but was turned into a monster from her remorse of a past betrayal. Appearing as an alluring woman to male victims (and a male to female victims), she then reveals her true, seething form and causes the victim to go insane. The Hashi Hime is quite fond of targeting happy couples.

Hassen. Native term for the Eight Immortals of Taoism (Pa Hsien).

Hearn, Lafcadio. (1850-1904). Writer who was born in Greece, raised in Ireland, but who later moved to America and, ultimately, Japan. His fascination with Japanese culture opened his adopted country's rich cultural heritage to Western readers. He became a Japanese citizen, took the name Koizumi Yakumo, and married a Japanese woman. Two of his books, "Kwaidan," and "In Ghostly Japan," are classics in the supernatural folklore field, the former being adapted for film.

Heike crabs. Crabs whose carapaces resemble the grimacing faces of deceased samurai. They are said to be the reincarnated souls of warriors who perished in the battle of Dan-no-ura.

Hidarugami. The spirit of hunger; an evil-possessing entity believed to be the spirit of someone who originally died of hunger and who now wishes to haunt the living and make them experience the same fate. They are believed to haunt trails, caves, and other frequented areas of a mountain. As prevention from being possessed, travelers are advised to eat well prior to climbing.

Hideri Gami. Human-headed creature believed to be responsible for droughts.

Himamushi-nyudo. Creature fond of drinking the oil from lamps; described as a hideous man with an unusually long neck that emerges from the edge of the elevated floor to feed.

Hitoban. Men with flying heads; known as Fei Tcheu in China. Sometimes associated with Rokurokubi.

Hitodama. The spirit of the newly deceased after it just left the body; said to be blue in color. These blue lights are often seen hovering above graves in cemeteries.

Hitotsume-kozo. Creature resembling a bald 10-year-old boy in traditional garb with a long tongue and a single eye in the middle of his face. Though generally considered benign, they are also notorious pranksters, running around, scaring people.

Hohkigami. Type of spirit said to inhabit old brooms. They are said to dust and clean a home at night.

Hoko. The spirit of a 1,000-year-old tree; said to resemble a black dog with an almost human face, but with no tail.

Hokusai, Katsushika. Recognized master of grotesqueries whose impressive sketches and woodblock drawings are collected in the 15-volume work, Hokusai Manga.

Hone Onna. Skeletal ghost who disguises herself as a beautiful woman in order to have intercourse with victims, only to suck their life-force out of their bodies.

Hotei. One of the Seven Gods of Good Luck (Shichi fukujin). Deity of benevolence and contentment; depicted as a rotund priest who often appears surrounded by many children. He carries a bag of treasures over his shoulder and wields a fan.

Hyaku monogatari. So-called "One Hundred Supernatural Tales." Seventeenth-century traditional storytelling game in which 100 lit candles were placed in lamp stands and hooded with blue-colored paper. Each of the assembled participants would then tell a ghost story, extinguishing a candle after each tale. The room would get dimmer with each story told. After the final candle is put out, something horrifying is expected to happen.

Hyakki yako. So-called "Night Parade of 100 Demons." Enormous procession of freaks, goblins, imps, animated objects, and ghosts marching down streets and the mountains on certain summer nights. The creatures would vanish by dawn.

Ikiryo. Spirit of a discarded mistress or wife. This apparition, the spirit of a still-living person created from her extreme rage or jealousy, can pursue the male victim and cause him to become ill.

Ikkaku Sennin. Wizard possessing a single horn (signifying his mother was a deer) who cornered a rain dragon inside a cave and brought drought upon the land. Popular subject of netsuke carvings.

Inu-gami. A malevolent spirit derived from the capture of the soul of a tortured and starved animal, most commonly a dog. This spirit is used by witches (inu-gami-moichi) to possess the body of a living person, causing them to become mentally and physically ill, and even causing them to behave like a canine.

Itako. Shaman spirit mediums who are traditionally old, blind women. Apprentices enter training as girls before their first menstruation and spend many years learning ritual prayers, fortune-telling, and chants. Upon completion of a ritual called kamitsuke, they are then considered qualified to practice their craft independently.

Jigoku. Term for hell.

Jiki-doku-gaki. Type of gaki; native term for the hungry ghost, or preta, in Hinduism and Buddhism. This kind is said to eat poison.

Jiki-fu-gaki. Type of gaki; native term for the hungry ghost, or preta, in Hinduism and Buddhism. This kind is said to devour wind.

Jiki-fun-gaki. Type of gaki; native term for the hungry ghost, or preta, in Hinduism and Buddhism. This kind is said to devour feces.

Jiki-ke-gaki. Type of gaki; native term for the hungry ghost, or preta, in Hinduism and Buddhism. This kind is said to devour smells.

Jiki-ketsu-gaki. Type of gaki; native term for the hungry ghost, or preta, in Hinduism and Buddhism. This kind is said to drink blood.

Jiki-ko-ki. Incense-eating goblins. Type of gaki; native term for the jungry ghost, or preta, in Hinduism and Buddhism. They are condemned by karma to seek their food in the smoke of incense. This is punishment for making bad incense and selling them for gain when they were alive.

Jiki-kwa-gaki. Type of gaki; native term for the hungry ghost, or preta, in Hinduism and Buddhism. This kind is said to devour fire.

Jiki-man-gaki. Type of gaki; native term for the hungry ghost, or preta, in Hinduism and Buddhism. This kind is said to devour the fake hair of wigs that adorn the statues of certain deities.

Jiki-niku-gaki. Type of gaki; native term for the hungry ghost, or preta, in Hinduism and Buddhism. This kind is said to devour flesh.

Jikininki. Type of gaki; native term for the hungry ghost, or preta, in Hinduism and Buddhism. Originally selfish or greedy individuals when alive, they are now cursed in the afterlife to go out at night and feed on corpses. This type belongs to the 26th class of pretas in Buddhist hell.

Jinmenju. "Human-faced Tree." Mysterious tree said to bear fruit that are actually human heads, complete with eyes, ears, noses, and mouths. They giggle at passersby, and some accounts even have them capable of speaking.

Jizo. Bosatsu is the guardian of those who suffer, particularly pregnant women and sickly children. Portrayed in statues as wearing a red bib and holding a staff in one hand and a jewel talisman in the other, he is said to help children who died young into the next world. These spirits include children who were aborted or miscarried.

Ju-chu-gaki. Type of gaki; native term for the hungry ghost, or preta, in Hinduism and Buddhism. This kind is said to have been born inside trees, punished by the growth of the grain within the wood.

Jurojin. One of the Seven Gods of Good Luck (Shichi fukujin). Patron deity of learning; one of the three stars, or gods, of longevity. He is generally depicted as having a high forehead and carrying a fan and a staff.

Kaibutsu. Umbrella term to describe imaginary or fantastic creatures.

Kaidan. Broad term meaning "ghost story." Usually refers to classic tales set during the historic Edo Period. It is made up of two characters: kai (meaning strange or mysterious) and dan (meaning talk). Japanophile Lafcadio Hearn used a romanized style for its spelling and referred to it as "Kwaidan" in his classic book.

Kami. Native Shinto deities; spirits believed to reside literally everywhere in nature (rivers, mountains, rocks, even household objects). This pantheon of gods is said to number over 8 million.

Kamikiri. Hair-cutting monster; creature with pincer-like hands that punishes the vain by cutting off locks of their hair.

Kanashibari. The infamous tie-down ghost; a pressing or choking spirit known for sitting on the chests of half-asleep people and suffocating them. Victims claim to be helpless during the experience, unable to move or breathe while staring at the spirit's hideous, laughing face. In recent years, it has been closely associated with the medical condition called sleep paralysis.

Kanro. Term for amrita, the ambrosia of the gods.

Kanshoshi. Native term for Han Hsiang Tzu, one of the Eight Immortals of Taoism (Pa Hsien).

Kappa. Nefarious river imp about the size of a small child; described as having the beaked head of a monkey and the body of a turtle. Although depicted in more recent times as being playful, they were originally quite feared, dragging washerwomen and children into the water, drowning them, and then drinking their blood. It likes cucumbers and wrestling. Its crown has a hollow that is filled with a liquid from which it acquires its strength and powers. Bowing to a kappa will cause it to bow back in return, draining the liquid from the crown and weakening it for an escape.

Kara-kasa. "Paper umbrella." Term for a type of supernatural lacquer-paper umbrella; described as having a single eye and a dangling tongue. In place of its handle is a single hairy male leg and foot. Together with the Bura-bura, they fly through the air and scare unsuspecting passersby. Like some tsukumo-gami, they were once believed to be household objects that became mischievous spirits due to their former owner's abuse or neglect.

Karako. Characters in art that resemble little Chinese children with two small tufts of hair on an otherwise bald head, wearing pajama-type clothes. They figure prominently in porcelain objects and traditional netsuke carvings.

Karasu tengu. One of two types of shape-shifting mountain goblins notorious for preying on the secret desires of pious monks and leading them astray. This type is literally half-bird, complete with a crow's head, a body covered with feathers, and claws in place of hands and feet. This type is also known for its martial arts prowess and is credited with teaching some of the country's best swordsmen.

Karura. Native term for the garuda. Also known as konjicho.

Karyobinga. From Kalavinka; celestial musicians with the heads of people and the bodies of birds.

Kappa

Kasenko. Native term for Ho Hsien Ku, one of the Eight Immortals of Taoism (Pa Hsien).

Kasha. Opportunistic ghoul known for stalking cremation grounds and stealing corpses to feed on.

Kawataro. Perhaps the earliest account of the kappa; described as a diminutive, naked figure with short hair, able to walk upright and speak with a human voice. Aquatic by nature, it is fond of stealing fruits and vegetables from the fields. It is also notorious for pulling livestock into the water to drink their blood through their rears. Like the kappa, it has a concave head, which, when filled with water, gives the creature great strength.

Keito. Term for dragon-like creature responsible for eclipses. Also known as ketu.

Kejora. Female ghost described as having unusual eyes and a face covered with hair.

Ki. The native term for chi, or energy.

Kichijoten. Female deity who sometimes replaces Jurojin or Fukurokuju as one of the Seven Gods of Good Luck (Shichi fukujin).

Kifuda. Small memorial tablets made of wood and placed on graves.

Kimnara. Native term for the kinnara. Celestial musicians with the heads of people and the bodies of birds.

King of Freaks. Misshapen being believed to visit households at 6 o'clock in the evening.

Kirin. The native version of the Chinese chi'lin, or unicorn. Described as having a fleshy singular horn on top of a dragon-like head and the scaly body of a deer, it is extremely benevolent with no harmful intent toward any living creature. It is used as a symbol of authority by the imperial court.

Kiten. Buddhist angels. Known also as tennin.

Kitsune. Native name for a fox spirit, which, in Chinese, Japanese, and Korean lore, is a trickster entity notorious of changing forms to seduce, frighten, or harass its victims. It's even been known to shape-shift into a beautiful woman to bewitch a man and drive him into madness. The kitsune is considered the messenger of the fertility god Inari, who descends from the mountains to assist in the cultivation of rice. Unlike its Western counterparts (where people become animals), the kitsune are originally animals that turn into people.
    A fox with nine tails, which it developed after living for several hundred years, is said to be endowed with magical powers.

Kitsune-bi. Literally, "fox fire." A tongue of red flame produced by the fox spirit, sometimes to lead men astray from the road when travelling. It's often been compared to the European Will-o'-the-wisp.

Kitsune-no-yomeiri. So-called "fox wedding." Unusual phenomenon where the presence of rain coincides with bright sunshine. It is said that a fox bride is then headed to the home of her groom in the forest.

Kitsune-okuri. "Fox expelling," annual festival held to avert the kitsune's mischief and mayhem for the coming year. Led by a priest, a procession of villagers carry straw effigies of foxes and people to the nearby mountain and bury them.

Kitsunetsuki. Fox possession; the entering of a fox spirit into a host body (usually a woman) and causing the person to behave irrationally, going as far as giving the victim abilities she didn't previously have. The person's facial expressions even begin to assume the likeness of the kitsune. The victim's diet also changes, taking on the spirit's cravings for tofu. This phenomenon, historically treated with exorcisms and even beatings, has long been associated with native psychosis and mental illness.

Koizumi Yakumo. The adopted Japanese name of writer Lafcadio Hearn.

Kokkuri. Type of native divination game popular in the 1880s. Uses an apparatus described as a round lid or tray balanced on three bamboo rods tied together to create a tripod. Invoking a spirit to occupy the structure, the participants gently place their hands on the lid and ask questions. The spirit responds by tilting the lid in a particular direction as specified in the question, lifting one of the tripod's legs on the opposite side.

Konaki Jiji. "Old man who cries like a baby." Supernatural entity believed to be an old man, who takes the form of a weeping baby seemingly lost in the woods. When an unsuspecting passerby picks up the "child," it reverts back to an old man and crushes the victim under his weight.

Konoha tengu. One of two types of shape-shifting mountain goblins notorious for preying on the secret desires of pious monks and leading them astray. This type resembles a mountain monk, or yamabushi, except it possesses an extremely elongated nose in place of a beak. It also has red skin and massive wings. Like the Karasu tengu, the Konoha tengu is known for its martial arts prowess. It is also known as Hanadaka tengu.

Konoyo. Term to describe the natural world in which we live.

Kosode no Te. "Hands in the sleeves." Term for a haunted kimono described as an empty robe, but with mysterious arms slithering out of its sleeves. It is believed to be the ghost of a woman longing for something. She is either a prostitute seeking a manly embrace or an old woman longing for her younger days. It is considered a type of Tsukumo-gami.

Kitsune

Koto-furunushi. Term for a type of musical instrument that has gained sentience and mobility over years of use. It is described as a traditional floor harp that is able to walk on its four legs. It is considered a type of Tsukumo-gami.

Kubikajiri. Type of ghost said to roam graveyards to feast on the heads of living and dead bodies. If it is unable to find one, it will then feast on the heads of other creatures. Its presence is said to be preceded by the pungent smell of fresh blood.

Kuchisake Onna. "Slit-mouth woman." Folklore character turned modern urban legend. Hundreds of years ago, there supposedly lived a beautiful but vain woman who was the wife of a samurai. Suspecting her of infidelity, her jealous husband slit her mouth from ear to ear and asked sadistically, "Who will think you're beautiful now?"

This character and story resurfaced in the 1970s, when a woman wearing a surgical mask was said to appear on foggy nights and ask passersby if she was beautiful. The woman was believed to be the disfigured victim of a botched surgery. If the passerby said "yes," she would then lift up her mask and show the person the ghastly incision and then repeat her question. If the person replied, "no," she would then kill him.

Kuchiyose. The practice of speaking in the voice of the deceased, as done by itakos, or shaman spirit mediums.

Kushii. The native version of the Loch Ness monster; described as a sea monster that has inhabited Lake Kushiro in Hokkaido.

Kwaku-shin-gaki. Type of Gaki, native term for the hungry ghost, or preta, in Hinduism and Buddhism. This type is described as "cauldron bodies" and is compared to a living furnace. Its body is filled with fire, causing its internal fluids to bubble like a boiling pot.

Long Arms and Long Legs. Extremely popular netsuke motif borrowed from China; two characters (Long Arms or tenaga, and ashinaga or Long Legs) embracing each other to symbolize the successful outcome of cooperation.

Maneki-neko. So-called beckoning or enticing cat; popular feline figure made of varying materials and depicted with one paw raised up in a welcoming gesture. It symbolizes a merchant's success in drawing in customers, as well as his good business fortune.

Manji. Native term for swatiska.

Meko pagoat. So-called "cat punishment." An old Ainu belief that the spirit of a dead cat can possess the living, causing them to imitate the movements of a cat before wasting away and dying painfully while mewing.

Mezu. Horse-headed demons in Buddhist hell.

Miko. Type of shaman (traditionally, unwed women) known for traversing the world of mortals and the gods, possessing wisdom and the power to heal.

Mikoshi nyudo. "Look-up Monk." Bald Buddhist priest said to have the ability to become taller by stretching its neck. It is known to look over room-dividers or menacingly stare at people in the face from above by leaning over their shoulders while standing behind them.

Mitsume kozo. Creature described as appearing like a priest, except possessing three eyes.

Mizuko. Literally, "water babies." A reference to aborted fetuses.

Mojabune. Type of Umi-bozu found off the coast of Honshu at Shiriyazaki; fisherman describe it as a towering sea monster. Locals mix miso paste with water and pour it into the ocean to drive the creature away.

Mokumoku Ren. So-called "myriad eyes." Spirits that manifest themselves as disembodied eyes seen in holes on torn shoji screens, the paper used for traditional sliding doors in Japanese homes.

Mononoke. Generic term to describe a natural spirit residing in an object; believed to be malevolent towards human beings. Often compared to poltergeists, they can be driven away by reciting Buddhist sutras.

Moryo. Diminutive creature fond of eating the livers of dead bodies. Red and black in color, it is said to resemble a person with long ears and red eyes.

Mujina. Native term for the badger. Like its fox (kitsune) and raccoon dog (tanuki) cousins, it is considered a trickster spirit in local folklore, capable of shifting forms to deceive people.

Mujina. Female spirit described in Lafcadio Hearn's book, "Kwaidan." Late one night, a traveler noticed a well-dressed woman weeping bitterly by herself. When he attempted to console her, he looked into her face and saw that she had no eyes, nose, or mouth at all. The frightened man screamed and ran to a roadside soba noodle seller. After he recounted his story to the vendor, the merchant revealed his own featureless face.

Namahage. "Blister-peeler." Term to describe horned demons that frequent homes during winter, looking for lazy children to punish. Adorned with fangs and a straw snow coat, they punish the idle in varying degrees, ranging from simple scolding to peeling the blisters off the feet of the idle warming themselves by the fire. Males have bright red skin while females have blue-green skin. Though fearsome in appearance and wielding farm implements, they are actually considered harbingers of good fortune.

Namazu. So-called "earthquake fish." A giant catfish believed to live deep beneath the streams of Japan. Its movements are said to cause earthquakes.

Nekomata. "Forked cat." A bakeneko (ghost cat) whose long tail has forked over a period of time. Besides being able to speak, it is feared for its abilitiy to raise the recently deceased simply by jumping over their heads. It then controls the reanimated corpse to exact revenge upon those who have wronged them. Aside from devouring the occasional person, they also have a fondness for drinking lamp oil.

Ni-o Guardians. A pair of fierce Buddhist guardians who stand guard inside temple entrances to ward off demons. Posing in dramatic fashion with one guardian with its mouth agape while the other with its mouth closed, these semi-clothed figures are known as Vajrapani in Sanskrit and Kongo Rikishi in Japanese Buddhism.

Ninso. Term for a sidewalk fortune-teller.

Nobiagari. Mysterious entity that appears in various guises along waterway paths, approaching unsuspecting passersby from behind. When the victim turns around to look, this creature then grows massively in size and gives chase, going as far as stretching its neck, limbs, and torso to inch closer.

Nodeppo. Creature described as a bat of extreme age that engulfs its victims with its wings and sucks out their breath until they die.

Nopperabo. Faceless ghost known for taking delight in frightening victims with his or her featureless visage. It is often associated with Lafcadio Hearn's story of the Mujina, the Japanese name for the trickster badger. Some theorize that this entity is actually a kitsune or tanuki imitating the human form.

Nue. Fierce composite creature imported from China; described as having the head of a monkey, the body of a tanuki, the legs of a tiger, and the tail of a serpent. It was considered an evil spirit and a harbinger of illness and bad luck.

Nukekubi. "Removable head." Supernatural being described as a person with the ability to completely detach his or her head and neck, allowing it to fly around and feed before reconnecting with its host body. It normally preys on insects and worms, but has also been known to devour human flesh. Failure to reattach its head to its body before sunrise means certain death and decay.

Nuppeppo. Anthropomorphic blob that hides beneath the eaves of temples. Resembling a jelly-like head with stubby arms and legs, it can be found walking aimlessly about on deserted streets and has been known to frequent abandoned temples.

Nure Onna. Wet Woman. Creature feared by coastal fishermen in northern Japan. She is described as a serpent with a woman's head; long, wet hair; sharp claws; and a flickering tongue. She is said to live among the shoreline rubbish and seaweed, feeding on offal and, occasionally, people.

Nurikabe. Kyushu. "Plastered wall." Type of spirit described as a mysterious wall that appears in front of passersby and prevents them from proceeding forward. Attempting to run away from it just causes it to appear in front of the victims again, mysteriously. Normally invisible to the human eye, they have been known to imitate the walls of a house or building.

Obake. Umbrella term for a myriad class of supernatural spirits, creatures, and entities.

Obariyon. Mysterious supernatural entity described as a featureless being that frequents lonely trails at night and appears behind unwitting travelers. Crying "Obusaritei," (meaning, "I want a piggyback ride,") it then proceeds to drop on the victim's shoulders, slowly increasing its size and weight and pinning the victim to the ground.

Obon. Traditional Buddhist festival to honor the dead. Families reunite and return to their ancestral places to clean and tend to the graves of their ancestors. Bon-odori (Bon dance) is also performed on this occasion. The festival itself lasts three days, culminating with the floating of lit paper lanterns down the river to signal the spirits' return to the underworld.

Odaisan. Folk male and female priests who can contact the dead and perform cures and miracles.

Ofuda. So-called "august scripts." Protective talisman described as white strips of paper inscribed with Chinese characters. They are attached to the doors of houses to prevent ghosts and other supernatural entities from gaining entry.

Oinigawara. Roof-tile motif using the semblance of an oni as a means of warding off evil, similar to the Chinese tao-tieh.

Oiwa. The vengeful spirit and lead character of perhaps Japan's most famous ghost story, the kabuki play, "Yotsuya Kaidan."

Okiku. The plate-counting ghost and lead character of the popular folktale, "Bancho Sarayashiki."

Okubyohgami. Term to describe a type of fear-inducing ghost, possessing its victims and causing them to be fearful of going anywhere.

Omamori. Protective amulet or talisman; described as a cloth brocade bag with a cord. Dispensed at different shrines and temples and ascribed to various Buddhist and Shinto deities, it contains prayers inscribed on paper or on pieces of wood and gives protection and luck for particular occasions and endeavors. Their designs are specific to where they were created. Omamori also ward off bad luck and have become part of mainstream culture, sporting the images of popular cartoon characters while dangling from purses and cell phone straps. If opened, these small amulets are said to lose their protective properties.

Oni. Demon or devil; extremely popular in folklore and described as having two horns, a furrowed brow, and claws in place of fingers and toes. Wearing a tiger-skin loincloth and sporting fangs, these neckless creatures represent malignant supernatural forces and are often vanquished by heroes.

Oni-bi. Demon fires; described by fishermen as pale, ghostly lights that hover above the waves and beaches. This is usually in reference to the restless spirits of the Heike warriors who perished in battle, but whose faces now appear on the carapaces of crabs.

Oni-yarai. Type of demon-expelling ritual performed at the Imperial Palace on the last day of the year; used to avert disasters caused by Oni.

Onibaba. "Demon hag." Nefarious old hag said to roam the mountains and forests in search of the livers of unborn children. According to legend, she was originally the nanny of a mute girl of wealth. When a fortune-teller prescribed the fresh liver from a living fetus as the remedy, this nanny set out to find such an item. Before leaving on this arduous quest, the nanny left her own daughter an omamori (amulet) for protection. After years of searching, the nanny eventually encounters a pregnant woman and proceeds to procure the liver and complete her mission. But she then sees the same omamori she left her daughter on this victim. The realization that she killed her own daughter and grandchild, in turn, drive her insane. She now prowls the paths with a kitchen knife in search of human entrails.

Onryo. A ghost who is able to return from the afterlife to exact revenge upon the living, particularly those who have wronged him.

Orochi. A giant snake deity that lived on mountain peaks and in deep mountains.

Otoroshi. Ferocious creature that guards shrines and temples, tearing apart impious visitors who enter sacred ground.

Rago. Term for Rahu, the sun-devouring, dragon-like creature responsible for eclipses.

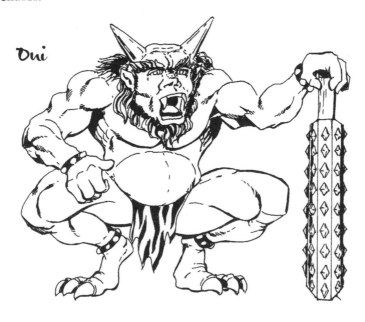

Oni

Rakan. Native term for lohan, an immediate disciple of the Buddha, on the verge of attaining enlightenment and becoming a bodhisattva.

Ransaika. Native term for Lan Ts'ai Ho, one of the Eight Immortals of Taoism (Pa Hsien).

Rikombyo. Literally, "ghost sickness." Old belief that when a person is stricken with intense grief caused by love, the sufferer will create a double of himself, the original staying put while the other joins the person being missed.

Rokurokubi. Female supernatural beings that have the ability to stretch their necks away from their body at great lengths, allowing their heads to snake about freely. Though normal in appearance during the day (appearing as attractive women dressed in traditional kimono), their true nature appears when they fall asleep and their heads begin to wander. Gentle in temperament, they are said to have a liking for absorbing male ki as well as drinking oil lamp fuel.

Ryotohin. Native term for Lu Tung Pin, one of the Eight Immortals of Taoism (Pa Hsien).

Ryu. Term for dragon. Classic mythological creature described as serpentine in appearance, possessing whiskers and a beard, but rarely wings. One of the guardians of the Four Celestial Directions (representing the East and the color green), it is most associated with water (oceans, mists, and clouds). Japan borrowed heavily from the classic Chinese model, including the use of its motif with the imperial institution. But unlike its Chinese cousins, Japanese dragons are said to possess only three fingers on each claw as opposed to five. Also known as tatsu.

Ryugu. Name of the Dragon King's underwater palace.

Ryujin (Ryu-o). Native term for the Dragon King, mythical character said to live in a majestic underwater palace called ryugu. He controls the sea by using his tide-ruling gems.

Saeno kami. Shinto highway deities; described as stones that either speak or make sounds. They are known to protect travelers, positioning themselves at entrances to villages to act as lookouts against bad luck or evil forces.

Sakasa-bashira. Literally "upside-down post." Tree trunk used as a pillar or support beam inside a house. Folk belief dictates that the trunk must be placed upright, as in the original orientation of the tree. Inserting it upside-down would bring bad fortune to the family, with the displeased spirit of the tree causing the pillar and its features to be fully animated, including groaning at night. This spirit will even leave the trunk and wander about the house, making faces at its occupants.

Seiryo. Term to describe the spirit of a living person who has temporarily left the body. Synonymous with shoryo.

Sennin. Generic term to describe a diverse class of fairies, wizards, and immortals who emerged from Taoist traditions in China, the most famous of which were the Eight Immortals of Taosim. Only a few are female and they are mostly depicted as mountain recluses in tattered robes. While many are said to exist only in legends, some are thought to be actual historical figures. Through their pursuit of longevity through alchemic, dietary, and sexual means, these beings achieved a state of transcendence.

Seto Taisho. "General Seto." Diminutive being said to be composed of discarded dinnerware. Its body is a teapot that wears an inverted soup bowl for a skirt, while its limbs are composed of various plates and spoons. Its head is a tokkuri bottle, which is used to hold sake. Capable of reassembling itself after a fall, this fierce being charges at its enemies with a spear tipped with a round ceramic jug.

Shachihoko. Roof ornament motif described as a dragon with a fish's body. The most famous one is made of gold and sits atop the Tokugawa Castle in Nagoya.

Shamisen-choro. Term for a type of musical instrument that has gained sentience and mobility over years of use. It is described as a floating traditional lute and it is considered a type of Tsukumo-gami.

Shichi fukujin. Seven gods of good luck. Extremely popular group of deities representing characters from Taoism, Japanese animism, and Indian beliefs. They are: Benzaiten, Bishamonten, Daikokuten, Ebisu, Fukurokuju, Hotei, and Jurojin.

Shiki-yurei. Mysterious phenomena where the surface of the ocean suddenly turns white at night. Sailing into it means losing the ability to move the ship.

Shikko-gaki. Type of gaki; native term for the hungry ghost, or preta, in Hinduism and Buddhism. This kind is said to eat corpses as well as cause pestilence.

Shikome. Grotesque demon hags that the creator goddess Izanami sent to pursue her husband Izanagi after he broke his vow not to look at her when he visited her in the underworld. Also known as Yomotsu-shikome.

Shin-ko-gaki. Type of gaki; native term for the hungry ghost, or preta, in Hinduism and Buddhism. This type is described as having a needle mouth.

Shinen-gaki. Type of gaki; native term for the hungry ghost, or preta, in Hinduism and Buddhism. This type is said to appear as wandering fires at night.

Shiryo. Spirit of a discarded mistress or wife. This apparition, the spirit of a woman who actually died from desertion or maltreatment, can cause the male victim to become gravely ill and lead, ultimately, to his death. This vengeful spirit has also been known to pursue the male victim's family.

Shishi. Mythological lion dog commonly seen as statues guarding the entrances to shrines and temples throughout Japan. They are often seen in pairs, with the male shishi (known as karashishi, or Chinese lion) depicted as having an open mouth and holding a ball, while the fiercer female (known as komainu, or Korean dog) has her mouth closed and is leaning her paw on a cub.

Shojo. Mythical, red-maned creatures said to be addicted to sake. Human in appearance (although they are sometimes depicted with the faces of monkeys), they live in coastal areas and drink alone or in groups.

Shokera. Monster that lives on rooftops and reportedly spies on the occupants of the house.

Shoki. Famous exorcist and demon queller; the native version of the Chinese Zhong-gui. He is depicted as a fearsome bearded warrior dressed in a Chinese scholar's robe and cap, wearing huge black boots.

Shoriken. Native term for Chung Li Ch'uan, one of the Eight Immortals of Taoism (Pa Hsien).

Shoryo. Term to describe the spirit of a living person who has temporarily left the body. Synonymous with seiryo.

Sokokukyu. Native term for Ts'ao Kuo Chiu, one of the Eight Immortals of Taoism (Pa Hsien).

Sorei. Ancestral spirit that guides and protects its descendants. This is a status attained from being a former aramitama through the consistent offerings of living relatives.

Stinking Monster. The spirit of the outhouse. It blows fecal matter upon people who have offended it.

Tanuki. A member of the dog family (Canis nyctereutes, procyonoides, or viverrinus) who resembles a raccoon, but is often incorrectly described as a badger. Like the fox (kitsune), it, too, is considered a trickster entity, capable of changing shape such as into a person and even into objects. It enjoys playing pranks, particularly with its immensely large scrotum.

Tate-Eboshi. Type of Umi-bozu found off the coast of Sado Island in western Japan; described as a towering 65-foot monster that tries to sink any boat it encounters in the ocean.

Tatsu. Term for dragon. Classic mythological creature described as serpentine in appearance, possessing whiskers and a beard, but rarely wings. One of the guardians of the Four Celestial Directions (representing the East and the color green), it is most associated with water (oceans, mists, and clouds). Japan borrowed heavily from the classic Chinese model, including the use of its motif with the imperial institution. Unlike its Chinese cousins, however, Japanese dragons are said to have only three fingers on each claw, as opposed to five. Also known as Ryu.

Tearai Oni. "Hand-washing demon." Type of oni said to be obsessed with washing its hands in rivers while bent over backwards and nearly upside-down. It is gigantic in size, with some accounts reporting a straddle of several miles wide.

Tekkai (Ritekkai). Native term for Li T'ieh Kuai, one of the Eight Immortals of Taoism (Pa Hsien).

Tengu. Shape-shifting mountain goblins notorious for preying on the secret desires of pious monks and leading them astray. Believed to be imported from China and India (sometimes linked with T'ien-kou and the garuda), they come in two forms: Konoha tengu (resembling monks, but with an extremely elongated nose), and Karasu tengu (a crow-headed being, complete with a body of feathers and claws for hands and feet). They are often associated with yamabushi, mountain priests thought to have esoteric powers, and have even been referenced in some sources as the teachers of the notorious ninja. Rural villagers give them offerings before cutting down trees in the mountain forest.

Tenjo Kudari. Type of goblin that drops from the ceiling at sunset.

Tenjo-name. "Ceiling licker." Folkloric creature described as tall and lean and possessing an extraordinarily long tongue that it uses to lick traditional wooden ceilings. It haunts the house at night when everyone is asleep and is blamed for mysterious stains seen on the rafters.

Tennin. Buddhist angels; often depicted holding lotus flowers or musical instruments while floating in the sky. Dressed in flowing robes and scarves, they are believed to have originated from Indian religious beliefs.

Tesso. "Iron Rat." A hybrid creature, part-human and part-rat, said to have originally been a Buddhist monk named Raigo, who died from a self-imposed hunger strike after his reward for praying for the birth of a royal son was ultimately denied. Reborn as the were-rat Tesso with the power to control rodents, he led an army of his brethren to devour the texts and sutras of his rivals' temples.

Tetsumonkai. Robed monk whose body is on display at the Churenji Temple located on Mount Yudono. Through a strict diet of rice and other grains, he literally mummified himself until his body dwindled to almost nothing. He later retreated to an underground chamber, sitting cross-legged in his own altar, and chanted until he died.

T'ien-kou. Chinese. "Celestial Dog." Shape-shifting demons that can take the form of men. Varying in form from different accounts (from shooting stars to mountain dog demons), they are notorious for abducting and devouring children. It has also been suggested that the T'ien-kou, upon arriving in Japan, combined with local lore and eventually became the notorious tengu.

Tofu Kozo. "Tofu boy." Supernatural entity described as a small boy dressed in a traditional conical hat, kimono, and wooden sandals. He also carries a plate with a block of tofu adorned with a single Japanese maple leaf. Encountered at night, anyone who tastes or consumes this tofu can suffer varying consequences, including death by virulent fungus.

Toire no Hanako. "Hanako in the bathroom." Apparition described as a uniformed elementary school girl who appears mysteriously in the women's bathroom, usually during the day when classes are in session. A

Tengu

popular theme in Japanese comics, students often dare each other to enter bathrooms frequented by this ghost.

Tommoraki. An evil messenger bird said to scream obscenities and vomit to foil the effectiveness of Buddhist ritual chants.

Torihada. "Chicken skin." Term to describe the feeling of getting goosebumps from fear.

Tsuchinoko. Scientifically unclassified snake chronicled in various historical accounts and documents; described as venomous with a triangular head with horns, and a main body that is thicker and wider than its head and tail (like a snake that has just eaten a meal). Measuring about 2 feet in length with the ability to leap short distances, it has been sighted all over the country and is also known as kansai, shikoku, and bachi hebi. Folklore contends that has the ability to speak and is fond of alcohol.

Tsuitate-danuki. Kyushu. Type of nurikabe, a mysterious wall that prevents villagers from walking along a particular path at night. According to folklore, the villagers held a ceremony and eventually imprisoned the entity into an obelisk.

Tsukumogami. Extremely diverse class of supernatural spirits that originated from various household objects and artifacts. In Japanese lore, objects that reach the age of 100 years are believed to come alive and be self-aware. These objects include tea kettles, lanterns, umbrellas, broken sandals, and scrolls. Developing eyes, appendages, and teeth, tsukumogami are generally considered harmless, although they have been known to exact revenge on abusive owners who discarded them after years of loyal servitude. The origin of these particular spirits is probably derived from Japan's native animist world view.

Tsutsuga Mushi. Blood-sucking vampire believed to exist in the mountains of Yagami during the 7th century. They were known to enter houses at night and suck the blood of its occupants.

Ubume. The spirit of a woman who died during childbirth. Often seen at crossroads clutching her baby, she is described as naked from the waist up, but with her lower extremities covered in blood. She is said to accost men, asking them to hold her child until she returns. But the infant, mysteriously, gets heavier in the man's arms, until he is unable to move from fear of dropping it. It is only when he recites a Buddhist chant that she returns, expressing gratitude for helping the child "return to this world."

It is a popular storytelling motif and is synonymous with kosodate-yurei.

Umibozu. So-called "priest of the sea." A type of mysterious supernatural denizen of the deep which is often described as a massive dome-like entity or octopus with glowing eyes that could tower above the largest ships. Encountered in the open ocean, its appearance sometimes coincides with atmospheric disturbances.

Ushi oni. "Demon bull." Type of sea creature that preys on fishermen.

Waira. Creature that feeds on children, prowling along quiet, lonely roads.

Wanyudo. One of Japan's oldest supernatural creatures; described as a flaming wagon wheel with an enraged human face in the center. According to legend, it was originally an abusive nobleman who was assassinated while touring the city in an ox-drawn carriage. The unfortunate who stare into its hypnotic gaze are run over and dismembered into smoldering pieces.

Yama Chichi. "Mountain father." This creature is described as a hairy bat of extreme age, with a pointed mouth that terminates into a beak. It is said that it sucks out the breath of sleeping victims, who, in turn, die several days later.

Yama-otoko. Mountain men who are considered uncivilized and unstable, and are said to have demonic animal companions.

Yama-uba. Hideous mountain crone with disheveled white hair in a tattered kimono; said to live in the deep forest. She preys on travelers, assuming the form of a beautiful maiden or a hapless old woman in distress, leading her victims astray or off-guard before finally devouring them.

Yamabushi. Mountain priests or ascetics; thought to have mysterious powers derived from the practice of animist rituals combined with Buddhism and Shintoism. Living in such a snowy and rugged environment, they purify themselves by fasting and meditating, as well as chanting beneath freezing waterfalls.

Yasha. Originally from Yaksha, a man-eating demon.

Yonaguni Monument. Controversial underwater site located off the coast of Yonaguni Island. Some scholars describe the towering rock structure as having unusually sharp corners and flat sides, along with staircase-like terraces not unlike a stepped pyramid. They have theorized that the monument is man-made, created sometime after the Ice Age and prior to sea levels rising. Other scientists, however, dismiss the unusual features as natural erosion, as evidenced by the shoreline cliff-faces degrading in the same manner.

Yanari. Invisible goblin said to mysteriously shake houses at night. The name also refers to a description of the sound a house makes during an earthquake.

Yotsuya Kaidan. Kabuki play and perhaps Japan's most famous ghost story. It centers around the disgraced ronin Iyemon, who murders his beautiful bride, Oiwa, in favor of another woman. Iyemon poisons Oiwa with a lethal tonic that horribly disfigures her face, which he mercilessly shows her in a mirror prior to her excruciating death. He then nails her body, and that of a servant whom Iyemon also slays, on a wooden door and throws it into a river.

Oiwa returns to haunt Iyemon with a vengeance, her gruesome visage appearing literally in the environment and objects around him. After a relentless retreat, he eventually withdraws to the mountains and, half-insane from his former bride continuing to manifest herself at every turn, dies at the hands of Oiwa's brother.

Yokai. Extremely broad term to describe a diverse class of monsters, demons, or spirits.

Yuki-Onna. Snow woman; described as a beautiful woman dressed in white who freezes her victims by blowing her frosty breath upon them. She also causes travelers to fall asleep, freezing to death in their tracks.

Yurei. Generic term for a ghost; most often depicted as a woman with long, unkempt hair, pale complexion, beckoning hands, and wearing draping white clothes that taper down to nothingness. Yurei are rarely shown as having feet.

Yurei

Zashiki Warashi. "Parlor children." The ghosts of children who were left to die or were disposed of after birth and have since returned to haunt houses. Sometimes playful and other times vengeful, they have been known to steal pillows and even press on the chest of sleeping people. This spirit can only be seen by children, and their stories are most common in northern Japan. They are sometimes associated with kanashibari.

Zokuzokugami. Term to describe a type of fear-inducing ghost that possesses its victims, causing them to be fearful of going anywhere.

Okinawa

Himpun. Traditional fence of Chinese origin placed in front of a house to conceal its interior as well as protect it from evil spirits.

Hinukan. Fire god; worshipped locally through a small shrine in the kitchen.

Ishigantuu. Stone tablet placed at dead-end roads to protect drivers and residents from evil spirits. Less than a meter tall, the word "ishigantuu" is inscribed on its surface.

Kaminchu. A female medium whose position is earned through heredity; taken up at middle age and kept until death.

Sanjinso. Male fortune-teller who uses the I-Ching and other similar books in selecting fortuitous days for various events, including funerals, marriages, and traveling.

Shisa (siisaa). Traditional architectural motif found on roofs and at gates. A cross between a lion and a dog, they are often found in pairs (one with its mouth open and the other with its mouth closed) and act as protectors against various evils. Said to be of Chinese origin (dating back to the 14th century), popular mythology held that a clay Shisa talisman once came to life and saved Okinawa from an invading dragon.

Yuta. Female psychic consulted for various occasions, including tragedies, economic hardships, and illness.

Korea

Chalk-chum. "Book divination." Type of divination used by a pansu. The pansu studies the hour, day, month, and year of the requestor's birth and determines an answer by comparing it to the Chinese characters that correspond with those dates.

Changsung. Road idol or spirit post. Ornate wooden posts placed in pairs at the entrance to villages for protection against evil spirits.

Ch'arye. One of three major types of rituals to honor the ancestral dead (chesa). This type involves an elaborate ceremony of offering and presenting food to ancestors at the table. It is generally performed only twice a year in the morning and honors the four preceding generations.

Chesa. Collective term for Confucian-based rituals or commemorations to honor ancestors. There are three main types: graveside commemorations (myoje), death anniversary commemorations (kije), and holiday commemorations (ch'arye). They generally involve offering food and drinks to the spirits, but vary in frequency and times observed.

Chibang. Term for a disposable ancestral tablet substitute made of paper and used during veneration rites. An ancestor's name, title, and birthplace is written on this paper in black ink, attached to a wall, and then later burned at the conclusion of the ritual.

Chollima. Mythical horse said to have originated in Central Asian beliefs, particularly from the Siberian tribes. Often portrayed as having wings, it is said to be so swift that riders are unable to mount it.

Chomjangi. Fortune-teller. Specialists well-versed in palm- and face-reading, as well as Chinese cosmology. They are regularly consulted

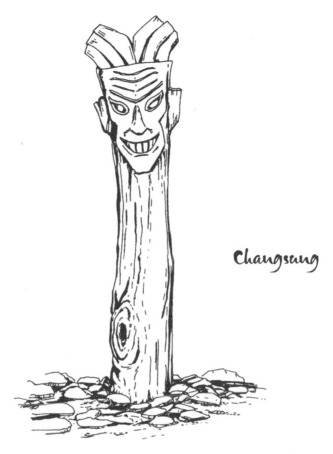

Changsung

for special events, important decisions regarding careers and marriages, funerals, and even the names of children.

Ch'onwang. Term to describe the four heavenly kings, guardians of the four cardinal directions.

Chosang. Term for ancestor spirit.

Haet'ae. Mythical creature said to swallow fire. Its protective stone statue adorns various structures and locations susceptible to being set ablaze.

Hanbang. Traditional healing brought over from China in the sixth century A.D. It consists of acupuncture, herbal medicine, moxibustion and pressure point massage.

Hanshik. Cold Food Day. A Korean custom that originated in China that commemorates the loyalty of a man who chose to die instead of being separated from his king. It is a holiday in which people clean the graves of their forefathers and perform ancestral rites. Per tradition, they eat only cold food on this occasion.

I-ee-go. Phrase of mourning or grieving.

Infant spirits. Spirits of deceased children believed to have mystical powers. They torment the living by possessing them, with some of their victims eventually becoming shamans. These spirits are also known to afflict their own mothers.

Kije. One of three major types of rituals to honor the ancestral dead (chesa). This type involves an elaborate ceremony of offering and presenting food to ancestors at the table. It is performed at midnight on the eve of the anniversary of the ancestor's death.

Kumgang shinjang. Term to describe the Vajras, a pair of ferocious-looking guardian deities painted on the doors of gates leading to temple grounds;meant to prevent evil spirits from entering. One guardian expels rays of light from its nostrils, while the other expels light from its mouth. These figures' countenance symbolizes the temple's full protection whether its gates are open or closed.

Kumiho. Fox spirit, the native version of the Chinese huli jing and the Japanese kitsune. Like its counterparts, it is a notorious shape-shifter, capable of transforming into a beautiful woman in order to seduce men.

Kut. Ceremony in which a mudang makes contact with the supernatural world in order to resolve issues of great importance (rites for a premature family death, curing illnesses, etc.). Varying in size, costuming, and pageantry, it is as much a dramatic performance as it is a healing ritual.

Kwe-yuk tasin. Term to describe the spirit of smallpox, the dreaded disease of childhood.

Kwisin. Generic term for a ghost or spirit.

Mangyong. Term used to describe a person's spirit immediately after his or her death, with the potential to later turn into other spirit types (kwisin or chosang). Synonymous with mangja.

Mongdal kwisin. The spirits of adults, particularly young women, who passed away prior to marriage. In traditional thought, it is believed that the deceased haunt the living because they are unhappy at not being able to marry. These spirits are greatly feared and considered very dangerous. Shamans hold many rituals and posthumous marriage ceremonies to placate them.

Mudang. One of four types of shamans in native Korean religion. This common type is created through a supernatural calling or possession, usually after an illness. Through ritual song and dance, mudangs act as an intermediary with the supernatural, invoking the spirits, performing blessings and exorcisms, curing illnesses, and even predicting the future. Synonymous with manshin. See also tan'gol, simbang, and myongdu.

Mudang

Musok. Term to describe indigenous shamanism, an animist religion and worldview that subscribes to the belief that spirits exist in all objects within the natural world.

Myoje. One of three major types of rituals to honor the ancestral dead (chesa). This commemoration occurs when one visits the grave of ancestral relatives and involves the offering of food and wine.

Myongdu. One of four types of shamans in native Korean religion. This shaman is created by receiving the spirit of a dead person, normally a deceased child.

Ohaeng. Native term for the five elements of nature (fire, wood, water, metal, and earth).

Paesonang. Goddess guardians of boats.

Paksu (pansu). Male version of the mudang; usually a man with fortune-telling and exorcism powers. He uses three systems for divination: san-tong ("number box"), ton-jun ("money divination"), and chalk-chum ("book divination").

Pujok. Protective talisman that serves to ward off evil and bad luck. Appearing as red characters on a yellow field, it is obtained from monks and shamans and, depending on its use, can be carried on one's person, sewn on clothing, or hung on a door or wall.

P'ungsu. Geomancy; native version of feng-shui.

San sin. Term for a male or female mountain spirit or the founding spirit of a town or village. These tutelary beings are worshipped in numerous shrines and temples on different occasions and festivals.

San-tong. "Number box." Type of divination used by a pansu; also known as turtle divination due to the shape of the box that contains metal rods or splinters. They are arranged in a notched sequence from one to eight. The pansu makes three throws for each rod. Based on the combination of notches, divines an answer to the requestor's question.

Shinju. Term for a wooden ancestral tablet used during veneration rites.

Simbang. One of four types of shamans in native Korean religion. Like the tan'gol, this shaman inherits her authority and status. It differs from the other shaman types, however, in its view of local gods and its use of divination as opposed to possession.

Spirit post. See changsung.

Tan'gol. One of four types of shamans in native Korean religion. This type inherits her authority and status, passed on from one generation to the next as determined by existing traditions and the established priesthood.

Tokkaebi. Famous horned goblin that appears in numerous native fairy tales. Boisterous and traveling in groups, they are believed by some to be wandering spirits of the deceased who haven't been granted permission to enter the world of the blessed. Tokkaebis live in the mountains and forests and are known to possess objects with magical properties (magic caps to render themselves invisible, wish-granting clubs, etc.).

Tokkaebi

Ton-jun. "Money divination." Type of divination used by a pansu. Similar to san-tong, the pansu throws three out of four coins from his hand and divines an answer based on the combination of characters that appear.

Um-yang. Native term for the yin-yang principle of dualism.

Wip'ae. Term for a wooden ancestral tablet used during veneration rites.

Yokwe. Generic term to describe a diverse class of native supernatural creatures.

Myanmar (Burma)

Ameindaw pyan. Ritual that involves the signing or reciting of a decree discharging a deceased government official from his post so that he doesn't haunt his old position. This is usually performed by the official's superior officer.

Aulan hsaya. Powerful male witch who employs ghosts and other spirits as a means to their malevolent ends, usually for a client.

Athtelan hsaya. Powerful "good" male witch who can cure or exorcise spirit-derived illnesses.

Bilu. Ogre-like guardian beings who supposedly devour people; often depicted with green skin and wielding a club. They figure prominently in traditional puppet theater and temple art.

Bo bo. Spirits believed to be sheltered within shrines located inside monastery compounds where worshippers make offerings.

Bo Bo Aung. A renowned master of the occult; highly revered for his supernatural prowess. He is enshrined in the Shwedegon Pagoda in Myanmar.

Bounmagyi. Native version of the rice goddess, a popular motif found throughout Southeast Asia.

Chintha. Term to describe a stylized guardian lion statue that protects temples.

Datloun. Object imbued with magical properties as a result of various alchemic processes; meant specifically for the prolongation of life.

Bilu

Gahta. Term for a spell or incantation.

Galon. Native term for the garuda.

Hintha. Mythical bird used as a decorative motif.

Hsei hsaya. Term for a traditional doctor or herbalist.

Hsutaun. Term for a prayer.

In. Paper divided into squares and inscribed with various mystical symbols; used as a talisman for protection against harm.

Lehpwe. Talisman or amulet used for protection against harm.

Leikpya khwade. Term for soul loss.

Leikpya. Human soul that remains after death to haunt the living.

Lokanat. Popular celestial deity regarded as a benevolent overseer and protector of the universe. Originating from several mythological sources, he is considered a symbol of peace and a patron of traditional arts and culture, particularly painting and sculpture.

Manok-thi-ha. Mythological entity whose statue acts as a guardian of Buddhist temples and monasteries. Often displayed in pairs, it is described as a man from the waist up, but with the hindquarters of a pair of lions literally connected at its trunk. Leaning forward on its arms, this fantastic creature is then supported by four rear legs, each pair positioned side-by-side. It is believed to roam Mount Meru, home of the gods.

Myousade. Spirits of those buried alive at the four corners of a city; meant to become protectors against evil spirits or people.

Nat. Diverse class of spirits that permeate Myanmar (Burmese) religion and culture. As much worshipped as they are feared, this pantheon of capricious beings include the ghosts of cultural heroes, ancestors, rogues, people who died a violent death, nature spirits, various devas, and even native versions of Hindu deities. The most important are collectively called the Thirty-Seven Nats, a more categorical than numeric classification from a royal list ordained by kings. The object of elaborate ritual worship, nats must be continuously placated with offerings at every occasion to avert their displeasure or anger. As much anguish as they can cause, nats can also take the role of protector if propitiated enough, particularly of villages, households, and even families. See also Thirty-Seven Nats.

Nat pude. Term to describe Nat possession.

Nat sin. Shrine for village nats.

Nat-thamee. Fairy spirits.

Naya. Mythical creature used as an architectural temple motif; described as a composite creature with the features of a lion, a bull, a dragon, a horse, and a snake.

Nekkhath-saya. Term for a native astrologer.

Ouktazaun. Spirits, who, as a form of karmic punishment for their excessive greed as human beings, guard buried treasure within existing pagodas meant for the construction of the Buddha's future domicile. Predominantly female, these beings are notoriously seductive, entrapping victims into aiding or switching roles with them to gain freedom. Having relations with these beings meant possession, soul-loss, and certain death.

Pyin-sa-yu-pa. "Five beauties." Mythological hybrid creature symbolizing music in Myanmar. It is described as having the antlers and hooves of a deer, the body of a snake, the trunk and tusks of an elephant, the tail of a fish, and the wings of a bird.

Soang. Native version of the Thai creature Phii krasu.

Soun. Lesser witch who uses spells and physical ingredients to implement and augment her inherent sorcery. Predominantly female, they act against victims out of personal malice. There are two types: wundwin soun (witches possessing inherent powers), and you-you soun (witches who learned or acquired their powers).

Soun pude. Term to describe witch possession.

Tasei (thaye). Deceased persons who have been reborn into ghosts as a consequence of their past evil actions. They are known as preta in Buddhism. Living around cemeteries to feed on corpses, they are also known to attack and devour people.

Taungbyon Festival. Famous festival held in August in honor of brothers Shwepyingyi and Shwepyinnge, two nats known collectively as the Taungbyon Brothers.

Taw. Term for supposed were-creatures that historically raided Lahu tribe villages on the northern Thai/Myanmar border. Described as half-human and half-animal, these hairy beings were believed to attack at certain times of the month, abducting or killing their victims.

Thabe. Ghosts of women who died during childbirth. They are particularly feared.

Thakinma. Legendary royal queen who sacrificed herself upon the creation of an irrigation system to become its supernatural guardian.

Thirty-Seven Nats (thounze khunna min nat). The most important nats (and overall spirits) of the Burmese supernatural pantheon as categorized in a royal list ordained by kings. They are linked to royalty and, with a few exceptions, consist mostly of the ghosts of deceased historical figures and cultural heroes who are believed to have existed between the 13th and 17th centuries.

The Thirty-Seven Nats are:

Thagya Nat
Mahagiri Nat
Hnamadawgyi Nat
Shwe Nabe Nat
Thonban Hla Nat
Taung-ngu Mingaung Nat
Mintara Nat
Thandawgan Nat
Shwe Nawratha Nat
Aungzwamagyi Nat
Ngazishin Nat
Aungbinle Sinbyushin Nat
Taungmagyi Nat
Maung Minshin Nat
Shindaw Nat
Nyaung-gyin Nat
Tabengshweti Nat
Minye Aungdin Nat
Shwe Sippin Nat

Medaw Shwesaga Nat
Maung Po Tu Nat
Yun Bayin Nat
Maung Minbyu Nat
Mandale Bodaw Nat
Shwebyin Naungdaw Nat
Shwebyin Nyidaw Nat
Mintha Manung Shin Nat
Tibyusaung Nat
Tibusaung Medaw Nat
Bayinmashin Mingaung Nat
Min Sithu Nat
Min Kyawzwa Nat
Myaukpet Shinma Nat
Anauk Mibaya Nat
Shingon Nat
Shingwa Nat
Shin-nemi Nat
(See also Nats.)

Thuyai-Thedi Medau. Buddhist term for the Hindu goddess Sarasvati.

Vyala. Auspicious mythical creature; described as a lion with an elephant's trunk.

Weikza. "Occult masters." Men who have acquired the power of prolonged life through various means in the anticipation of future events, particularly the arrival of the future Buddha. They are also said to possess other supernatural powers.

Wundwin soun. Witch with inherent supernatural powers. She is capable of shape-shifting into animals and can also fly (headless if flying at night and as a vulture or bat during the day). She is very fond of eating human excrement, detaching its head to the ground to feed.

Yokthe pwe. Traditional marionette theatre.

You-you soun. Witch who learned or acquired her supernatural powers. She is especially fond of eating human excrement, detaching its head to the ground to feed.

Zawgyi. Magician or sorcerer.

Cambodia

Apsaras. Sanskrit for "Daughters of Joy." Term for female celestial nymphs or dancers who are the companions of the gandharvas. One of the many Indian divinities that permeate Southeast Asian art, religion, and mythology, they are often depicted dancing or playing musical instruments while in the presence of gods, kings, and those who died valiantly in battle. According to the Ramayana, apsaras emerged from the ocean when it was churned to obtain amrita. Known as Tepanom in Khmer.

Arak. Khmer spirits of disease.

Apsara

Arei ap. Ghoul or sorceress that wanders about at night as only a head with its alimentary canal trailing behind it, searching for and feeding on excrement.

Daerechhan. The spirits of beings who are condemned to be reborn in the shape of animal for seemingly no reason.

Devata. Sanskrit for the word "deity." Spelled regionally in Southeast Asia as dewata, jewata, thewada, and diwata.

Dvarapala. Sanskrit term for divine, club-wielding guardians placed at entrances and doorways to ward off evil spirits. One of many Indian divinities that permeate Asian art, religion, and mythology, these fierce-looking guardians often come in pairs and are believed to represent opposing forces of nature. Known as Ninwang in Chinese, Ni-O in Japanese, and Inwang in Korean.

Gandharva. Class of minor deities that live in heaven and are charged with guarding the soma, the sacred drink of immortality extracted from a plant. One of many Indian divinities that permeate Southeast Asian art, religion, and mythology, they appear as irresistibly handsome men as well as celestial musicians and singers. Their wives are said to be the apsaras, whose union at the beginning of time produced Yama and Yami, the first pair of human beings.

Gatiloke. Khmer. Collection of ancient Buddhist folktales recorded in writing at the end of the 19th century. Its numerous stories have been used traditionally to impart lessons in morality, ethics, and the "correct" way of living.

Kala. Sanskrit term for "black" or "death." It is a guardian motif found throughout Asia, depicted by a grinning monster with bulging eyes appearing over doorways, lintels, and shrine arches, sometimes spewing complex garlands from its mouth. According to Indian mythology, Kala is the god of time and is, therefore, also the god of death, sometimes associated with the god Shiva. It is a variation of the kirtimukha, or the "face of majesty."

Kennar. Male version of the kenarey or kinnaree.

Kennorey. Native version of the kinnaree, a musical entity that is a beautiful woman from the waist up, but a bird from the waist down. Also known as kenor.

Khmoch. Native term to describe a spirit or ghost.

Khmoch chhav. Khmer for the "raw dead." Spirits of people whose lives were prematurely ended by suicide, murder, drowning, or pregnancy.

Khmoch pray. The wandering ghosts of stillborn babies and of women who died during childbirth. Offerings are made as protection against them because they sometimes possess relatives and require an exorcism to drive them out.

Kruth. Native term for the garuda.

Makara. Hindu, Pan-Buddhist Asia. Sanskrit term for a hybrid water monster that figures prominently in sculpture and architecture. It is most commonly depicted as a creature with the jaw of a crocodile, the snout of an elephant, the tusks of a boar, the body of a fish, and the tail of a peacock. It is a common decorative motif, found around doorways, gateways and balustrades, and sometimes alongside two Nagas. It is known as chu-srin in Tibetan.

Makara

Neak-ta. Collective term for a diverse class of earth spirits that permeate all facets of Cambodian culture. Residing in objects, rocks, trees, bodies of water, and villages (often taking the name of their associated area or object), these tutelary beings protect their territories as long as offered befitting worship. While some are ancient in age, new spirits can be instantly created if invited to reside in an object or area previously unoccupied. Neak-ta can take many forms (including spirits of the dead as well as aspects of Brahmanic divinities), and occasionally communicate through female mediums.

Norok. Term for hell, describing the eight levels of the native afterlife in which the guilty are punished for their crimes, but are then allowed to be reborn once they have atoned for their sins.

Rahu. Sanskrit term for a monster demon often depicted in South and Southeast Asian architecture as a dragonhead swallowing the sun or moon. It is cited as the cause of eclipses, with some cultures ritually making loud noises for the creature to release the heavenly bodies. According to Hindu mythology, the monster demon once impersonated a god just to drink the wine of immortality. The god Vishnu beheaded him for this transgression, but Rahu's now-immortal head rose up to the sky and now, occasionally, swallows the sun and moon in revenge.

Reachea-Sey. Architectural motif depicting a lion that possesses the ability to leap and fly through the air.

Reamker. Cambodian version of the Indian epic, Ramayana.

Simha. Khmer architectural motif depicting a lion with four arms.

Tevoda. Native term for devata.

Tha-mop. Native version of the Thai creature phii khamot.

Yakshas (Yaksas). Pan-India, Southeast Asia. Minor gods in Hindu mythology that follow Kuvera, the god of riches. Living in the Himalayas and guarding hidden treasure, these nature spirits can assume many diverse forms and are fierce protectors of their masters' palaces. Though generally benevolent, they are also known to exhibit wicked and vengeful behavior. In Southeast Asian architecture, they are depicted as ogre-like temple guardians and semi-divine protectors of Buddhism and its principles. In Khmer mythology, they are associated with plants and trees. They are known as Yecha in Chinese, Yasha in Japanese, Yak in Thai, and Yeak in Cambodian. Female Yakshas are known as Yakshinis.

Yakshini. Pan-Indian, Southeast Asia. A female Yaksha. She is a forest spirit, often described as a seductive and voluptuous woman who leads men astray on paths. Some yakshinis are depicted as having a horse's head.

Hmong

Txiv neeb. "Person with a healing spirit." Shaman who acts as an intermediary with the supernatural world; often used to retrieve lost or wandering souls.

Dab. Generic term for a class of malevolent spirits who cause various illnesses when encountered or offended. They've been known to kidnap the souls of newborn babies, sit on the chest of Hmong males to press the breath out of them, and even intentionally cause accidents among drivers. They can be placated by a txiv neeb (Hmong shaman) with animal sacrifices using cows, chickens, or pigs.

Dab ntxaug. Spirit that lives in the jungle and causes epidemics when disturbed.

Hu plig. Soul-calling. Ceremony held on the third day after a child's birth. Prior to this, the baby is not considered a full human being and thus is undeserving of full funerary rites. It is believed that newborn babies' souls are vulnerable to evil spirits and wanderlust, so this ceremony is performed to placate the soul with offerings and a good name thus settling the baby within his or her new body.

Thailand

Ajaan sak. Art of magical tattooing; applied by revered masters who are said to imbue the designs with mystical properties derived from the supernatural, thus making its wearer invulnerable to physical harm. A tradition dating back several hundred years, its wearer must adhere to certain codes of behavior if the potency of the design is to be maintained. Also known as khru sak. Tattooing has also spread to clothing, where the mystical designs are applied to shirts, sparing its wearer from the painful process of the needle without losing the designs' magical protection.

Apsonsi. Mythical creature described as a beautiful woman from the waist up, but possessing the hips, legs, and tail of a lion. It is used as a decorative motif.

Baaramii. Term used to describe supernatural energy, karma, and psychic power.

Bangfai Payanak. Mysterious balls of fire attributed to a fire-breathing naga (paya nak) seen rising at night from a section of the Mekong River bordering Laos. Despite religious and scientific explanations for the unusual phenomenon, its legend persists and now attracts tourists.

Caw phii. Guardian spirit of the forest; entity whose permission and protection must be obtained in order to cut down trees or hunt animals within its particular domain. Shrines are erected in its honor for worship and offerings. Also referred to as cau phau or cau mae.

Chaatrii. Term to describe a native sorcerer.

Chang samkhan. White elephant. Important symbol of royalty and prestige. It is derived from a centuries-old tale in which the once-barren Queen Maya miraculously became pregnant with the future Buddha when she dreamt that a white elephant had entered her womb. Possessing a great number of white elephants has since become a defining measure of a king's status.

Chao Mae. Term for a female spirit or goddess.

Chao Mae Sao Hai. Principal character in a popular folktale. A log floated up a canal one day and came to rest on the shore of a village. When local men began hearing a voice from the log crying for help, they tried to haul it out of the water, to no avail. A villager then dreamt of a woman who claimed she was trapped in the log. If he could bring it out of the water, she would reward him with riches. Tying a sai sin cord around the log and praying, he was able to remove the log with surprising ease. The spirit, Chao Mae Sao Hai, kept her promise and made him wealthy.

Chao Mae Sarmmook. Principal character in a popular folktale. Chao Mae Sarmmook was a poor girl who fell in love with a man from a rich family. His parents, however, refused to let him marry her, and she threw herself over a cliff in anguish. But instead of her body being carried out to sea by the tide, it mysteriously remained at the base of the cliff. Local villagers placed her body inside a cave, where, miraculously, it became filled with golden cutlery and dinnerware. When people began borrowing the utensils and not returning them, Chao Mae Sarmmook became offended and sealed the cave. Realizing their offense, the villagers built her a shrine at the foot of the cliff.

Chao Mae Tuptim. Female spirit that inhabits banyan trees.

Chao Por Prakan. The spirit of death. If its emissary, the owl, is seen flying westward over a house, someone in the household will die.

Chao Thii. "Lord of the place." Guardian spirit of a specific tract of land that needs to be placated with offerings before building any structure on the property. Its home shrine can now be found in department stores.

Chedi. Native term for stupa.

Doo lai meu. "Looking at the lines of the hand." Term for a practitioner of palmistry.

Farang ghosts. Phenomenon reported immediately after the 2006 tsunami that decimated coastal Thailand, Western Malaysia, and countries that bordered the Indian Ocean. Ghostly farangs (Thai term for "foreigners," meaning Europeans or Americans) were sighted walking about after the catastrophe. Some locals claimed that they heard voices and laughter when there was no one there; others saw them strolling along the beach and even catching rides as if still alive, only to later disappear. The sightings were later attributed to trauma and mass hallucination, particularly in coping with the tsunami.

Ghilen. Native term for the Asian unicorn.

Ham yon. "Testicle yantra." Ornate wooden lintel placed over the doorway of an inside room to protect the owner against evil spirits. The elaborate carving represents the genitals of a buffalo.

Hamsa. Mythological swan or goose that was the mount of the Indian god Brahma. Popular as a decorative motif in native sculpture and architecture, it is also known as hongse.

Hasadiling. Mythical creature that combines the body of a swan with the head of an elephant. It is used as a decorative motif.

Hera. Mythological creature used as an architectural motif at the end of arches. It is described as having the body of a naga, with its teeth meeting its nostrils. The creature is also depicted in various ways: spewing flowers, another creature, or even flames out its open mouth.

Himaphan. Pan-Asian. Term for a mythical forest said to be the home of fantastic animals that inspired artisans from all over Hindu and Buddhist Asia. Located somewhere in the Himalayas, it is said to be invisible to mortal eyes. Also known as Himavat.

Hun krabok. Native version of marionette puppetry.

Khawng-khlang. Collective term for protective amulets and charms. They are divided into four major categories: Khuruang-rang (objects from nature that have been transformed into stone or copper); Phra-Khruang (various figurines representing lessons and episodes within the life of Buddha); Pluk-sek (the process of awakening magic within objects through the use of magic symbols or incantations); and Wan ya (medicinal plants and herbs).

Khon. Refers to the ornate mask or the traditional masked drama of the Ramakien in Thai theatre.

Khon song. Spirit medium. Human host chosen by spirits to communicate to the living, possesses the body usually against the host's will. Also known as mau song.

Khru sak. The art of magical tattooing.

Khu. Lisu Highlander. Term to describe the so-called "calamity spirit."

Kumanthanung (Kumantong). "Golden Boy." Beloved spirit whose statue adorns the altars of many occult specialists. Considered a playful child in need of attention, he is said to be beneficial in exorcising spirits, bringing prosperity to businesses, and even predicting the future. Originating from an 18th century Thai literary classic, it tells of two rivals (the handsome but poor Khun Phan (K. Phan), and the ugly but rich Khun Chang) vying for the love of a woman. When K. Phan is banished by the king due to his rival's treachery, he goes in search of items to protect himself from his enemies. He eventually meets and marries Buakhlee, the beautiful daughter of a bandit. But when the pregnant girl's father convinces her to betray him, K. Phan takes revenge by killing her and removing the unborn child inside. Drying the fetus out over a fire while chanting mantras, K. Phan imbues it with magical properties that enable it to grow into a boy known as "Golden Boy," who, in turn, saves his father from his enemies.

Khuruang-rang. One of four types of protective amulets and charms. This pertains to numerous objects found in nature (meteoric fragments, fruit seeds, animal horns or tusks) that have been transformed into stone or copper. It is said to leave its wearer invulnerable.

Khwan. One of two souls believed to exist in a person, the other being the winyaan. It is described as the essence or spark of life itself, a personal spirit that can run away from the body if curious or afraid. Once lost, the khwan must then be ritually lured back to protect the weakened body from spirit possession. Said to be comprised of 32 souls that inhabit different parts of the body, it is best kept in check by the topknot of hair on top of the head.

Kinnanorn. The male counterpart of the Kinnaree. Also known as kinnara.

Kinnaree (kinnari). Among the most beautiful of Thailand's extensive supernatural pantheon, she is described as a beautiful woman from the waist up, but possesses the lower abdomen, legs, wings, and tail of a swan from the waist down. Renowned for her grace and skill in singing and dancing, she is celebrated in traditional sculpture, artwork, and architecture. In India, they are considered minor heavenly musicians, or gandharvas.

Kruang. Term to describe a native amulet.

Lak Muang. City pillar. Spiritual wooden post or pillar revered as the home of a city's guardian animist spirit.

Kinnaree

Loy Krathong. Popular holiday in November to honor Mae Khong Kha, the goddess of waterways and rivers. Krathongs (banana leaf bowls holding a lit candle) are floated on the water at night.

Luuk Krawk. Stillborn Ghost. A dead infant whose spirit is trapped inside its corpse, keeping the body from deteriorating, as if it were still physically alive. It is greatly prized by sorcerers, who can draw out the spirit and manipulate it for monetary gain. Also known as Luug Kraug.

Mae Kong Ka. "Mother of the waters." Goddess of the sea; honored in the Loy Krathong festival for her bounty in providing water for the Thai livelihood.

Mae Naak. "Lady Naak." Immensely popular spirit said to be based on an actual person who lived in the 18th or 19th century. The daughter of a wealthy village chief, Mae Naak fell in love with the lowly family gardener (Mark) and eloped against the wishes of her father, who had already prearranged her marriage to a rich man. Becoming pregnant and giving birth while her husband was away on military service, she and her baby died due to complications. But she shunned the afterlife for the love of her husband and returned among the living to visit him at his military post. Though delighted to be reunited with his family, Mark soon realized that he was indeed living with a ghostly corpse. He fled to a Buddhist temple, where a monk imprisoned the pursuing Mae Naak in a ceramic pot and disposed of her in a river. As with most stories, this tale has evolved to have many different endings.

Over the years, her legend had grown in popularity, touching upon the themes of youthful passion, unrequited love, and revenge. She is now considered a protective spirit, warding off ills and disasters as well as aiding gamblers with lucky numbers.

Mae Phra Phai. Goddess of the wind.

Mae Phra Plerng. Goddess of fire.

Mae Phra Toranee. Mother Earth.

Mae posop. Rice Mother. Native version of the popular rice goddess motif in Southeast Asia. Ritually invoked and worshipped for a bountiful harvest, she is considered a benevolent guardian spirit whose respect and approval are constantly observed.

Mae Naak

Mae Toranee Pradtoo. Mother Earth of the Doorway; a spirit said to reside inside the raised threshold of a door.

Mae Torranee. Mother Earth goddess; said to bestow fertility upon women who ask for children.

Mau Phii. Spirit doctor; an intermediary with the supernatural world. Synonym for sorcerer, medium, and healer.

Mau song. Term to describe a spirit medium.

Moo. Term to describe a shaman or specialist proficient in many areas, including herbalism, divination, sorcery, and even exorcism.

Mor doo. "Look doctor." Term to describe a fortune-teller.

Naga-Makara. Pan-Southeast Asian. Decorative motif that combines the forms of a naga and makara into a unified design.

Nak. Native term for the naga.

Namman prai. Corpse oil. A mystical aphrodisiac obtained by ritually harvesting the oil secretions from the chin of a fresh female corpse and placing it inside an earthen pot. A single drop rubbed against the desired girl's skin or mixed in her food and she will then find its user irresistible, at times fatally. Also known as namman phraaj.

Nang Takian. "Lady Takian." Beautiful spirit maiden who makes her home in the Takian tree, punishing offenders who deface or chop down her home. She is known to shriek when her tree is cut down.

Nang talung. Native version of shadow puppetry.

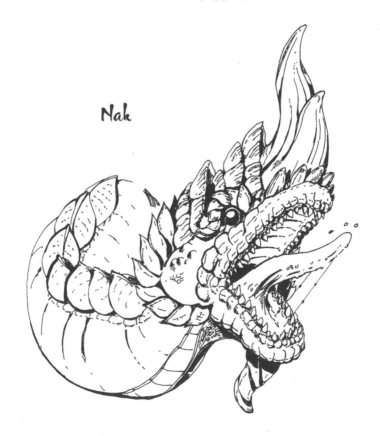

Nak

Nang Tani. Lady Banana Ghost. Female tree spirit that emerges as a beautiful maiden if the banana tree dies as it is blossoming.

Nech ma juama. Lisu Highlander. Term to describe an herbalist, known as a "medicine woman." Her skills are passed on along the same gender, from female teacher to student, from mother to daughter.

New Year's Fun Ghosts. Possessing spirits that induce children to dance and behave outrageously during New Year's festivities.

Ngan Duan Sib. Tenth Lunar Month Festival. Traditional festival meant to honor the Phii Pret, or the hungry ghosts. Celebrated with ornate parades, floats, foods and temple pilgrimages, these offerings are meant to feed the starving spirits, who are released to earth by the king of hell for one day.

Ngyak. Thai, Pan-Southeast Asia. Term to describe a mermaid that appears in legends, stories, and decorative motifs throughout the region.

Nìphà. Lisu Highlander. Term to describe a native shaman who is recruited for the role by a spirit.

Padaung women. Karen. Kayan. So-called "giraffe women." Women with elongated necks supported vertically by brass rings that extend above their shoulders. A rapidly disappearing custom beyond tourist areas, it is believed to have originated as protection against tiger attacks.

Phi phu. Shan. Term to describe a witch or a sorcerer. Its spirit is literally contagious among anyone exposed to it over a period of time. Once a person becomes a host to this spirit, he or she gains the ability to turn into an animal as well as have a spirit double.

Phii. Generic term for spirit or ghost.

Phii Baan. Village guardian spirit whose shrine must be placated regularly. It is usually considered the founder of the city.

Phii Baaw. Spirit of an unmarried man.

Phii Ha. Spirit of epidemic diseases, most specifically cholera. This phii is often blamed for rampant unexplained deaths, particularly among villagers.

Phii Ka. So-called "spirit in human form." Ghost that possesses a living person and causes him to feed voraciously on human entrails. It can only be exorcised from its human host through a severe beating with a magical item in the hands of a sorcerer or medicine man. Once free, the host suffers no physical harm afterwards.

Phii Khamot. Glowing spirit, a sort of will-o'-the-wisp, that appears in swamps and causes its victims to lose their way, luring them from place to place with its light. Known as tha-mop in Cambodian.

Phii Kong Koi. Described as having only one leg and foot, this reclusive jungle spirit is known to suck blood from the toes of people wandering in the forest. The victim will then weaken and eventually die.

Phii Krahang. Male version of the Phii Krasue. It is believed that a person who becomes adept in magic will grow wings and eventually become a Phii krahang. He will use two long pestles for his legs and another for his tail.

Phii Krasue. (Phii Krasyy). Malevolent spirit that resides inside an old woman by day, but then emerges through her mouth as she sleeps at night. It prowls about as a flying head with its bodily entrails trailing behind it. Emitting a glow as it soars through the air, it is notoriously fond of eating human excrement, blood, and the intestines and placenta of pregnant mothers. This creature is known to lurk beneath the thatched floor of a pregnant woman's room in an attempt to feed. The host of this spirit passes itself on to another body by spitting into the mouth of its successor.

Phii Lang Kluang. Wandering spirit said to approach strangers to show them the hollow in its back, which contains millipedes.

Phii Mae Mai. Widow ghost. Malevolent female ghost said to sit on men's chests, suffocating them or causing massive heart attacks.

Phii Pa. Generic term for a class of diverse forest or jungle spirits.

Phii Paub. A malevolent ghost that possesses unwitting sorcerers who fail to follow proper protocols when dabbling in black magic. Once it occupies a body, it can then transfer from person to person through the exchange of saliva.

Phii Phoang. Malevolent glowing spirit fond of raw or pungent foods; believed to originate from a man who carries or ingests medicinal or poisonous unknown herbs called "wan." Like the Phii Krasue, this creature is fond of prowling beneath the thatch floor of a pregnant woman's room in an attempt to feed.

Phii Poang Khang. Nocturnal jungle spirit said to resemble a monkey and lives near salt-licks.

Phii Prai. Malevolent ghost of a pregnant woman who dies in childbirth. Special burial rituals must be strictly followed to prevent this ghost (and her child) from returning after death to haunt the living. These two spirits are sometimes put in the service of magicians as ghostly guardians of property.

Phii Pret. Native term for the classic preta, or hungry ghost. Originating from the Buddhist cosmology of the afterlife, they are described as thin and bony; possessing a long, dangling tongue with a swollen belly; and a mouth the size of a pin's head. Inhabiting cemeteries and other areas of death, they suffer a fitting fate of karmic retribution, desperately looking for any offerings that would earn them enough merit for eventual rebirth.

Phii Pu Ya. Spirits of family ancestors, referred to as grandfathers and grandmothers.

Phii Puu Njaa. Term for ancestral spirits of the northern Thai.

Phii Ruan. Spiritual guardian of the house; usually the soul of a deceased resident who remained behind to look after the welfare of the family. This phii is held in high regard, often worshipped with flowers and food.

Phii Saaw. Spirit of an unmarried woman.

Phii Tai Hong. Terrifying class of malevolent ghosts of those who died a painful or unexpected death.

Phii Tai Thang Klom. Ghost of a pregnant woman who died in childbirth. It is particularly feared because of the compound ghost of mother and fetus. This type of Phii Tai Hong was considered so powerful that pregnant women were historically buried alive under important structures so they would return as spectral guardians.

Phii Pret

Phra-khruang. One of four types of protective amulets and charms. This pertains to various figurines cast or carved representing lessons and episodes within the life of the Buddha.

Phra Phum. "Lord of the land." Male angel whose home shrine can now be found in department stores. It is said to have originated from Bhramanism as developed in Khmer traditions.

Phra Phum Wat. Lord of the land. Temple guardians thought to be the spirits of past occupants, protecting different areas of the compound. Shrines in their honor are found throughout cities and villages.

Phra Sai. Male angel that inhabits banyan trees.

Phra Siam Devathirat. The guardian spirit of Thailand.

Phwu swi. Lisu Highlander. So-called "were-animal spirit," acquired by close association with or contamination by someone who possesses it. Once infected with this spirit, the host cannot remove it. If the host is killed, then the spirit transfers to the murderer. This spirit sometimes acts on its own malevolent volition and transforms its host into a were-animal against his will.

Phya Nahk (Payanak). King of the nagas.

Phyiphe. Lisu Highlander. So-called "witchcraft spirit," acquired by close association with or contamination by someone who possesses it. Once infected with this spirit, the host cannot remove it. If the host is killed, then the spirit transfers to the murderer. This spirit sometimes acts on its own malevolent volition to cause misfortune to others, even without its bearer's permission.

Pluk-sek. One of four types of protective amulets and charms. This pertains to the process of awakening magic within various objects through the use of mystical symbols, inscriptions, tattoos, or incantations.

Preuksathewada. Type of guardian spirit that resides in a city's central pillar, protecting it from invaders.

Rajasingha. Royal lion, derived from Hindu mythology.

Ramakien. Native version of the Indian epic, Ramayana.

Red String Ghost. Popular Internet ghost story in which a heart surgeon and a nurse encounter a deceased former patient as he tries to board their elevator. The surgeon immediately closes the door as the man approaches, noticing that he is wearing a red string around his wrist, a tag only given to dead bodies. When the surgeon explains his actions to the nurse, she raises her wrist and reveals her own red string.

Sai sin. Sacred white cord used in Buddhist ceremonies for blessings and to ward off evil spirits.

San phra phum. Spirit house. Term for a spirit altar common in Thai houses and businesses. Resembling a dollhouse in the traditional architectural style, this shrine acts as a home for the spirit of the land, who protects the property from harm and brings about prosperity if properly placated with offerings. Over the years, it has developed from a simple animist shrine to an expensive status of wealth.

Saiyasat. The magical and supernatural arts.

Singh. Native term for the mythological lion in Hinduism and Buddhism.

Souls. Every person is believed to possess two souls, the khwan and the winyaan.

Tantima. Mythical bird wielding a staff. Coming in pairs, they are considered guardians of temple entrances.

Thep. Native term for a deva.

Thepchumnum. Artistic device that adorns native temples in sculptural or illustrated forms, depicting rows of yakshas, devas and garudas posed in worship or adoration.

Thephanom. A celestial deity or deva in the pose of worship, as depicted in traditional art.

Thepparak. Guardian spirit of a specific tract of land that resides in a large tree. It needs to be placated with offerings before building any structure on the property.

Thewada. A celestial deity, guardian angel, or deva with its palms together in prayer, as depicted in traditional art.

Thotsakan. "Ten necks." One of the principal characters of the Ramakien, the villainous demon king of Longsa (Sri Lanka) who possesses many arms and heads. He is known as Ravana in the Indian version of the Ramayana.

Tsao Muong. Shan. Term to describe a residential spirit of a specific area whom villagers and residents must placate with offerings in order to coexist peacefully.

Tua yeua. One of several unclassified hominids seen throughout the forests of Southeast Asia, this one known to hill tribes in southeast Burma. Described as having red fur and living in the forest, they have been compared to orangutans, although orangutans in that region have been extinct for centuries.

Thewada

Topknot. Strands of hair cropped at the crown that were ceremoniously cut at a young age; meant as a rite of passage before puberty. It was originally believed to contain the khwan soul from escaping through the top of the head.

Wan ya. One of four types of protective amulets and charms. This pertains to the use of medicinal plants and herbs, particularly in folk medicine.

Wat. Buddhist temple complex of worship.

Whispering Ghost. Spirit who whispers about the future into its master's ear.

Winyaan. One of two souls believed to exist in a person, the other being the khwan. It is the soul that journeys into the afterlife, carrying the karmic merit that is weighed and judged to determine its ultimate fate. However, it is particularly vulnerable right after death, and if not carefully tended to with specific rituals, may return as a malevolent ghost.

Yaa sanee. So-called "love magic." Type of magic that practitioners manipulate through charms to induce approval, compliance, or persuasion from others to achieve their own personal goals.

Yang tree. Dipterocarpus alatus. Towering forest tree believed to be the abode of a male godling spirit and a female wood nymph. Wood-cutters are often reluctant to chop down Yang trees for fear of offending its residing spirits.

Yi khwu juapha. Lisu Highlander. Term to describe a sorcerer, known as an "incantation man."

Yom Phra Baan. Native term for Yama, the Hindu god of death.

Vietnam

Ba Hoa. Fire Goddess. Malevolent entity known for starting fires or inducing others to do so.

Ba Thuy. Water goddess. A water spirit that can both cause and remove noi (see entry). Often associated with Long Than (The Dragon King), boat-dwellers hold rituals in her honor for favorable weather, safe passage, and even clean water.

Con hoa. Malevolent ghosts of victims who originally died by fire. Like the fire goddess Ba Hoa, they are greatly feared for setting thatched houses ablaze, or inducing others to start it. Rare rhinoceros or goat horns are sometimes used as protective talismans against them.

Da Trang Crabs. Famous allegory for moderation and common sense. A hunter, Da Trang, is given a pearl by a magical serpent who grants him the power to speak to wild animals. Gaining favor with a king for his beneficial insight, he unexpectedly loses the pearl in the ocean and, despite efforts to extend the beach forward to the spot where he lost it, his progress is washed away by the tide. Da Trang eventually dies in his diligence to retrieve it. Beach crabs, creating mounds in the sand only to have them be washed away, are said to embody his spirit and persistence and serve as a lesson in moderation in our everyday actions.

Den. Term to describe the temple of a deified hero.

Giai. Legendary giant fresh-water turtle said to be able to demolish dikes.

Goddesses of the Nine Heavens. Entities associated with falling stars. Shrines in their honor are constructed at the base of trees that the meteor is believed to have used to descend to earth after disappearing in the glade.

Luoi cam set. Axe wielded by the thunder spirit Thien Loi (see entry); said to come in bronze and stone forms. Found beneath the ground where lightning has struck, it is believed to be a potent talisman if located.

Ma. Generic term for a ghost or phantom.

Ma A Phien. The dreaded opium ghost; associated with addiction.

Ma cho. Dog ghost. Harmless animal spirits believed to flock to the fields after sunset, scurrying between the legs of unsuspecting passersby.

Ma da. Malevolent ghosts of the drowned who cannot find peace until they find a replacement for their suffering. Prowling in the water or hovering above it as a nondescript black mass while wailing, "It's so cold," they wait for victims, particularly kin and children. Children are sometimes given metal bracelets as protection from being dragged into the water.

Ma dung. Collective term for harmful ghosts associated with oxen, buffalo, and horses. They are often blamed for unusual occurrences within a village.

Ma heo. Pig ghost. Harmless animal spirits believed to flock to the fields after sunset, scurrying between the legs of unsuspecting passersby.

Ma meo. Cat ghost. Harmless animal spirits believed to flock to the fields after sunset, scurrying between the legs of unsuspecting passersby.

Ma Than Vong. Tightening Knot Ghost. Spirit that compels people to commit suicide by whispering in their ears, "co, co (neck, neck)."

Ma troi. Wayward ghost of a drowned person whose body has not been recovered. Manifesting itself as a glow over water or near fire to warm itself, its appearance is believed to be a sign to family members to continue their search for the body and restore it to the family tomb. If unsuccessful, a sorcerer (Ong Thay Phap) is then called to perform a ritual to retrieve the soul, keep it in a jar, and place it on the altar of the ancestors.

Ma-lai. Native version of the Thai creature Phii krasu.

Mistresses of the Spirits. Entities associated with falling stars. Shrines in their honor are constructed at the base of trees that the meteor is believed to have used to descend to earth after disappearing in the glade.

Noi. A curse that compels the victim to submerge his face in water, drowning and spreading the curse to his kin. Entire families have been known to perish from this curse, with the drowning depth being as shallow as a cup of water.

Nguoi Rung. One of several unclassified hominids seen throughout the forests of Southeast Asia. Said to inhabit the wilderness between Vietnam and Laos, it is described as being 6 feet tall and almost completely covered with hair.

Ong Thay Phap. Master of Sorcery. He specializes in exorcising evil spirits, deriving his powers from his supernatural patron, Ong Thay Thuong ("the supreme being").

Quy. Malicious supernatural beings that live in trees and appear as human shadows.

Thien Loi. Thunder Spirit, sent to earth to exact punishment against criminals and evil spirits. He wields an ax called luoi cam set, using a bronze one against human beings and a stone one against evil spirits and animals. Such an ax is said to be found beneath the spot where lightning has struck and can be utilized as a potent talisman.

Thuong-luong. Mythical red-crested sea serpent described as being 100 feet long and covered with scales. This ferocious creature is known to cause waves that overturn boats and to abduct women to bring back to its kingdom as wives.

Tien. Benevolent and cheerful supernatural entities capable of bestowing beneficial gifts, attributes, and knowledge upon people. They have been compared to djinns.

Tinh. Soul-stealing ghost. Malevolent supernatural entity that tricks its victims into opening their mouths, drawing out their soul, and leaving them insane.

Wave spirits. Spirits said to lie at the bottom of large rivers, rising occasionally and causing large waves.

Yeu. Malicious demons that live in trees and appear as human shadows.

Malaysia and Indonesia

Abangan. Indonesian. Traditional Javanese religious system; centered around peasantry and animism.

Adat. Indonesian. Sacred beliefs or customs passed down by ancestors.

Adu zatua. Indonesian. Sumatra. Nias. Carved wooden figurines of dead ancestors; believed to represent their continued contact and influence among the living. Tied together in clans, these seated figurines are present in all Nias homes and are given offerings on special occasions.

Amok. Malaysian term for "frenzied" or "killing" madness.

Anak kerak. Malay, Indonesian. According to popular belief, it is the dead, aged fetus of the first-born child of parents who are both first-born. Either still-born or killed before its first birthday, the fetus, or infant, is then smoked and shrunk. Possessing great power to heal and harm, this spirit must be treated like a living child and fed milk daily from a bottle.

Ananta. Indian. Hindu. Boundless, infinite, eternal. Mythical serpent that the Hindu god Vishnu rests upon between cosmic periods. Also known as Shesha and Vasuki.

Arupahadtu. Indonesian. Borobodur monument. "Realm of formlessness." The top level or tier that divides the temple into three sections, corresponding to the three steps of Buddhist thought that lead to Nirvana, or enlightenment. This level represents the highest level, where, upon receiving instruction from teachers seen on previous tiers, the man has no more need for external guidance.

Asu. Indonesian. Borneo. Kenyah term for a decorative dragon dog motif.

Babainan. Balinese. Term to describe possession by an evil spirit.

Badé. Balinese. Formal term used to describe a nobleman's ornate cremation tower; used to transport the deceased to their place of burning. It consists of a platform that supports the three levels of the Balinese universe, along with a monstrous winged Bhoma to ward off evil spirits.

Bajang. Malay, Indonesian. Malevolent male spirit said to take the form of a mewing pole-cat. Particularly dangerous to children, the appearance of this demon foretells danger and disease. It is believed that it can be enslaved by a person as a familiar and made to do its master's bidding. Kept in a bamboo container, it is fed eggs and milk.

Bajasa. Indonesian. Borneo. Bare'e Toradja. Type of woman (or a man who poses as a woman) shaman who takes spiritual journeys to the underworld or to the sky to cure those afflicted with soul-loss, also known as tadu.

Bali. Indonesian. Borneo. Kenyah term for spirit.

Bali akang. Indonesian. Borneo. Kenyah term for the spirit of bravery.

Bali matei. Indonesian. Borneo. Kenyah term for the spirit of death.

Bali statues. Indonesian. Borneo. Carvings of spirits used to scare away sickness-carrying ghosts.

Bali uma. Indonesian. Borneo. Kenyah term for guardian house spirit.

Balian. Malay, Indonesian. Term for a native male or female shaman with the ability to heal as well as to communicate with spirits.

Balian panengen. Balinese. A practitioner of white magic.

Balian pangiwa. Balinese. A practitioner of black magic.

Bangsa alus. Malay, Indonesian. Umbrella term for the entire class of Malay supernatural entities.

Banten. Balinese. Term for offering.

Bapu. Indonesian. Flores Island. Nage. Term to describe malevolent free spirits that can harm human beings. With the ability to disappear at will and even shape-shift into various animals and people, these mischievous entities can bring about illness and death and have been known to capture souls.

Barak. Balinese. Character in the Calonarang mask drama. Red-colored apprentice Leyak, who arrives from the south, a direction most associated with plagues and storms.

Barich. Indonesian. Borneo. Dayak term for female shamans who specialize in the so-called "treatment" of paddy fields.

Barong. Balinese. Mythical protector of the island and dual enemy of Rangda, queen of the Leyaks. Described as a cross between a lion and a tiger, he is said to have originated from Bali's animist past rather than from Hinduism, although he is sometimes associated with Banaspati Raja, the lord of the forest from Hindu mythology. Greatly revered, he represents white magic and the forces of the right. In the barong play, he is depicted in two forms: towering two-legged puppets (barong landung), and the two-man-operated four-legged type (barong ket). He is portrayed as having the temperament of a playful puppy, but is fierce in battle.

Barong bangkal. Balinese. The pig motif of a barong puppet.

Barong gadja. Balinese. The elephant motif of a barong puppet.

Barong landing. Balinese. Human-shaped holy barong puppet.

Barong matjan. Balinese. The tiger motif of a barong puppet.

Barong Play. Balinese. Mask drama involving giant sacred puppets in a procession, seeking out and expelling evil spirits. It dramatizes barong versus rangda, the battle between good and evil.

Barong singha. Balinese. The lion motif of a barong puppet.

Basir. Indonesian. Borneo. Ngadju Dyak. Term to describe an asexual shaman or hermaphrodite used by divinities to communicate with the living. Basirs both dress and behave like women.

Batutut. Malaysian. One of several unclassified hominids seen throughout the forests of Southeast Asia. Said to have inhabited the Malaysian state of Sabah, it is known primarily from distinct footprints.

Bedawang Nala. Balinese. Gigantic mythical turtle said to support the entire world on its back. Its movements are believed to cause earthquakes and other volcanic activity. It is supported by two enormous nagas (Naga Basuki and Naga Anantaboga) that act as its foundation.

Bedayo Ketawang. Indonesian. Javanese. Sacred dance performed in reverence to Nyai Loro Kidul on the anniversary of the Sultan's coronation. Comprised of nine virgins in wedding attire, it is said that Loro Kidul sometimes appears with the group as the tenth dancer.

Begu. Indonesian. Sumatra. Batak term for a spirit.

Begu ganjang. Indonesian. North Sumatra. Regional term to describe a dangerous malevolent spirit.

Belawing. Indonesian. Borneo. Apo kayan. Ornate totem pole crowned with a fierce warrior carving; used to protect villages and drive away evil spirits.

Berhantu. Malaysian. Term for spirit-raising, as practiced by pawangs.

Bersih desa. Indonesian. Javanese. "Cleaning the village." Ritual ceremony used to cleanse villages of evil spirits.

Beruang rambai. Indonesian. One of several unclassified hominids seen throughout the forests of Southeast Asia. It is said to inhabit the Sarawak/Kalimantan border in central Borneo.

Beruwa. Indonesian. Borneo. Kenyah term for the human soul; one of two components believed to complete a human being (the other being luhan, or body). Once it leaves the body at death, the beruwa then joins the other ancestral spirits and becomes a bali matei, or spirit of death. Such ancestral spirits must be placated with offerings, or they will tempt the spirit of the weak, such as children, to leave its host, ultimately causing that person to die.

Bhatara. Balinese. "Lord." Generic title given to a god.

Bhoma (Boma). Balinese. So-called "son of the earth." Demonic head carving appearing over doorways; described as having bulging eyes, large tusks, and a draping tongue. The offspring of Vishnu and Ibu Pertiwi (mother earth), this villainous demon fought against the gods and was ultimately slain by Krishna (an avatar of his father Vishnu). In death, Boma was transformed into a positive guardian, frightening demons above the main gate that leads to the central courtyard of a traditional temple.

Bhur. Balinese. In the native cosmology, the underworld.

Bhuta (Bhut, Buta). Pan-Indian, Southeast Asia. Malevolent, impure spirit whose main purpose is to annoy, pollute, and corrupt human beings, thereby disturbing the balance between good and evil. Said to be the ghosts of men who died violently, they are known to possess victims, destroy crops, and even cause epidemics. Haunting lonely places like cemeteries and dark forests, they must be regularly propitiated with offerings. They are often blamed for mysterious lights, whistling, and events that cannot be explained. It's believed that they are afraid of fire and possess no shadow.

Bhuta Yadnya. Balinese. Ritual sacrifice meant to appease the polluting Bhut spirits, which are capable of bringing sickness, misfortune, and even death.

Bhuwa. Balinese. In the native cosmology, the visible world.

Bomoh. Malaysian. Traditional medicine man or sorcerer; employs spells, charms, and native remedies to cure the afflicted.

Boogie man. Term said to have been derived from historical encounters with the Bugis, a fearsome sea-faring tribe in Southeast Asia. Embodying the classic pirate archetype, they were the scourge of the Mollucan archipelago.

Buto Ijo. Indonesian. Javanese. Term to describe a spirit who can be commanded by its master to look for wealth. The master must provide it a charm in the form of a human soul.

Calonarang. Balinese. Rarely performed mask drama used to exorcise afflicted villages by challenging the offending witches, magicians, or leyaks to match their abilities against that of Rangda, queen of the leyaks, and the goddess of death. If successful, the defeated spirits must cease their activities.

Celuluk. Balinese. Character in the Calonarang mask drama. Bald-headed with protruding teeth and a large belly, she is almost a comedic leyak in performance.

Cenoi. Malaysian. Semang. "Nephews of god." Celestial spirits; a type of intermediary to the divine, invoked by the hala shaman in curing the afflicted.

Dalang. Indonesian. Term for a Wayang puppeteer.

Danjang. Malay, Indonesian. Protective guardian spirit; very similar to a demit in terms of function. However, danjangs are considered to be actual historical figures that are closely related to a specific site (i.e., the founder of a village, etc.).

Datu. Indonesian. Sumatra. Term to describe a high-ranking priest whopossesses supernatural powers to exorcise spirits and heal the afflicted.

Daya beruri. Indonesian. Borneo. Dayak term for male shamans who specialize in healing.

Demit. Malay, Indonesian. Spirit confined to a specific area (usually holy sites or pundèns), catering, and protecting its inhabitants.

Deva (dewa). Malay, Indonesian. Term for a male deity; celestial beings said to inhabit the lower levels of Buddhist heaven.

Devi (dewi). Malay, Indonesian. Term for a female deity; celestial beings said to inhabit the lower levels of Buddhist heaven.

Dewi Durga. Balinese. One of three goddesses that comprise the Hindu female trinity (along with Dewi Saraswati and Dewi Sri). Unlike her classic Indian counterpart, however, the Balinese Durga is considered a beneficent entity. Although she is the ruler of the graveyard and of the underworld, she also represents the recycling of the physical body back into the cosmos. The role of the goddess of destruction in Bali is played by the evil Rangda, with whom Dewi Durga is sometimes associated. She is also the consort of Siwa (Shiva), one of the three gods that comprise the Hindu male trinity.

Dewi Saraswati. Balinese. One of three goddesses that comprise the Hindu female trinity (along with Dewi Durga and Dewi Sri). The patron deity of students and artisans, her four arms represent creativity, wisdom, devotion, and meditation. She is also the consort of Brahma, one of the three gods that comprise the Hindu male trinity.

Dewi Sri. Balinese. Rice Goddess. One of three goddesses that comprise the Hindu female trinity (along with Dewi Durga and Dewi Saraswati). But unlike the classic Indian model, she replaces Lakshmi as Wisnu's (Vishnu) consort. She is perhaps the island's most famous deity, a living embodiment of rice, whose appeasement and blessings are necessary for a bountiful harvest. Shrines and rice-stalk effigies (called Dewi Cili) of her image are present in every rice field.

Djènggès. Indonesian. Javanese. Type of sorcery similar to tenung, except that sharp objects added to the spirit offerings are magically transferred to the stomach of the intended victim.

Djeró Gedé Metjaling. Balinese. Fanged black demon who lives on the small island of Nusa Penida. It is believed to arrive in Bali in the waning months of the rainy season, exploding on shore like a fireball and spreading its evil. Also known as I Macaling.

Djimat. Indonesian. Javanese. Term for a protective amulet or charm; appearing as written Arabic.

Djinn (Jin, Jinn). Middle East, South, Southeast Asia. Arabic umbrella term for a class of Islamic spirits said to have been created by God from "smokeless fire" prior to human beings. Living in an intermediate state between angels and humans, these innumerable illusionary spirits can assume any form, including animals, and exist in communities similar to that of living people. They can reside virtually anywhere (markets, graveyards, deserts, ruins) and have been known to harass victims with pranks, sickness, and possession. The leader of all Djinns is Iblis, a former angel who was cast out from heaven for refusing to bow to Adam at Allah's command. There are two types of Djinns: Djinn Islam, spirits faithful to Islam, and Djinn Kafir, infidel spirits. The singular term for Djinns is jinni, from which the Western name "genie" is said to have been derived.

Djinn Islam. Middle East, South, Southeast Asia. Spirits faithful to Islam.

Djinn Kafir. Middle East, South, Southeast Asia. Infidel spirits.

Djrangkong. Malay, Indonesian. A skeletal spirit; literally a man without flesh.

Dukun. Indonesian. Javanese. Generic term for a diverse class of sorcerers whose magical and curative powers encompass a wide variety of skills and functions.

Dukun cabul. Indonesian. Javanese. Term to describe a so-called "immoral practitioner," a dukun who engages in despicable and depraved activities such as murder and rape.

Dukun palsu. Indonesian. Javanese. Term to describe a so-called "false practitioner," a dukun who engages in deceptive or fraudulent activities.

Dukun santet. Indonesian. Javanese. Term to describe a feared practitioner of black magic (ilmu gaib).

Duwe. Balinese. Wild animals that "reside" in temples, affectionately referred to as their owner.

Ebu gogo. Indonesian. Flores Island. Mythological pot-bellied hominid that has been compared to an elf. Described as being 1 meter tall and covered in hair with protruding ears. The recent fossil discovery of Homo floresiensis on this island has caused speculation about the possibility of this creature's existence.

Gaib. Indonesian. Javanese. Umbrella term to describe supernatural phenomena.

Gamang. Balinese. So-called invisible people; spirits said to inhabit areas free of human habitation, including rivers, ravines, rocks, and trees.

Gendam. Indonesian. Javanese. Type of sorcery that induces a victim to go to a specific place against his will.

Gendruwo. Malay, Indonesian. A male memedi, playful—and, at times, dangerous—spirit that frequently inflicts mischievous pranks upon its victims. They have been known to abduct people, assuming the form of family members to lure them away. If the intended victim eats the food offered by the gendruwo, he will then become invisible.

Genie. Middle East, South, Southeast Asia. See Djinn.

Gergasi. Malay, Indonesian. Term for a giant-tusked ogre.

Guna. Indonesian. Javanese. Type of sorcery described as a form of love magic, inducing reluctant victims to come to one's bed.

Guna-guna. Indonesian. Javanese. Term to describe black magic.

Hala (halak). Malaysian. Semang. Traditional medicine man who invokes the cenoi spirits for curing the afflicted. He also uses quartz crystals (called chebuch) in determining the cause of an illness.

Hampatong. Indonesian. Borneo. Kalimantan. Dayak. Wooden ancestral figurines carved to honor the dead as well as protect the community. Coming in two types (tajahan, which commemorates the deceased, and pataho, which guards the living), they appear in various human, animal, and supernatural forms.

Hantu. Malay, Indonesian. Generic term for evil spirit. It is the inverse of "Tuhan," which means "God."

Hantu ayer. Malay, Indonesian. A type of water spirit.

Hantu bakal. Malay, Indonesian. A type of jungle spirit.

Hantu bandan. Malay, Indonesian. So-called "spirit of the waterfall." Most often seen lying prone in the water with the currents raging down between the rocks.

Hantu belian. Malay, Indonesian. A tiger spirit believed to take the form of a bird.

Hantu b'rok. Malay, Indonesian. So-called baboon demon. A simian spirit capable of possessing dancers and temporarily giving them incredible climbing powers.

Hantu bukit. Malay, Indonesian. Spirits that haunt hills and hilly areas.

Hantu bungkus. Malay, Indonesian. See pocong.

Hantu denei. Malay, Indonesian. So-called "demon of wild beast tracks." A type of jungle spirit.

Hantu gharu. Malay, Indonesian. Spirit of the Eagle-wood tree, one of numerous plants and trees in the Malay forest said to be haunted. This powerful spirit must be properly propitiated with sacrifices. Failure to follow proper protocol can result in death to the transgressor.

Hantu-hantuan. Malay, Indonesian. So-called "echo spirits." A type of jungle spirit.

Hantu hutan. Malay, Indonesian. Generic term for the entire class of Malay forest spirits.

Hantu kubor. Malay, Indonesian. So-called "grave demons." Cemetery-haunting spirits said to prey upon living victims.

Hantu Jarang Gigi. Malaysian. "Snaggle-toothed ghost." One of several unclassified hominids seen throughout the forests of Southeast Asia. Said to inhabit the jungles of Johor in Malaysia, these towering, hairy bipeds are described as herbivorous and covered in black fur. This creature is also known as Orang Mawas.

Hantu jepun. Malay, Indonesian. Spirits of World War II Japanese soldiers, which are quite common throughout Southeast Asia.

Hantu kapur. Malay, Indonesian. Spirit, or "bisan," of camphor trees; one of numerous plants and trees in the Malay forest said to be haunted.

Emitting a shrill sound at night, this spirit must be properly propitiated; otherwise, obtaining the camphor gum would be difficult.

Hantu kertau. Malaysian. Supernatural creature described as having the head of a deer and the body of a boar.

Hantu laut. Malay, Indonesian. A type of sea spirit.

Hantu lilin. Malaysian. So-called "candle ghost." Entity that carries around a candle wherever it goes.

Hantu longgak. Malay, Indonesian. Spirit whose gaze is said to be locked upwards. Its victims foam at the mouth.

Hantu (orang) mati di-bunoh. Malay, Indonesian. The spirit of a murdered man.

Hantu pemburu. Malaysian. The legendary Spectre, or Wild Huntsman, a hunter who roams the vast Malay forests in search of his animal quarry. Accompanied by a pack of ghostly dogs and covered with an overgrowth of orchids, he is said to be the harbinger of death and disease. A wild bird called a baberek is also said to fly in flocks at night prior to his arrival.

Hantu pusaka. Malaysian. A hereditary spirit kept by a pawang and used as a familiar.

Hantu raya. Malay, Indonesian. So-called "great" demon; described most commonly as a spirit double for its malevolent magician master, assuming its master's form even after his death to haunt victims.

Hantu rebut. Malay, Indonesian. Storm spirit that howls and revels within its torrential winds.

Hantu rimba. Malay, Indonesian. So-called "deep forest demon," a type of jungle spirit.

Hantu samambu. Malay, Indonesian. Spirit of the Malacca Cane plant, one of numerous plants and trees in the Malay forest that is said to be haunted. Like the camphor tree, it also makes noises at night. The stick insect is believed to be the spirit's physical manifestation.

Hantu sawan. Malay, Indonesian. Malevolent devil said to cause convulsions.

Hantu songkei. Malay, Indonesian. Spirit associated with the loosening or untying of animal snares and traps. Described as having a lengthy nose and wide-set eyes that allow it to see all around its body. It is also invisible from the chest down.

Hantu tetek. Malay, Indonesian. So-called "breast ghost," a spirit infamous for having ridiculously enormous breasts that it uses to smother its victims.

Hantu tinggi. Malaysian. So-called "tall ghost," known for changing its size and growing tall before its victim, locking the person's neck up permanently in place.

Harimau kramat. Malay, Indonesian. Term for a ghost tiger, the guardian spirit of sacred areas.

Hariti. Sanskrit. Originally, the mother of the Yakshas. Described as a horse-headed, child-eating ogress, she was later converted by the Buddha and became the patron goddess for the welfare of children and childbirth. She is known as Kishimojin in Japanese.

Homo floresiensis. Indonesian. Controversial human remains found on the island of Flores in 2004. Dubbed "Hobbits" (after the diminutive characters created by fantasy author J.R.R. Tolkien), the meter-tall hominids are believed to have lived about 18,000 years ago. Evidence of stone tools suggest they were proficient in hunting. In scientific circles, however, there is disagreement about whether this population truly represents a new dwarf species in the human family tree, or if it actually suffered from various physical and glandular disorders.

As of this writing, similar fossils have also been found on the Pacific island chain of Palau.

Hudoq. Indonesian. Borneo. Kenyah-Kayan. Term to describe an ancestral spirit, a visual motif carved on masks, doors, beams, and panels. Hudoq-style masks portray both human and animal characteristics (with fangs and tendril-like ears) and are repainted in various colors for different occasions.

Ikan duyong. Malay, Indonesian. Term for a native mermaid. "Duyong" is actually the root word for "Dugong," describing the marine mammal related to the manatee.

Ilmu. Malay, Indonesian. Term for "magic," as practiced by bomohs. It also refers to knowledge, particularly esoteric knowledge of Islamic nature.

Ilmu ghaib. Malay, Indonesian. Term for a type of native sorcery or black magic.

Ilmu hitam. Indonesian. Javanese. Term to describe so-called "evil-working" magical substances.

Ilmu leak. Indonesian. Javanese. Term to describe a type of witchcraft.

Ilmu pengasih. Malaysian. Term to describe so-called "love magic."

Imam. Islamic term to describe the head of a mosque district.

Jaba pura. Balinese. Realm of the ground spirits.

Jaran Guyang. Balinese. Character in the Calonarang mask drama; described as a powerful witch who specializes in creating spells that cause people to cry and scream. She is also capable of shifting forms, particularly a horse.

Jatayu. Son of garuda and the fearless king of birds. In the Mahabharata, he fought on the side of Rama and was ultimately slain by Ravana, the villainous ruler of Sri Lanka. He embodies the ideal loyal friend.

Jauk. Balinese. Masked demon dancers of the Barong play.

Jelangkung. Indonesian. Often referred to as the native form of the Ouija Board, it is generally described as a ritual that uses a prop to summon and communicate with the spirits of the deceased. This prop is a doll-like figure inside a bucket or basket which the conjurer invites the spirits to inhabit. This ritual is said to be most effective when held in tombs with a particularly gruesome history.

Jenglot. Indonesian. Mysterious supernatural creature often on display in museums. It is described as being the size of a small doll and corpse-like in appearance, but with unusually joined feet and extremely long hair. They are said to be uncovered by psychics after having performed supernatural ceremonies and are fed blood by its keeper.

Jimat. Indonesian. Javanese. Term to describe a mystical talisman or amulet.

Jin Laut. Malaysian. So-called "spirits of the sea."

Jin Tanah. Malaysian. So-called "spirits of the earth."

Jogormanik. Balinese. Yama's minister of hell; described as bald with a huge belly and blemished skin. He is a character from the Bhima Swarga, a Balinese folktale based loosely on an episode from the Mahabharata.

Kala. Balinese. Malevolent, impure spirit whose main purpose is to annoy, pollute, and corrupt human beings, thereby disturbing the balance between good and evil. Haunting lonely places like cemeteries and dark forests, they must be regularly propitiated with offerings.

Kalpavriksha. Term for the sacred wishing-granting tree.

Kamadhatu. Indonesian. Borodbodur monument. "Realm of desire." The lowest level or tier that divides the temple into three sections, corresponding to the three steps of Buddhist thought that leads to Nirvana, or enlightenment. This level represents the state of man prior to his knowledge of the Buddha's teachings.

Kampel-kampelan. Malay, Indonesian. Mild possession similar to kesurupan, except that the possessed isn't evidently sick and only acts strangely on occasion. A bath is said to cure it.

Kampir-kampiran. Malay, Indonesian. Type of spirit possession similar to kesurupan, except that the invading spirit hails from a distant location, encountering its host while traveling from place to place.

Karang asti. Balinese. Similar to the karang tjuring motif, except that this is described as the jawless head of an elephant.

Karang bintulu. Balinese. Popular motif used in various carvings; described as a head with a singular eye and a row of upper teeth, complete with extended canine fangs.

Karang sae. Balinese. Term to describe a type of ornate door guardian.

Karang tjewiri. Balinese. Gate decoration described as having a monster face with long canines and a hanging tongue.

Karang tjuring. Balinese. Architectural corner motif described as a singular eye with a toothed upper bird's beak.

Kecak. Balinese. Famous monkey chant dance, in which up to a hundred men sit together and chant collectively. Originally a male warrior dance, it is an imitation of Hanuman and his monkey army from the Ramayana.

Kemomong. Malay, Indonesian. Spiritual possession based on a voluntary pact with a spirit, imbuing the host with new powers in a symbiotic partnership.

Kenyalang. Indonesian. Borneo. Ornate wooden hornbill carving once significant to ritual ceremonies that preceded native head-hunting expeditions.

Keramat. Malaysian. Term to describe a village's sacred shrine.

Keraton. Indonesian. Javanese. Term for a palace that serves as the spiritual center of a kingdom.

Kesurupan. Malay, Indonesian. Most common type of spirit possession, in which a local spirit temporarily occupies a victim as evidenced through seizures. A dukun is summoned to placate the spirit, which, in turn, leaves the host body. The victim usually has no memory of the possession upon recovery.

Khaki besar. Malaysian. One of several unclassified hominids seen throughout the forests of Southeast Asia. This one has been called the country's resident Bigfoot and is described as being 8 feet tall and creating 18-inch footprints with its four-toed feet.

Ki Blorong. Malay, Indonesian. The male version of the nyai blorong.

Kiwa (Left). Balinese. Negative forces of magic.

Kokokan. Balinese. Native white heron who congregate in the thousands upon the rice fields. It is considered sacred and is, therefore, left undisturbed.

Kris. Malaysia, Indonesia, and southern Philippines. Double-edged ritual sword or dagger found in straight or wavy-bladed forms. It is often ascribed with magical powers and abilities and is even said to individually possess a spirit.

Krobongan. Indonesian. Javanese. Ceremonial bed located in the center of prominent homes in central Java; meant to be a place of rest for the rice goddess Dewi Sri when she visits that particular home. At the foot of the bed sit a pair of figurines called loro blonyo, statues representing Dewi Sri and Sadono, her consort.

Kumbha Karna. Gigantic younger brother of Ravana, the villainous ruler of Sri Lanka. Known for sleeping half a year and only waking up for a single day, he was desperately awakened to fight the god-king Rama. Only after drinking 2,000 bottles of liquor did he feel ready for action. He was ultimately beheaded by Rama in battle.

Langsuir. Malay, Indonesian. Malevolent spirit said to originally have been a beautiful woman who died upon hearing that her child was stillborn at birth. Dressed in a green robe with long nails, she has long black hair that conceals a hole on the back of her neck. It is through this hole that she is said to suck the blood of children. She is able to fly, and has often been compared to a banshee or a White Lady.

A woman can potentially turn into a langsuir if she dies during or after childbirth. To prevent this, eggs must be tucked under each armpit and her palms pinned down with needles. Glass beads must also be placed inside her mouth. These measures prevent her from shrieking and flying off upon transformation.

The langsuir has also been known to take the form of a night owl. Her stillborn child is the dreaded pontianak.

Lelembut. Malay, Indonesian. Spirit that possesses a person. Believed to enter victims through their feet, it may induce sickness, insanity, and even death. Only a dukun can remove this invading entity from the body.

Leluhur. Balinese. Term to describe deified native ancestors.

Lembu. Balinese. Cow-shaped sarcophagus, or coffin, for the dead.

Leyak. Balinese. Shape-shifting class of malevolent witches. Appearing as mysterious flames, shadows, white cloths, or unusual animals, they feed on fresh corpses, drink the blood of sleeping victims, and are fond of children's entrails. They are said to frequent lonely roads and cemeteries and are blamed for all the ills of the island. Leyaks have even kept up with modern times, shape-shifting into vehicles and other modes of transportation.

Leyak Mata Besik. Balinese. Character in the Calonarang mask drama; a one-eyed Leyak who is a student of black magic under Rangda.

Leyak Poleng. Balinese. Character in the Calonarang mask drama whose specialty is bringing about plagues.

Lontar. Balinese. Dried and pressed palm leaves upon which ancient Hindu teachings are written. The script and language of the teachings are called kekawin.

Loro blonyo. Indonesian. Javanese. "Inseparable couple." A pair of statues that sit at the foot of the Krobongan, representing Dewi Sri and her consort Sadono. They have also become known as "marriage figures," which are displayed before a wedding and are meant to receive the goddess' blessings for a fruitful union.

Macaru. Balinese. Offering to appease demons.

Mae. Indonesian. Flores Island. Nage. Local term to describe the human soul.

Mahisa Wedana. Balinese. Character in the Calonarang mask drama. A powerful witch created from a human umbilical cord, she can change her form into a white water buffalo. The flapping of her ears is the only sound she makes.

Mambang kuning. Malaysian. So-called mischievous "yellow spirits." Entities active at sunset and used by bomohs for their own purposes.

Mamuli. Indonesian. Traditional silver amulet given to the bride by the groom's family. Shaped like female genitalia, it is a protective talisman for the married couple.

Manang. Indonesian. Borneo. Sea Dayak term for a type of shaman that employs a magical box containing quartz crystals that the practitioner uses to diagnose and cure soul-loss.

Mbitoro. Indonesian. Irian Jaya. Mimika. Term to describe a native spirit pole which is displayed during burial rituals.

Memedi. Malay, Indonesian. Generic term for a diverse class of spirits that frighten their victims. Generally considered harmless, they are often encountered in dark and isolated areas at night. They are also notorious for assuming the form of family members or relatives to deceive and lure their victims.

Mentèk. Malay, Indonesian. Type of tuyul that lives in rice fields; described as a small naked child capable of stealing rice grains for its master.

Menyantet. Indonesian. Javanese. Term to describe black magic.

Meru. Balinese. Tower-like structure or shrine meant to represent the legendary Mount Meru, abode of the gods.

Mount Agung. Balinese. The island's most sacred mountain.

Mukene. Indonesian. Seram. Nuaulu. Pia. Spirits that possess the insane, afflicting the victim's body and causing it to deteriorate physically.

Nabau. Indonesian. Borneo. Mythical serpent said to grow to gigantic size; described as dragon-like with seven nostrils. It also has the ability to change forms.

Naga Anantaboga. Balinese. One of two gigantic nagas that support Bedawang Nala, the mythical world turtle. This naga represents food, shelter, and clothing.

Naga banda. Balinese. Serpent that conveys the soul to heaven; ritually prominent in the ngaben cremation ceremony.

Naga Basuki. Balinese. One of two gigantic nagas that support Bedawang Nala, the mythical world turtle. This naga represents protection and safety.

Nau. Indonesian. Seram. Nuaulu. Term to describe a local form of divination.

Ngaben. Balinese. Elaborate and heavily ritualized Hindu cremation ceremony used to free the spirit and help it ascend to the next world.

Ngeb. Balinese. State of mental shock and emotional distress upon seeing something traumatizing or horrific, such as ghosts.

Ngeleyakin. Balinese. Term to describe a native form of witchcraft.

Ngerebeg. Balinese. Ritual exorcism ceremony usually held the day before a temple festival; meant to purify the village and balance the positive and negative forces. Varying in appearance from area to area, this procession of puppets travels to different temples and surrounding villages. Its young participants are dressed up as supernatural beings, making loud noises to pacify the invisible entities that might disrupt the forthcoming festival.

Ngerit. Balinese. Term for mass cremations.

Ngerupuk. Balinese. Demon-scaring ceremony and ritual exorcism held the day before Nyepi, the Hindu-Balinese Day of Silence. In modern times, it involves Balinese youths creating and parading giant demonic dolls (ogoh-ogoh) around the village, screaming and banging on gongs in an effort to scare evil spirits away.

Ni Lenda Lendi. Balinese. Character in the Calonarang mask drama. Durga-worshipping Leyak who was created from a shadow and specializes in turning into a crow.

Nitu. Indonesian. Flores Island. Nage. Term to describe malevolent free spirits that can harm human beings. With the ability to disappear at will and even shape-shift into various animals and people, these mischievous entities can bring about illness and death. Nitu are specifically known to make people lose their way and to even abduct them.

Njunjung. Indonesian. Javanese. Community ritual occasion that involves cleaning and honoring the graves in a graveyard.

Noa. Indonesian. Flores Island. Nage. Term to describe malevolent free spirits that can harm human beings. With the ability to disappear at will and even shape-shift into various animals and people, these mischievous entities can bring about illness and death and have been known to capture souls. Noas are specifically known to inflict disease upon livestock and pestilence on crops. See also nitu, bapu.

Nuhune. Indonesian. Seram. Nuaulu. Female ancestral guardian spirits that inhabit menstruation huts (or bosune) and who are blamed for congenital abnormalities if not properly placated.

Nuraga. Indonesian. Javanese. Type of sorcery that compels victims to do one's will.

Nutu. Indonesian. Seram. Nuaulu. "Mother of the corpse." Term to describe a spirit that causes madness, afflicting the sides of the trunk and the pelvic region.

Nyai Loro Kidul. Indonesian. Javanese. Goddess of the southern ocean. Highly revered nature spirit to whom the Javanese royalty trace their lineage. According to legend, she was once a beautiful maiden who contracted leprosy and threw herself into the ocean. She was then transformed into the goddess of a vast underwater kingdom. It was by communing with her and gaining her help that the founder of the old Majapahit Empire and his succeeding Mataram descendants secured major victories in their ascent to power.

Referred to sometimes as a mermaid queen, she is fearfully respected and still receives prayers and annual sacrifices from devotees. She is said to rule over spirits in an underwater palace and uses her ministers to recruit drowning victims to repopulate her kingdom with men. She is also a goddess of the volcano Gunung Merapi, making her a dual personification of the land and the sea. Aging with the moon, she is believed to be only young at the start of the lunar cycle.

As a symbolic wife and patroness of the ruling class, Javanese royalty today continue to make offerings in her honor. A sacred dance called Bedayo Ketawang, comprised of nine virgins in wedding attire, is still performed in reverence to her on the anniversary of the ruler's coronation.

Nyi (Nyai) Blorong. Malay, Indonesian. Malevolent creature described as having the upper body of a beautiful woman, but the torso and lower half of a serpent. Possessing razor-sharp teeth, it crawls along the ground on its clawed hands. She is also called the snake demoness of riches, known for seducing men seeking to become rich.

Ogoh-ogoh. Balinese. Giant demonic dolls created and paraded by Balinese youths; meant to scare away evil spirits during Ngerupuk, the day of purification held before Nyepi, the Hindu-Balinese Day of Silence.

Oko-jumu. Andaman Islands. Traditional shaman initiated into the practice by dying and then returning back to life. Besides possessing knowledge of medicinal cures and the weather, these spiritual intermediaries can also expel demons from the afflicted.

Ora. Indonesian. Komodo Island. Local term for Varanus komodoensis, the Komodo Dragon monster lizard. Growing to 11 feet long and weighing up to 500 pounds, it feeds on wild pigs, goats, deer, and, occasionally, people.

Orang bunian. Malay, Indonesian. Invisible spirits that live deep within the Malay forests. Possessing supernatural powers, they are believed to live in communities very similar to that of their human counterparts, befriending people, and even helping them in times of need. They are also known, however, to abduct people to live in their world.

Orang bunyi. Malay, Indonesian. So-called invisible voice spirits.

Orang darat. Malay, Indonesian. So-called "land folk," or land spirits, for whom sacrifices must be made in order to use their domain.

Orang Mawas. Malaysian. One of several unclassified hominids seen throughout the forests of Southeast Asia. It is also known as Hantu Jarang Gigi.

Orang minyak. Malay, Indonesian. Infamous "oily man" of Malaysian supernatural lore; a man believed to have made a pact with the devil and then went on a rampage of raping virgins. His naked, oil-drenched body makes him elusive, but his attacks on women have been recorded for several decades.

Orang Pendek. "Short person." Indonesian. General term for someone of short stature. In cryptozoology, however, it refers to one of several unclassified hominids seen throughout the forests of Southeast Asia. Said to inhabit the island of Sumatra, it is described by various witnesses as being short in stature with gray or reddish-brown fur. It is also known by its distinct footprints.

Panaspati. Malay, Indonesian. Fire-breathing spirit that walks on its hands with its head located in its crotch.

Pandawas. Indonesian. The heroes of the Mahabharata are the five sons of Pandu. The semi-divine brothers are Arjuna, Bhima, Nakula, Sahadewa, and Yudhisthira.

Parekan. Balinese. Comedic attendants of the main characters from the "Bhima Swarga," a Balinese folktale based loosely on an episode from the Mahabharata. Demons Twalén, described as a pensive, witty black monster with a pot belly, and his son Merdah (Mredah) are the retainers of the

Orang Pendek

good or "right" magic (tengen), while demons Délam, described as red with a big mouth and stubby legs, and Sangut represent the bad or "left" magic (kiwa). The two sides fight humorously through magic, with Twalén and his "right" magic always prevailing in the end.

Patulangan. Balinese. Cow-shaped sarcophagus used for burying nobility.

Pawang. Malaysian. Shaman or sorcerer possessing knowledge of traditional spells, charms, and medicine. They also function as intermediaries with spirits and have the ability to transform into tigers.

Pedanda istri. Balinese. Term for a female high priest.

Pelesit. Malay, Indonesian. A malevolent cricket that is the familiar of the dreaded Polong. It usually precedes its master and enters the body of its victims. It is occasionally caught and fed with a pinprick of blood. The pelesit is described as having sharp, bloody teeth and causing prolonged illness and death. It comes in two types: domesticated (owned and tamed by a master), and wild or undomesticated.

Pemangku (pamangku). Balinese. Keeper of the temple; commoner or lay priest who performs all its daily duties and rituals.

Pemangku-dalang. "Priest-puppeteer." Balinese. Term of reverence for the Wayang Kulit puppeteer, who is seen as a mystic, a priest, and a storyteller.

Penanggalan. Malay, Indonesian. Horrific malevolent spirit that appears as a head flying through the air with its bodily entrails dangling behind it. Fond of drinking the blood of women during childbirth, this vampire was originally a woman herself who was so startled by a passerby during religious penance that she separated her head and organs from her body while leaping onto a tree branch. Because of her draping intestines, she is particularly fearful of thorns. This spirit has also been described as a mysterious ball of fire that streaks across the forest.

Penengen. Balinese. Counter "right" magic used as protection against Leyaks and the dreaded Pengiwa.

Pengiwa. Balinese. The initiation of a disciple in transforming into a dreaded Leyak.

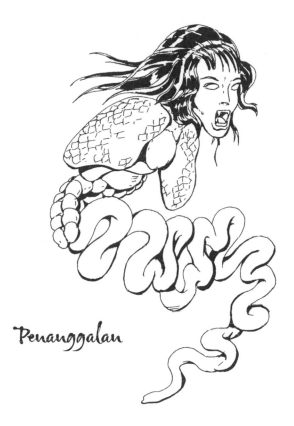

Penanggalan

Penunggu. Malaysian. Type of restless spirit; a person who died unexpectedly, leaving unfinished business with the living. It's been compared to a poltergeist.

Peri. Malay, Indonesian. Generic term for the supernatural class of fairies and elves.

Pinam notune. Indonesian. Seram. Nuaulu. Somori. Spirit of a mother and child who died during childbirth and, who, in turn, will afflict another mother and child with the same fate.

Pisatjis. Malay, Indonesian. So-called wandering spirit children without a family or a home who are always searching for people to live inside.

Pocong. Malay, Indonesian. Ghost described as an animated jumping body wrapped in a Muslim burial shroud. It is also known as hantu bungkus.

Pokok berhantu. Malaysian. Collective term for "haunted" trees in the Malay forest that are said to be inhabited by spirits. They include the Jelotong, Berombong, and Jawi-jawi trees.

Polo. Indonesian. Floes Island. Nage. Term to describe a male or female malevolent witch whose sole purpose is to cause harm. It possesses a special type of soul, called a wa, that is capable of leaving its body at night in search of victims. Appearing in either human or animal form, it must return to the witch's sleeping body if it is to wake up.

Polo dhuki. Indonesian. Flores Island. Nage. "A witch presses down." The act of a witch pressing down on its victim, immobilizing him helplessly in place and unable to cry out.

Polo kaka mae. Indonesian. Flores Island. Nage. The act of a witch capturing a human soul.

Polo muzi. Indonesian. Flores Island. Nage. So-called "new" witches, those who have just acquired their mystical powers. Considered more dangerous than polo olo, or "old" witches.

Polo olo. Indonesian. Flores Island. Nage. So-called "old" witches, those who have possessed their mystical powers for a long time, passed on from generation to generation.

Polong. Malay, Indonesian. A bottle imp, described as a small female figure the size of a finger joint. It is said to originate from the blood of a murdered man that is contained inside a bottle. After days of worship and prayer, the man who wishes to enslave this spirit must cut his own finger open and allow the developing creature inside the bottle to suckle on the blood. Once developed, it is able to fly and enter its master's intended victim. This spirit has its own familiar, called a pelesit, that precedes its arrival.

Pontianak. Malay, Indonesian. Perhaps Malaysia's most famous and dreaded spirit. Said to be the stillborn offspring of the dreaded langsuir, she is described as a blood-thirsty vampire dressed in white that feeds on the blood of children. Any stillborn offspring can potentially turn into a pontianak, and the preventive measures that apply to its langsuir mother also apply to this vampire. Over the years, however, the pontianak's origin

Pontianak

and appearance have been used interchangeably with that of the langsuir, a woman who died at childbirth. The pontianak has been a popular subject of local folklore, and has been made more famous in movies.

Like the langsuir, she has been known to take the form of a night owl and has also been referred to as Matianak.

Poyang. Malaysian. Beruan, Jakun. Type of shaman that passes on his art to his son seven days after his death. If the son desires to inherit his father's powers, he must burn incense while watching the corpse alone. The father will reappear to him on the seventh day in the form of an attacking tiger. If the son continues to burn incense without showing fear, the tiger will disappear and will be replaced by two spirit women. These spirits, in turn, will become his familiars. The inheritor will then be initiated after losing consciousness. Failure to perform this ritual correctly traps the father's soul inside the tiger forever.

Puchau. Indonesian. Borneo. Iban term for a quiet chant or prayer that is uttered in times of emergency or as protection against disease.

Punti. Indonesian. Borneo. Iban term for charms that, when buried under the ground, will cause pain when stepped over by the intended victim.

Pupuk. Indonesian. North Sumatra. Batak. Magical substance placed on the crown of the Tunggal panaluan magic wand, among the tufts of hair or feathers of the figure that sits astride its top. This substance is said to come from the brain of a captured enemy's child and used to power the wand.

Pura. Balinese. Native temple where offerings are made to the gods for protection. Within its walls, the gods reign supreme and evil spirits are rendered helpless.

Pura Besakih. Balinese. The most significant religious complex on the island, consisting of 22 puras, or temples, scattered throughout the southern slopes of sacred Mount Agung.

Pura dalem. Balinese. Term to describe the temple of the dead; situated near the cremation grounds.

Pusaka. Indonesia. Term to describe a sacred heirloom.

Raksasa. Malay, Indonesian. Term for a giant male demon; seen in traditional architecture as stone statues guarding the temple gates.

Raksasi. Balinese. A giant female demon.

Rangda. Balinese. Dreaded widow queen of the Leyaks; a blood-thirsty cannibal and devourer of children. She is the dual opposite of Barong, representing black magic and the forces of the left. Her origin is varied. One version holds that she was originally a queen in old Java who was accused of practicing witchcraft and exiled by the king. Maintaining her innocence, she made a claim to the throne when he died without an heir, but was rejected. She began studying black magic in earnest, becoming so powerful that she nearly destroyed the kingdom. She is sometimes associated with Dewi Durga.

Rangda is depicted in the Calonarang as having enormous tusks, a draping tongue, drooping breasts, and 6-inch fingernails.

Rarung. Balinese. Character in the Calonarang mask drama and the chief servant of Rangda. Created from human blood, she can turn herself into a bird or a tiger. This Leyak specializes in disposing objects, particularly bodies.

Ratu Pedanda. Balinese. High priests; present in all ceremonies and occasions and revered as spiritual and cultural leaders.

Ravana. Indian. Demonic king of Sri Lanka (old Ceylon) and principal villain of the Indian epic Ramayana. He abducted the beautiful queen Sita and was ultimately defeated by the god-king Rama and his loyal brother Lakshmana, with the help of Hanuman and his monkey army. Ravana is often depicted as having 10 heads and 20 arms.

Rangda

Ri. Indonesian. Papua New Guinea. New Ireland. Modern-day mythological creature said to resemble an unattractive mermaid; human-like from the waist up, but with a fish tail from the torso down. Local sightings by fishermen date back to the early 1980s.

Roh halus. Indonesian. Javanese. Term to describe spirits who afflict victims with illness. These powerful beings are also invoked in traditional ceremonies.

Ropen. Indonesian. Papua New Guinea. Bismarck Archipelago. Modern-day mythological creature said to resemble a pterosaur, a prehistoric flying reptile with leathery wings and sharp teeth. Some accounts claim they have crested heads, while others say they have a clover-tipped tail. These nocturnal creatures are said to inhabit the remote caves of New Britain and Umboi and have been sighted by missionaries and investigators as emitting a red glow from its chest while in flight over the night sky.

Rupadhatu. Indonesian. Borobodur monument. "Realm of forms." The middle level or tier that divides the temple into three sections, corresponding to the three steps of Buddhist thought that lead to Nirvana, or enlightenment. This level represents the state of man in which he becomes more enlightened about the meaning of life, self-sacrifice for the sake of others, and the ultimate reward of escape from rebirth through right behavior.

Ruwata. Indonesian. Javanese. Ritual occasion that involves warding off evil from vulnerable children.

Sakti. Balinese. Magical energy that one accumulates to resist the power of evil.

Samar. Balinese. Invisible spirit armies said to reside in temple precincts.

Sanghyang. Balinese. Local gods or ancestral spirits.

Sanhyang dedari. Balinese. Ritual exorcism of spirits in which two young girls enter a trance-like state (possessed by the heavenly nymphs dedari Supraba and Tundjung Birú) and are brought to a temple in a procession. While still entranced, the two dance in synchronicity to a chorus of singing men and women. When the singing stops, the two fall to the ground and are soon revived to consciousness, having no memory of what had just transpired.

Santèt. Indonesian. Javanese. Type of sorcery in which the victim is rubbed with pepper grains and contracts incurable diarrhea.

Santri. Malay, Indonesian. Religious system based on Islamic traditions.

Saruana. Indonesian. Seram. Nuaulu. Ancestral spirits summoned by mediums to remove illnesses.

Sebel. Balinese. State of magical weakness in which one becomes vulnerable to the attack and influence of evil.

Sedapa. Indonesian. One of several unclassified hominids seen throughout the forests of Southeast Asia. Said to inhabit the central Sumatran highlands, it is described as having hair down to its waist and arms that extend to just above its knees.

Semangat. Malaysian. Term to describe the vital, active spirit, or "life-force," in a person.

Serana. Balinese. Term for a protective charm.

Sétan (Sheitan). Malay, Indonesian. Generic term for devil or evil spirit.

Sétan gundul. Malay, Indonesian. So-called "bald devil," appearing with its head completely shaven, except for a traditional topknot on its crown.

Sétanan. Malay, Indonesian. Spiritual possession similar to kampel-kampelan, except that the invading spirit is deeply imbedded in the victim. Only a dukun can extricate it from the host.

Shesha. Indian. Hindu. King of all the nagas and ruler of the underground realm of Patala. Wrapped around the world and residing in the primeval world ocean, Shesha serves the god Vishnu, who reclines upon his chest. He was also used as the rope when the gods decided to churn the ocean of milk to obtain Amrita, the elixir of immortality. In traditional paintings, Shesha is also the multiheaded naga that is seen shading Vishnu as he rests during the stage between cosmic periods. He is frequently identified with the nagas Basuki, Anantaboga, and Taksaka.

Si gale gale. Indonesian. Lake Toba, north Sumatra. Life-size marionette puppets created to appease the spirits of wealthy men who died without having a son. They are used in elaborate death rituals before being destroyed. Their broken pieces are then collected for their magical properties.

Sibaso. Indonesian. Sumatra. Batak. Type of shaman, usually a woman, whose sole purpose is to protect the soul from abductions by demons.

Sida Karya Putih. Balinese. White-faced character that appears at the end of the Topeng perfomance, warding off evil spirits that might try to disturb the occasion.

Sikir. Indonesian. Javanese. Generic term for sorcery.

Simpan jinn. Malaysian. Term to describe spirits owned by a master and made to do his bidding.

Singa. Indonesian. Sumatra. Batak tribe. Serpent buffalo carved in pairs and used as an architectural motif in houses. This creature is said to live in the underworld.

Sirep. Indonesian. Javanese. Type of sorcery described as inducing victims into a deep sleep while being robbed.

Suangi. Indonesian. Seram. Nuaulu. Term to describe a sorcerer capable of causing illness through magical means.

Suangi. Indonesian. Irian Jaya. Term to describe a woman who is possessed by a malevolent witch spirit that causes death or illness to others in the community.

Sundel bolong. Malay, Indonesian. "Prostitute with a hole in her." A naked female spirit whose long black hair conceals a hole in the middle of her back. She has been known to castrate suitors who were lured by her beauty.

Suratma. Balinese. Yama's record-keeper of hell. He is a character from the "Bhima Swarga," a Balinese folktale based loosely on an episode from the Mahabharata.

Swah. Balinese. In the native cosmology, the celestial world.

Swastika. "Well-being." Sanskrit term for a traditional Indian symbol found throughout Hindu and Buddhist Asia, although seen independently in many cultures throughout the world. Symbolically representing various meanings (wellness, the sun, the cosmos, etc.), this ancient mandala was graphically distorted by Adolph Hitler, reversing its branches and then tilting it 45 degrees, to represent Nazi Germany in World War II.

Tabu rah. Balinese. "Pouring blood." Cockfighting ritual for the sole purpose of purification; spilling blood on the ground as an offering to the malevolent butas and kalas.

Tadu, Indonesian. Celebes. Bare'e Toradja. Type of woman (or a man who poses as a woman) shaman who takes spiritual journeys to the underworld or to the sky. They also deal with curing those afflicted with soul-loss and are known as bajasa.

Tajen. Balinese. Term for native ritual cockfighting.

Taksaka. Hindu. Naga king of the underground world of Patala.

Taksu. Balinese. Term to describe a deity that protects a native temple.

Tanana (*Panjak hana-tan hana*). Balinese. Umbrella term for various supernatural beings beyond the scope of human eyes and perception. This includes *bhutakalas, wong samar, tonya, and gamang spirits*.

Tau-tau. Indonesian. Toraja. Life-size statues carved and painted in the likeness of the deceased, even getting dressed in that person's clothing. They are placed on the death-cliffs, balconies carved from the cliff-face itself, while the actual bodies are stored alongside in rectangular vaults hollowed out from the rock.

Tawur. Balinese. Offerings made to the ground spirits.

Teluk. Indonesian. West Javanese term to describe a dangerous, malevolent spirit.

Tengen (Right). Balinese. Positive forces of magic.

Tenget. Balinese. Term used to describe when a mask becomes supernaturally charged with divine energy.

Tenung. Indonesian. Javanese. Type of sorcery in which a dukun makes offerings to evil spirits to induce violent illness upon the intended victim.

Thethekan. Malaysian. Ghost named for its distinctive-sounding footsteps ("thek-thek-thek"). It is known for abducting children playing outside their homes at night.

Toa mali. Indonesian. Flores Island. Nage. Term to describe a native magician or diviner who is capable of detecting and identifying witches and witchcraft.

Togtogsil. Balinese. One-eyed demon from hell. Character from the "Bhima Swarga," a Balinese folktale based loosely on an episode from the Mahabharata.

Tondi. Indonesian. Sumatra. Batak term for soul.

Tonya. Indonesian. Balinese. Spirits of people who died an unfortunate or accidental death.

Triloka. Balinese. The division of the universe into three sections: buhr (the underworld), buwah (the visible world), and swah (the celestial world).

Tukang santet. Indonesian. Javanese. Term to describe a feared practitioner of black magic (ilmu gaib). Acquiring his powers from an elder family member, this sorcerer has the ability to inflict so-called "enlarged stomachs" against those with whom he has quarreled. This affliction involves bloody diarrhea and vomiting, with contents that include dirt and hair. It is believed that if the sorcerer does not use his acquired powers for malevolence, the power will destroy him. Also known as dukun santet.

Tukang tawur. Indonesian. Borneo. Ngadju Dyak. Class of sorcerers used by spirits of the dead to communicate with the living.

Tumbal. Balinese. Amulets against witches; ornate drawings of symbols, monsters, or exaggerated divinities illustrated on flags.

Tumpek Uduh. Balinese. Birthday for trees and plants, particularly coconut palms.

Tunggal malek. Indonesian. North Sumatra. Batak. One of two types of magic wands used by East Karo Batak priests. This wand is described as having a single figure riding a horse at its crown, while the rest of the body is smooth. These wands were used to create sickness and death for enemies, along with other magical purposes.

Tunggal panaluan. Indonesian. North Sumatra. Batak. One of two types of magic wands used by East Karo Batak priests. This wand is described as having a single figure riding a horse at its crown, followed by carvings of people and animals that run the length of its body. This particular type contains tufts of hair and feathers on its figure's head, where a substance called "pupuk" is placed. These wands were used to create sickness and death for enemies, along with other magical purposes.

Tugal

Tuyul. Malay, Indonesian. Famous Malay spirit; described as a bald ghost child with a large belly that can be employed by human beings to acquire money without detection. They can be summoned either through meditation and fasting or by entering a pact with the spirit world. The wealth of certain families has long been attributed to the help of tuyuls. In exchange for their services, the master need only provide modest food and lodging.

Ubat kebal. Indonesian. Borneo. Iban term for protective amulet; used to guard against physical harm.

Ukur kepeng. Balinese. Life-size dolls made of yarn and coins that are cremated with the corpse. For the upper class, an ukur selaka (similar doll, but made with silver wires and plaques) is used alongside the ukur kepeng, but is not cremated. It is instead used repeatedly and is considered a family heirloom.

Undagi tapel. Balinese. Mask carver; usually a hereditary profession in which the artisan must undergo a purification process and fully comprehend the rituals involved in the specific masks created.

Upacara. Balinese. Daily offerings of incense and flowers to the gods and goddesses, accompanied with quiet mantras.

Uwil. Malay, Indonesian. The spirit of a former Buddhist soldier.

Uyan. Malaysian. One of several unclassified hominids seen throughout the forests of Southeast Asia. Said to inhabit the Malaysian state of Pahang, the males are described as naked with curly hair, fully proportioned but only three feet tall.

Vasuki (Basuki). Indian. Hindu. King of the nagas. It was used as a rope by the gods and demons to churn the ocean of milk in order to retrieve the amrita, the nectar of immortality. Also known as Ananta and Shesha.

Vyalakas. Indonesian. Heraldic, prancing lions used as a decorative motif in native art.

Wa. Indonesian. Flores Island. Nage. Term to describe a witch's wandering soul. See polo.

Wadah. Balinese. Cremation towers used to transport corpses to their place of burning. They can be simple or very ornate, depending on one's status. A nobleman's tower is referred to as the more formal badé.

Wali songo. "Nine saints." Indonesian. Javanese. The group believed to be responsible for spreading Islam throughout Java in the 15th century. They are said to possess magical abilities.

Wayang golek. Indonesian. Javanese. Traditional wooden doll puppets, said to have originated from 13th century Chinese sources. Like its Wayang kulit cousin, this puppet theater recreates stories from the Indian epics Ramayana and Mahabharata, along with local Javanese stories and characters.

Wayang kulit. Balinese, Javanese. Traditional leather shadow puppet theater, performed for entertainment, to invoke blessings, to educate, and to ward off evil spirits. Ritual stories revolve around the Indian epics Ramayana and Mahabharata. The puppeteer (dalang) is very highly regarded, as much a priest as an entertainer and storyteller.

Wayang topeng. Balinese. Mask drama that reenacts royal court life and historical episodes from the old Balinese and Javanese kingdoms, maintaining ancestral links to the modern world with the help of dance and song.

Wayang wong. Balinese. Mask drama that reenacts the old stories of the Ramayana, emphasizing the triumph of virtue and justice over vice.

Wedon. Malay, Indonesian. Term for a type of spirit covered up in a white sheet.

Weretiger. Pan-Asian. The Asian counterpart of the European werewolf. Varying culturally from region to region, tigers in general were always closely associated with souls, whether it was the animal's own or its victim's. Their strength, ferocity, and sheer presence were often associated with magical powers and attributes, including the absorption of their victims' souls into their own. It was believed that this soul transfer could influence the tiger's demeanor, whether refraining from attacking the living relatives of a victim, finding a replacement for an entrapped soul, or executing divine justice after death.

Weretiger

It is this reverence for its power that prompted native peoples to identify with the animal. The belief in the existence of weretigers throughout Southeast Asia was a given fact. In old Malaysia, they were said to live in the Korinchi district of Sumatra, living in their own town deep in the jungle and behaving much like regular people. They hunted prey (which occasionally included humans), and were identified by the lack of a cleft above their upper lip. Malay shamans were also believed to commune with tiger-spirits, developing the ability to transform into the big cats. They reverted to their human forms after death. Some styles of the Malay/Indonesian martial art of silat even imitate the attack and movements of tigers.

In Chinese lore and cinema, werecats often replaced werewolves, and their transformations were more often attributed to sorcery and magic than infection through the exchange of blood.

Wéwé. Malay, Indonesian. A female memedi who is married to a gendruwo; often seen carrying children around like a living human mother.

Widiadara. Balinese. Term to describe a handsome male celestial youth.

Widiadari (bidadari, bededari, dedari). Balinese. Most likely derived from the Sanskrit widyadari, meaning angel or heavenly nymph; known in public mythology as beautiful winged maidens bathing in a river. The celestial children of the god Indra, bidadari are the very essence of beauty itself. They are most commonly seen now as wooden carvings in Balinese craft stores, hung over children's cribs to act as protective guardians.

Wong samar. Balinese. So-called invisible people, spirits said to inhabit areas free of human habitation, including rivers, ravines, rocks, and trees. Wong samar are known to abduct victims and bring them into their world. They sometimes interact with people by assuming human form or communicating through spirit mediums.

Wurake. Indonesian. Borneo. Bare'e Toradja. Term to describe a class of spirits believed to live in the atmosphere.

The Philippines

Abat. Tausug. Native term for a malevolent spell or hex; referencing mysterious ailments of a supernatural cause.

Abat (Awok). Visayan. Type of self-segmenting witch who detaches her upper body from her waist and flies out at night in search of victims. Alighting on the thatched roofs of native houses, she uses her thread-like tongue to devour unborn children from the wombs of sleeping women. She must return to the lower half of her body before sunrise or perish in the daylight. The abat is sometimes considered a type of ghost.

Abyan. Ally spirit that aids a sorcerer or shaman in performing his skills and functions.

Ada. An indigenous fairy said to live in the forest.

Agboboni. Tinguian. Term for a native spirit medium.

Aghoy. East Visayan. Enchanted beings said to live in the trees near villages, described as diminutive people in stature, but not dwarf-like in bodily proportion. Having fair skin and hair, they have blue or green-colored eyes and communicate with villagers through whistling.

Agimat. A talisman or amulet; usually in the form of a stone or a gem. It is believed to give its owner extraordinary abilities as well as protect him from harm or detection.

Agtà. Term for supernatural dark-skinned people of gigantic size; said to live inside balete trees and smoke a large pipe. Although generally friendly, they are also known to kidnap victims or play practical jokes on them.

Aklan. Province located on the island of Panay in Central Philippines, notorious for being the home of the feared aswang creature.

Al-allia. Ilocano. Regional term for a ghost or spirit.

Alan (Aran). Tinguian. Horrific spirits said to live in the wood of trees, described as having wings, but with its toes positioned at the back of its feet. Its long fingers are pointed backwards and attached at the wrists. Like bats, they hang upside down on tree limbs.

Albularyo. Derived from the Spanish "herbolario." Folk-healing herbalist who specializes in using medicinal plants to cure illnesses.

Allawig (Al-alaowig). Ilocano. Term for a ball of fire that leads those who follow it astray. Found in isolated swamps and fields, it comes in different colors and doesn't burn its immediate surroundings.

Almos. Bilaan. Native term for a shaman, priestess, or spirit medium.

Amamanhig. Capiz. A deceased person who refuses to lie down in his coffin and die, opting instead to walk among the living until resolving the unfinished business he or she incurred while still living. Known as maranhig in Kinaray-a.

In some accounts, it is a female vampire, sucking blood from victims by inserting its sharp tongue into their necks. It is afraid of water and cannot bend its legs due to rigor. This type is said to be eager to pass on its vampiric qualities to relatives so that it can die in peace.

Ampas. Samal. Type of protective talisman; described as a stringed pendant worn by children around their necks until the age of 10.

An-annong. Ilocano. Painful (albeit temporary) headache believed to be inflicted upon people by supernatural beings.

Anani. Ibanag. Term to describe a type of malevolent goblin.

Andagaws. Mandaya. Type of spirit that lives in caves.

Angel statues. Free-standing ornate cement sculptures that adorn building lobbies; said to sometimes come alive at night when no one is around, leaving their post and tracking marks on soft surfaces.

Angelito. Type of love charm retrieved from a dead female infant. Battling evil spirits in procuring it is said to make the bearer irresistible to women.

Anghel. An angel from the Christian heaven.

Angngalo. Ilocano. Mythological giant said to be the reason why the ocean is salty. Towering to the sky, he created the seas, the mountains, and the lakes with his bare hands and feet. One day, when he lowered his massive legs across the sea to help people gather salt in baskets, red ants began to bite them. This caused him to dip his legs into the water for relief, making the people spill their bushels of salt into the water, making the ocean salty forever.

Angyaw. Cebuano. Term to describe a native form of sorcery that involves binding the victim's name on the leg of a black chicken after it has been taken to a so-called "sacred place," where the sorcerer communes with spirits. Securing the bird's leg to the branches of specific trees and reciting his curse, he then dips three darts into a noxious solution and with a blowgun, fires them under the bird's throat and wings. Depending on the sorcerer's ally spirit, the intended victim may experience pain on the dart's corresponding entry points, or fall prey to accidents. This ritual should ideally be performed at noon or at 8 p.m. on Fridays.

Ani-ani. Zambal. Towering hairy man several meters tall who is often seen smoking while sitting on the branch of a tree at night. With the ability to turn into animals, this pungent, bearded giant is known to block the path of passersby.

Aninga-as. Ilocano. Term for a shadow, meaning a ghost.

Anito. Indigenous nature spirits or ancestors that are venerated; usually represented as idols among their worshippers.

Anituan. Aeta. The ritual healing of those afflicted with supernatural maladies.

Aniyani. Pangasinan. Regional term for a spirit or ghost.

Annani. Filipino. Ibanag. Enchanted beings that eat the food of humans. If offended, they are propitiated with various meats, sweets, and pastries, as well as betel nuts.

Annong. Filipino. Ilocano. Term to describe mysterious events or afflictions associated with sorcery.

Ansisit. Ilocano. Type of dwarf that lives underground or inside anthills, inflicting illness upon those who disturb its home. People are told to refrain from sweeping out dirt from the house at night for fear of accidentally irritating this being's eyes and offending it.

Anting-anting. Native talisman, charm, or amulet believed to grant its bearer extraordinary—and even mystical—powers of strength, immunity, and deception. Coming in a multitude of sizes, shapes, and materials, they are often passed on from generation to generation, usually upon the passing of the previous wielder. In some situations, however, it can be obtained by defeating the supernatural creatures that guard it.

Antiwil. Cebuano. Term to describe a native form of sorcery that deals with infidelity or unfaithfulness. Killing two turtles in the act of mating, the sorcerer will then take its conjoined organs and mix it with other ingredients. Wrapping the potion in a small piece of cloth, it is then secretly attached to the victim's garments. If this person proceeds to have sexual intercourse while wearing this clothing, the participants will be unable to separate from their partners. However, if the first person to see the attached couple were to disrobe immediately, the curse would lose its potency.

Apuyanon. Pangasinan. Native term for a folk healer or quack doctor.

Aralan. Cebuano. Term to describe a native form of sorcery that involves striking a representation of the intended victim with a chopping blade after it has been covered with the seven leaves of specific trees and then wrapped in a black cloth. Though not meant to pierce the fabric during striking, it will nonetheless induce aches and pains on the victim's body.

Aran. Ibanag. Type of dwarf that lives underground; described as a diminutive old man with its feet pointing backwards. It is known to be mischievous, occasionally stealing and courting village maidens.

Arowak. Lanao. Term to describe the souls of the deceased.

Asugui. Native term for the element Mercury, carried as protection against evil spirits.

Aswang. Broad term for a category of malevolent supernatural creatures that are extremely popular in local supernatural lore. Appearing in both flying and terrestrial forms, these creatures are notorious for feeding upon the unborn fetuses of pregnant mothers, the livers of unsuspecting victims, and even corpses that have just been buried.

People can become aswangs through heredity, the consumption of infected food, or the transfer of essence to a person upon the creature's death. Once converted, aswangs are said to have the ability to turn into dogs or large black pigs. The weapon historically used against them is the dried tail of a stingray.

There are said to be five basic types as classified by noted folklorist Maximo D. Ramos: vampires, hex-casting witches, malevolent ghouls, weredogs, and body-detaching flying witches. Perhaps the most famous aswang of all is the dreaded Manananggal.

At-ato. Tinglayan Igorots. Circle of stones believed to be the meeting place of anitos, or spirits.

Avuhan. Humanoid creature that lives in the forest; gray in complexion and often portrayed as cannibals in myths.

A-way. Bontoc Igorot. The spirit of a person who died a natural death.

Awan-ulo-na. Ilocano. Headless supernatural being often seen under large trees; said to have the power to change its shape and size.

Awog (awug). Type of charm hung on plants to prevent thieves from stealing them. Robbers who take the protected plants will find their stomachs mysteriously enlarged. This charm is also known to disorient the thieves until they're caught. A variation, the awug hatud, simply coerces the perpetrators to bring back what they've stolen.

Ayag. Ifugao. Spirit-summoning ceremony performed when a person's sickness has been diagnosed as the result of soul-loss. Returning to where the afflicted is believed to have lost his soul (usually from a previously trodden path), the mumbaki, or shaman, ritually sacrifices and cooks a chicken. After consuming the bird, participants recite incantations and strike gongs, hoping to call the lost soul back.

Ayo-ayo. Surigao del Norte. Ritual that involves proposing a contract with residing spirits prior to clearing the land for use.

Ayok. Term to describe a type of witch that attacks pregnant women to retrieve her child.

Babato ti saba. Type of talisman that gives its bearer the power of invulnerability, particularly against bullets or hacking attacks. It comes from a banana plant, and the bearer must defeat supernatural beings in procuring it.

Babaylan (Baylan, Baliang). Term to describe a native female shaman or a high priestess.

Bagat. Ritual praying or offerings made to spirits to cure spiritual afflictions is usually held in the original place where the illness was contracted.

Bagat. Central Panay. Term for a shape-shifting demon that takes the form of ferocious-looking animals. Appearing at dusk and at a full moon in fields and along roads, it is said to possess its victim's soul from the encounter and then causes him to suffer and, ultimately, die from physical distress. These beings are sometimes considered to be the pets of supernatural entities.

Bakunawa. Mythical serpent, crocodile, or dragon said to cause lunar and solar eclipses, swallowing the moon or the sun. Only by shouting or making loud noises will the creature release the celestial bodies.

Balangobang. Isneg. Native term for ghost.

Balawa. Tinguian. Type of elevated spirit shrine used in the say-ang ritual of contacting the dead. Towering over nine feet in height, the structure contains a top shelf in which food is kept and offered. The agboboni (spirit medium) enters the shrine and ritually summons a spirit, falling into a trance as its body is occupied and becomes capable of giving guidance to those assembled around it.

Balbal (Barbalan). Type of aswang said to have the ability to fly, alighting on the thatch rooftops of houses that contain a dead body. It then retrieves the corpse and leaves a banana trunk facsimile in its place. It is also known to hide under houses and positioning itself directly beneath its victim. It then proceeds to invisibly devour the victim's liver or drain the body of blood.

    People are said to turn into balbals when a mysterious small bird enters the host body and develops inside, inducing the victim into seeking fetuses and fresh corpses. It can also turn others into balbals simply by touching the food they ingest. Those infected have a desire to fly or to see pregnant women. In some accounts, balbals are said to have the ability to shape-shift into animals and is recognized by its unique quacking sound.

Balete tree. Local term for the banyan tree, often considered the home of mysterious spirits and entities commonly associated with the supernatural.

Balungbunganin. Batak. Nature spirits that inhabit bagtik or almasega trees.

Ban-ok. Cebuano. Term to describe a native form of sorcery, in which a spirit inserts foreign objects (animal hairs, stones, insects, leaves, glass) into a victim's body, causing severe physical ailments and even insanity.

Banbano. Pangasinan. Term to describe mysterious events or afflictions associated with sorcery.

Bangat. Tagbanuwa. Powerful charm given to dogs for hunting, making them effective, but extraordinarily dangerous to be around.

Bangungot. So-called "night terrors" in which a person who has just consumed a heavy meal suddenly experiences intense nightmares simply by falling asleep right afterwards. It is said to only affect Filipino males and can lead to cardiac arrest and, ultimately, death.

Bannog. Ilocano. Mythological giant bird that nests in cliffs or large trees; said to be capable of lifting a water buffalo, a horse, or a cow with its massive talons to feed its young.

Banwa-anon. Visayan. Invisible beings who might be offended if one dumps hot water in their direction without first asking to be excused. They are also said to be offended if silence isn't observed during the tolling of church bells.

Barang. Cebuano. Dreaded form of native witchcraft which involves the use of various small, specially bred insects (also called barang) to enter the body and internal organs of the intended victim to induce pain and even cause death. The practitioner is called a mambabarang.

Baras. Pangasinan. Tall. Term for a tall, dark giant known for abducting women at night and bringing them back to its home in the forest. Seeing the giant's face in the morning is said to drive its victims insane. It is also known as kirbas.

Batibat. Ilocano. Malevolent spirit known for sitting on the chest of victims who have fallen asleep after a big meal, immobilizing them and choking them in place. Some accounts say that it lives inside the trunks of trees that have been cut down and used as a support post, entering and leaving through a knothole. Only by wiggling the victim's big toe and biting his thumb will the person be freed an the spirit driven away.

Baton. Type of supernatural illness that affects infants in the form of fevers and restlessness; believed to be caused by sunlight or moonlight seeping in from the rafters and casting directly on the child while it sleeps. Rubbing mother's milk that has been exposed to the same light on the infant's abdomen is the cure.

Bato'y bunot. Pangasinan. Protective talisman that makes its bearer impervious to blows; described as a stone found inside a coconut husk.

Batungbayanin. Batak. Nature spirits that inhabit the mountains.

Bawa. Pets of supernatural entities; described as chickens that play in stoves and eat hot embers. They make clucking noises called ugtak.

Bawa. West Visayan. Mythical bird said to be the cause of lunar and solar eclipses, flying from its cave above the clouds to swallow the moon or the sun. Only by singing or playing music to the mountains will the creature release the celestial bodies.

Bawanen. Pangasinan. Term for a native witch who can act as an intermediary with supernatural entities and cure spiritual afflictions.

Bawo. Supernatural demon or entity described as a large, muscular man dressed only in a loincloth.

Beheaded Spanish priests. Ghostly clergymen; described as robed priests, but without heads. They are believed to have been executed during the Spanish and Japanese occupations of the country.

Bekat. Isneg. Female giant in mythology. She was outwitted by two boys who she tried to deceive and from whom she stole food. Unable to swim, she ultimately drowned when she thought the boys were hiding in the water.

Bengat. Tiruray. Type of charm or spell cast upon a field for protection. Anyone who steals food from this field and devours it will see his stomach burst.

Berberoka. Apayao. Malevolent man-eating giant ogre said to use his body to dam a river. When unsuspecting villagers come out to try and catch the stranded fish, the ogre rises up and snatches them in the sudden deluge and devours them. Ironically, though, the ogre is afraid of little river crabs.

Biangonan. Batak. Small spirits said to inhabit trees and rocks, possessing talons that they use to tear at the throat of their victims. They also paralyze them with long, piercing shrieks.

Binangenan. Luzon. Supernatural spirits that live in the balete tree; said to inflict sickness and even death as a form of punishment.

Binangunan. Pinatubo. Creature similar to a tikbalang which is, described as being horse-like, but possessing flames that run the length of its head and tail.

Binobaan. Malevolent ogre that lives in the woodsand is said to invite lost hunters to its home to drink wine. When his victims become intoxicated, the ogre then devours them. His wife, however, is kind and helps the victims escape.

Bisnag. Apayo. Game played by people who keep vigil over the deceased. Participants expose their thighs and take turns slapping each other's thighs as hard as they can, stopping only when the players have reached their physical limits.

Blanga. Bilaan. Term to describe a feared flesh-eating demon.

Blugul. Bilaan. The souls of wicked men believed to have gone to a soul-devouring demon. This demon is said to sleep constantly; its movements, although dormant, are the cause of earthquakes.

Bolo-bolo. Visayan. Siquijor. Folk method for curing ailments performed by a mananambal. Inserting a straw into a glass jar of water containing a magical stone, the specialist then blows into the straw while motioning the jar over different parts of the patient's body. It is believed that this action literally blows away the body's impurities, which would appear as various particles floating on the water's surface.

Bong-ar (bogwa). Ifugao. Bone-washing ritual. Illness suffered by the death of a loved one (over a period of time), which a shaman attributes to the deceased's offended spirit. The spirit is believed to be demanding an animal sacrifice and a secondary funeral for its existing bones. The original wrapped corpse is exhumed and picked clean of remaining flesh and hair. It is re-wrapped and brought back to the home of the afflicted, where the participants eat a meal that includes the sacrificed animal. This ritual is repeated in several homes, with relatives and neighbors invited to participate.

Bo-ot. Unknown type of sea creature used against aswangs. Burying this creature beneath an aswang's house is said to cause the witch severe itching, prompting it to leave its domicile.

Boroka. Derived from the Spanish "bruja," meaning witch. Type of self-segmenting witch who detaches her upper body from her waist and flies out at night in search of victims' livers. She must then return to her lower half before sunrise, or perish in the daylight.

Bowing trees. Tall trees that are said to mysteriously bend down to the ground as if blocking the path of unwitting passersby.

Bruha. Derived from the Spanish "bruja." Generic term to describe a witch.

Bulul. Ifugao. Popular decorative and architectural motif usually depicting a seated male or female figure with its arms folded. Often appearing in pairs on native artifacts, they represent nature deities summoned at various rituals.

Bungisngis. Tagalog. Enormous cyclops with a pair of tusks protruding from its mouth; fond of snickering and playing jokes on passersby. His upper lip is said to be so enormous that it covers his eye when he is laughing.

Buni. Tinguian. Type of ritual to cure the supernaturally afflicted using various foods offered to the spirits.

Buntot pagi. The dried tail of a stingray, the classic weapon of choice used to whip and strike against malevolent spirits and evil witchraft.

Burial jar. Ceramic or limestone urns used by ancient Filipinos to house the bodies of their deceased. After the initial burial, the body is exhumed, cleaned, and stored in these ornate jars in a seated position, its arms folded across its chest. The lids are often decorated with carvings of human heads or figures. These relics have been found throughout the northern and central Philippines, the most famous being the Manunggul Jar from Palawan, which dates back 3,000 years.

Buringkantada. Bicolano. Mythological giant who lived in a house with many rooms. When two boys entered its home and became trapped when the giant arrived home, they were able to fool it by cleverly pretending to be an intruder larger than the giant itself by using of household objects. The giant ultimately ran away, and the boys retrieved its treasure.

Burihay (Burikay). Isneg. Term for a native ogre.

Busaw (busau). Mandaya, Bukidnon, Manobo. Malevolent, blood-thirsty forest ogres described as having coarse black hair, bristles on its body, and a hooked, upturned chin to catch the blood dripping from its mouth. They are black in color, prowl around at night, and tower at 12 feet in height. The chiefs of this species are said to possess a single ivory horn on their forehead, while the females have only a single eye. Some live in huts; others live inside large trees. They are afraid of metal and fire.

Buso. Bagobo. Diverse class of malevolent demons that include disease spirits and the souls of the dead. They are said to be fond of human flesh, living on the volcanically active Mount Apo and sending out illness to their victims in order to kill and devour them. They must consistently be propitiated in order to ward off their attacks. Most likely a regional variation of the busaw.

Butabuta. Cebuano. From "buta," meaning blind. Term to describe a native form of sorcery that makes the intended victim go blind. This is achieved by placing a representation of the victim inside a shell and covering it

Busaw

with a toxic compound. The shell is then heated on a stove that burns the branches of specific trees.

Buwaya. Term for a crocodile, once worshipped by ancient Filipinos.

Buyagan. Type of witch said to possess the so-called "evil tongue," or buyag; sorcery derived from envy in which the practitioner (intentionally or inadvertently) curses a prosperous victim with a verbal compliment, reversing the good fortune and resulting in financial or even physical decline. They are also said to have dark tongues. Buyagans gained their power through heredity or contamination.

Cahoynons. Capricious fairies that live in trees and forests. They are divided into wealthy and poor social classes, with the latter considered harmful. The batanguon (ugly) and pequet (invalid) fairies belong to the poor class.

Caibaan. Ilocano. Term for earth spirits that live in ant mounds or underground, inflicting maladies on those that desecrate or step over their homes without permission.

173

Calag. Hiligaynon. Type of flesh-eating ghoul. By merely touching the deceased person's coffin, they can cause the body's belly to burst.

Cama-cama. So-called "spirits of the well." Diminutive entities that pinch the bodies of people who bathe in their waters, leaving black and blue bruise marks on their skin.

Capiz. Province located on the island of Panay in the central Philippines; notorious for being the home of the feared aswang creature.

Caragat. Gadang. Malevolent spirits known for stealing souls of the living. Formerly human beings, they are known for bringing death and disease to people.

Caratua na pinatay. Gadang. Souls of the dead; capable of harassing their descendants if not properly placated with offerings.

Crucifix. Holy symbol depicting Jesus Christ hanging on the cross. A sacred image among Catholics, they are often hung on the wall to bless a house or to protect it against evil spirits.

Dadawak (mandadawak). Igorot. A shaman or medicine man who practices the art of dawak. Wearing a protective talisman bead called an arubo and a bark-cloth turban, this shaman adorns the location of healing with flowers and leaves to guard against the entry of evil spirits. He or she then summons good spirits to aid in the recovery, chanting and offering an animal sacrifice. A mana-abig (fortune-teller) then helps the dadawak by examining the bile and liver of the sacrificed animal to see what type of spirit has caused the affliction. These entrails are later offered to the spirits.

Dagau. Manobo. Mischievous spirit known for stealing rice from granaries. It is also known as nakabuntasai, or "can cause hunger."

Dagpi. Cebuano. Term to describe a native form of sorcery that causes the intended victim to fall ill and for his body to swell. This is done with the sorcerer placing a type of powder under his nails, reciting an invocation of evil, and then touching the victim.

Dalakitnon. East Visayan. "Those who live in the balete tree." Enchanted beings said to live in mansions in the deep woods that appear as the balete tree to human eyes. They are more European in appearance, having fair skin and hair, and are extremely wealthy, attending expensive colleges and traveling to foreign countries.

Danag. Isneg. Ancient gods who long ago descended to earth and began cultivating taro alongside human beings. When a person accidentally received a sliver in his finger, one of the deities offered to remove it by sucking it out. It found the taste of human blood so enjoyable that their race gave up planting their crops and became blood-drinking vampires.

Darudar. Ilocano. Supernatural phenomenon said to occur on the first month of the year, when the mysterious mass revelation of people's best-kept secrets is said to take place. Those dining out under the moonlight during this occasion are particularly vulnerable to its influence.

Dawak. Igorot. Type of sorcery associated with healing victims who are believed to be suffering from soul-loss.

Dawendi. Leyte. Solitary supernatural entity the height of a building or a tree who wanders about at night. .

Dayamdam. Agusanon. Enchanted beings who appear as miniature people and hop around leaves and fallen trees in the forest. Their permission is required before cutting down any tree in their area of residence.

Demonyo. Generic term for a devil or a demon.

Diablo. Generic term for the devil.

Dikay dalin. Pangasinan. Term for earth spirits that live in ant mounds or underground, inflicting maladies on those who desecrate or step over their homes without permission.

Diwata. Term for a native god or deity. It is a variation of the Sanskrit term "devata," which appears in various forms throughout the Southeast Asian archipelago.

Dongsol. Cebuano. Term to describe a native form of sorcery that uses a sea creature of that same name. Creating a figure of the intended victim using parts of specific trees, the sorcerer bundles the representation in a black cloth and inserts it into the mouth of the said sea creature. This magic causes the victim to quietly hemorrhage inside, particularly when touched.

Dururakit. Isneg. Term for a native shaman who presides over ceremonies and performs healing rituals. They are predominantly female.

Duwende. The native version of the classic dwarf or gnome, said to reside underground or within ant mounds, harboring treasure. Short in stature with a beardand wearing a hat, these reclusive beings are unpredictable in nature and are dealt with cautiously. A person must also ask for permission to pass if he encounters an ant mound along a path, or the duwende living inside might take offense and exact punishment.

Ebwa. Tinguian. Type of ghoul known to steal and devour corpses after they have been buried. Fire is kept burning by families around the fresh grave for several days to keep this creature at bay.

Engkanto. Enchanted, fair-skinned beings encountered in remote areas who occasionally dabble in the lives of ordinary mortals. Dangerously unpredictable, they are said to live in luxurious homes and domiciles that appear to the human eye as unusual trees or boulders. They occasionally court human beings, play tricks on unsuspecting passersby, and even bring unsuspecting children into their world. They curiously avoid salt, , however.

Espiritista. Generic term for a spirit medium.

Espiritu. Generic term for a spirit.

Fagad. Tiruray. Term for a spirit giant known for devouring corpses after burial.

Faith healing. Broad term to describe the various methods of native folk healing with practitioners using massage, herbs, and religious prayers to cure the physically or spiritually afflicted.

Falimu. Tiruray. Type of charm that induces everyone who meets its bearer to be friendly to him.

Duwende

Falulud. Tiruray. Type of charm that brings about great wealth for its possessor.

Falusud. Tiruray. Type of love charm that induces affection from a woman to its bearer.

Fangablang. Buhid Mangyan. "Those who are encountered." Term for ferocious and hideous spirits.

Faramanis. Tiruray. Type of charm that imbues its bearer with great physical beauty or handsomeness. This is done by saying a prayer and placing an egg inside a bowl of oil while the moon is full.

Fekimoy. Tiruray. Type of protective charm that paralyzes an enemy in place while attacking.

Feliyos. Tiruray. Type of protective charm that makes an enemy miss his mark while in the motion of attacking. It is procured from a certain type of grass.

Felungkang. Tiruray. Type of charm that mystically causes an enemy's extreme anger to calm or subside.

Ferirung. Tiruray. Type of charm that mystically renders its bearer invisible.

Funi (Buni). Ifugao. Umbrella term for a diverse class of native sorcery or witchcraft; commonly believed to be the cause of numerous illnesses.

Gabà. Illness attributed to supernatural beings; said to be a form of punishment or divine retribution for moral, social and ecological offenses.

Gahoy. Type of supernatural illness said to be contracted from the drifting scent of a sweaty traveler who just returned from a long journey. The cure requires the victim to chew several roots and peppers.

Galap. Jama Mapun. Term for sea devils.

Galing-galing. Ilocano, Pangasinan. Native term for protective talisman; synonymous with the anting-anting.

Gargasi. Jama Mapun. Native term for a giant.

Garuda. Maranao. Hideous ogre that grows wings when in pursuit of its prey; said to live in three mansions under the sea, each of which is occupied by a princess who was abducted from the creature's plundering of kingdoms. It is also known to live high in the mountains.

Gatu-i. Ifugao. Predatory deity known for snatching souls and mating with, devouring, or enslaving them.

Gawigawen. Tingguian. Mythological giant described as having six heads and wielding an axe and a spear that spanned half the sky.

Gayuma. Tagalog. A love charm or potion with the power to arouse a person's affection for its bearer.

Gibuang. Cebuano. "To cause someone to become insane." A native form of sorcery that involves retrieving three hairs from the intended victim (one from the top of the head and one from each temple). These hairs are in turn placed inside a container and then swirled in a counter-clockwise direction. A variation involves taking these same hairs, tying them to a small piece of wood or other floatable object, then inserting it into a whirlpool on the river.

Gilangkatan ug spirito. Phenomena in which a person's soul is attracted to the supernatural and leaves the body. The conscious person is said to lose interest in people and in work.

Gimukod. Bagobo. Native term for a soul, two of which are believed to exist in a human body. Gimukod takawanan is the "good" soul, which appears as the shadow on the right side of one's path. Gimukod tebang, the so-called "bad" soul, appears on the left, as well as in one's reflection in the water.

Ginam-mol. Ilocano. Native term for protective talisman, synonymous with the anting-anting.

Ginayang. Ifugao. Term for the souls of murdered victims.

Gisal. Cebuano. "To fry." Term to describe a native form of sorcery that induces a painful burning sensation on the intended victim. This is done by inserting a representation of the victim inside an extremely sour citrus fruit that has been slit open. Securing it shut with the barb of an unborn stingray, the sorcerer then recites his curse to the victim and then proceeds to fry the object in the lard of a pig slaughtered during the novena for a deceased person. Once the fruit is cooked, it is wrapped inside a black piece of cloth and hung over the hearth. The victim will experience painful burning throughout his body.

Gisurab. Isneg. Benevolent mythological giant who lived in a cave with his two wives (Gungay and Surab), and a third wife in the clearing (Sibbarayungan). He grew and stored his own food in the wilderness, and was friendly to his human neighbors.

Gohad. Filipino. Ifugao. Method of native sorcery, described as employing different spiritual beings (particularly lennagwa or linawa, celestial beings of the moon, sun, and stars) as a means to achieve an end.

Guban-on. Visayan. Spirit guardians of the forests and mountains. They are known to remove the paths of offending travelers to make them lose their way.

Guinguinammol ti nuang. Type of talisman or anting-anting that gives its bearer extraordinary strength. It is spewed from the mouth of a water buffalo, and the bearer must be quick to retrieve it, or face the wrath of the charging animal.

Gukas. Subanon. Death rite performed exclusively for a deceased village headman, meant to say farewell and placate his spirit. Observed five to nine days after the passing, it involves the building of a two-tiered receptacle (binulod) meant to display food on top and the deceased's belongings below it. This structure is then attached to a corner post in the house. The baliang (shaman) drinks rice wine and performs various rituals before the bereaved family and visitors to the sound of gongs and music. The binulod is later disposed in another location, and rice wine poured over its spot.

Guni-guni. Broad term to describe the imaginary or the unreal, mysterious events or occurrences that usually involve the unexplainable.

Gungutan. Mythological man of the forest, described as heavily built and hairy. Occasionally helping people in need, he is said to have the ability to change himself into different animals.

Habak. Type of protective amulet described as a piece of paper inscribed with a Latin prayer, wrapped in a black cloth, and worn to protect against evil spirits and influences.

Habay-habay. Tausug. Type of protective amulet derived from unusual-looking objects in nature (stones, teeth, leaves, etc.), worn to give its wearer courage and invulnerability.

Hakawhaw (hagoho). Ifugao. Method of native sorcery that sends animal spirits (various mammals, reptiles, birds, and even insects) as a sign to attack the enemy.

Halimaw. A fearsome ghost, monster, or supernatural entity, usually encountered in the dark or in remote places at night.

Halimon. Tausug. Native term for a protective talisman.

Halopey. Ifugao. Method of native sorcery, described as taking the soul of the enemy and imbuing a chick with it. After piercing the little bird through its ears with a stick, burning it inside a furnace and flinging it to the ground, the sorcerer buries it with its beak exposed in a location that the enemy frequents. When the victim passes over the beak, he is said to fall on the ground and die.

Hampan. Tausug. Protective necklace talisman given to infants and worn until puberty, described as a white piece of cloth inscribed with Malay or Indian words written in Arabic.

Hantorah. Composite liquid solution made of various oils and herbs that is said to react and bubble when brought within the vicinity of supernatural entities.

Haplit. Cebuano. Term to describe a native form of sorcery that involves tying a representation of the intended victim near the tip of the candle with a black cloth. After pouring special oil on the fabric, the sorcerer then temporarily renounces God (because he intends to kill someone) and lights the candle. If he is successful, the cloth will bleed and the intended victim will collapse.

Hapod. Ifugao. Method of native divination to determine sorcery. It involves balancing an egg on end while naming the possible culprits. If the egg balances on a specific name, that identifies the specific sorcerer.

Haposeng. Ifugao. Form of divination that uses rice floating in a cup of water made of a coconut shell.

Hilan. Cebuano. Term to describe an unpopulated and uncultivated area that is believed to be infested with supernatural entities.

Hilo (hilu). Cebuano. "Poison." Type of sorcery that involves the use of snake venom to attack a victim. It requires the sorcerer to use this craft against a member of his family. The practitioner then goes to a so-called "enchanted place" and makes an offering to a spirit, asking for it to summon snakes to his altar, which is surrounded by sharp bamboo blades. The blood and venom left from the writhing snakes are then collected and mixed with the parts of venomous trees. This blend in turn is secretly mixed with the victim's food or beverage, causing the target to suffer severe physical ailments. The blend can also be transferred via a seemingly harmless pat on the back.

Hilo-an. Visayan. Type of sorcerer who uses poisons derived from plants.

Himalad. Visayan. Native term for palmistry, fortune-telling by reading the lines of the palms.

Ho-ulig. Ifugao. Term to describe a form of counter-sorcery.

Hokhok. Visayan. Type of lethal sorcery that enables a practitioner to kill with a simple touch of the hand, or by breath.

Hoklub. Cebuano. Term to describe a native form of witchcraft where the sorcerer creates a doll made of wood that represents his victim. Wearing black clothing, the sorcerer also dresses the doll in black, tying a red belt around its waist and a red sash diagonally across its chest. He then takes a stick and proceeds to strike the doll at the corresponding parts of the victim's body, specifically at the area he wants to attack.

Hukluban. Bicolano. Type of malevolent male or female witch that uses insect familiars to do its bidding, similar to a mambabarang. Gaining the ability to fly by rubbing ointment on its body, it is notorious for turning corpses into banana tree trunks. It is also known as para-suniyaw.

Hukluban. Powerful witch said to have the power make unconscious or kill a victim with a simple greeting.

Habit. Visayan. Term for a sorcerer's spell.

Hunab. So-called "evil air," undercurrents of air controlled by the lamang-lupa or spirits beneath earth, believed to cause illness and misfortune.

Hunghung. Method of folk healing in which the practitioner whispers prayers over the afflicted area.

Ibiris. Tausug. Islamic counterpart of the Christian devil, the consummate tempter and source of all evil.

Igdalaut. Cebuano. Mixture composed of various toxic ingredients used extensively in the implementation of magic or witchcraft.

Ikugan. Manobo. Enormous monkey with an unusually long and prehensile tail. Waiting for its victims high in the trees, it uses its tail to drag them up the branches and choke them, before dropping the bodies to the ground below.

Imod. Ifugao. Type of love potion said to make its bearer irresistible to the opposite sex. It is composed of women's hairs collected by swimming lizards who frequent bathing areas, leaves, the sex organs of the lizard itself, as well as parts of a native bird. Then it is wrapped in a cloth bundle and carried around. Unlike other love potions, which require contact with the victim in order to work, this particular type is also effective from a distance. It must be discarded or passed on to someone else upon marriage, for keeping it afterwards makes its bearer sterile or barren.

Impakto. A malevolent fiend or demon, sometimes referenced as coming from the depths of hell.

In-annapet. Ilocano. Ritual meant to appease offended spirits; involves pastries made of sticky rice, offered by a folk witch on behalf of the victim at the location of contact.

Inikadowa. Maranaw. The so-called, "other person within a person." It is a type of secondary soul common to all people and is believed to be responsible for spirit possessions.

In-innapet. Tinguian. Ritual offering of food to spirits for various occasions of celebration, including a bountiful harvest and the curing of the afflicted.

Inlablabuut. Ifugao. Malevolent, shape-shifting giant known for assuming the guise of a handsome man to lure its female victims to its home. Once the deception is successful and the victim is trapped, the inlablabuut reveals its true hideous form and devours her.

Iqui. Batangas. Type of self-segmenting male witch who detaches his upper body from his waist and flies out at night in search of other male victims' livers. It is said to alight on thatch rooftops and use its thread-thin tongue to quietly consume its meal.

Itongol. Ifugao. Method of native divination that uses the gall of a chicken.

Jampan. Tausug. Term for a charm worn as protection from enemies or evil spirits.

Japanese soldier ghosts. Apparitions of former occupying soldiers from World War II. They are often seen at old buildings, going about their previous roles or activities as if still among the living.

Jin islam. Tausug. "Moslem spirits." Spirits that obey the commandments of God.

Jin kapil. Tausug. "Non-believer spirits." Potentially harmful spirits who do not follow the commandments of God.

Jinan. Tausug. Native term for a spirit medium.

Kabibi. Bagobo. Term to describe a type of love potion.

Kadaolat sa miatai. Maranao. Type of funeral or pre-burial dance where six or more participants line up and sing and dance on the path that leads up to the grave of the dead. This is believed to cause the deceased to rise one last time and visit his family and relatives.

Kagkag. Romblon. Type of ghoul that resides in the deep forest. It hunts for fresh corpses at night, keenly attuned to its brethren and its nocturnal environment, and having the ability to turn itself into animals.

Kakarma. Ilocano. Regional term for a ghost or spirit.

Kalag. Visayan term for a ghost, although it actually references a human soul.

Kalanget (caranget). Ifugao, Gaddang. So-called "lice of the ground," a dwarf-like entity said to reside in anthills, underground, or in secluded areas. It is described as having a small body and a large head.

Kalapaw. Isneg. Mythological giant known for his great strength; able to uproot coconut trees with his bare hands, as well as traverse great distances with a single stride. Too large to marry a normal woman, he ultimately married his giant sister and bore a son. He is known as Sappaw in Apayo.

Kalariot. Pampanga. Term for a tall, dark giant known for abducting attractive women from their houses at night and bringing them back to his home in the woods.

Kalaw. A native hornbill bird (Buceros hydrocorax), believed to be the sentinels of engkantos. They are dangerous if ridiculed.

Kaldero'y kaibaan. Pangasinan. Mystical pot said to be derived from spirits of the earth, capable of giving unlimited amounts of food.

Kaluluwa. Tagalog. The human soul.

Kama-kama. Ilonggo. Dwarf-like entity similar to a duwende, said to reside in anthills, underground, or in secluded areas.

Kamanan-daplak. Zambal. Enchanted beings that reside in trees that overlook mountain streams. These miniature, fair-haired beings are said to smell as sweet as flower blossoms, and harmlessly call villagers' names out loud at sunset.

Kamatu. Tiruray. Native term for a ghost.

Kapamagarowak. Lanao. All Souls' Day, observed during Ramadan, when the arowak (the souls of the deceased) are believed to visit the living. Prayers and an exchange of food are held in observance of this occasion.

Kapamangaingai sa tonong. Maranaw. The ritual invitation of local and neighboring spirits to partake in food offerings, meant to gain their blessings and permission prior to working on or occupying a specific area.

Kapre. Towering, cigar-smoking giant said to reside in massive banyan trees, sitting on the branches and waiting to scare unwitting passersby. Besides having the ability to change its height, it is also known to turn into various animals.

Kaskas. Term to describe a type of shape-shifting witch or aswang, named after the sound that it makes.

Katao. Maranaw. Type of love potion, a love-inducing drink derived from the doka tontoi gum, which is extracted from plants from the group's secret ancestral jungles.

Kataw. Visayan. Regional term for a mermaid, described as a beautiful, dark-haired woman from the waist up, but having a fish's tail for a torso or legs.

Kaykay. Visayan. Type of lethal sorcery that enables a practitioner to kill simply by pointing his finger at his victim and running him through from a distance.

Kapre

Kebel. Tiruray. Type of protective charm that imbues its bearer's skin with great invulnerability, particularly to physical attacks.

Kibaan. Ilocano. Enchanted, fair-skinned beings that appear as miniature people who are only a foot tall. Living in trees frequented by fireflies at night, they sing beautifully in a high-pitched voice and are known to have bright gold teeth. Occasionally prone to stealing, they leave footprints that point in the opposite direction from which they're walking.

Kiki. Type of shape-shifting aswang, capable of turning itself into a fierce small bird.

Kinabagat. Ifugao. Wooden figure carved in the central post of a traditional Ifugao house.

Kinakasihan. Type of spirit possession, described as being inhabited by a good spirit that mentally empowers the person. This spirit may also act as a messenger, but can inadvertently inflict illness upon the body if the body is not prepared to be occupied.

Kirbas. Ilocano. Term for a tall, dark, and hideous giant known for abducting attractive women from their houses at night and bringing them back to its home in the forest. Seeing its face in the morning is said to drive its victims insane. It is also known as baras.

Kiwig. Aklan. Type of shape-shifting aswang, described as a person who can turn into a cat, dog, or a pig and who viciously attacks its victims. In its animal form, it is stooped in stature, with its arched tail pointing backwards.

Kiyamorkaan o manga lokus. Maranaw. "Cursed by his ancestors." Term to describe the haunting of a living descendant by his ancestors, usually because of issues regarding family honor.

Kubot. Type of witch said to resemble a huge bat or large umbrella. It captures its victims with its wings and spirits them up in the air to be brought home and butchered.

Kulam. Umbrella term for malevolent witchcraft or sorcery, usually involving the casting of spells and the pricking of voodoo-style dolls. A practitioner is a mangkukulam.

Kumao. Isneg, Iloko. Term for an ogre described as a large man who devours people.

Kurita. Maguindanao. Term for an ogre that haunted Mt. Kabalanan; described as having many limbs.

Kutob. To have an ominous premonition or intuition, usually of forthcoming events. It literally means "heartbeat."

Laga. Cebuano. "To boil." Type of sorcery that involves carefully wrapping the personal effects of a victim (hair, clothing, saliva, feces) in a leaf, bringing it to a so-called "enchanted place," invoking a spirit to attack, and then boiling the packet in a pot of extremely noxious ingredients mixed on a Good Friday. If successful, the intended victim will suffer severe physical ailments.

Lagtaw. Tausug. Mysterious witch said to possess the ability to stretch and expand its limbs to great lengths and heights, even growing tall enough to reach towering coconuts. Touching its feet meant gaining incredible knowledge.

It is also known as a towering, dark giant who frightens children at night. With enlarged eyes, ears, and nose, it is said to live inside the holes of trees.

Laho. Term for a dragon that swallows the sun or moon and causes eclipses, most likely derived from the Sanskrit Rahu, a mythical dragon with the same function. Making a lot of noise will cause the monster to disgorge the celestial bodies and bring light back into the world.

Lakay. Dwarf-like entity similar to a duwende, said to live inside termite mounds.

Lamang lupa. Mysterious beings or spirits said to literally live in the ground. Care must be taken not to offend them, lest visitors or residents on their land be punished for their transgressions.

Lambus. Tiruray. Type of protective charm worn around the neck or waist.

Lampong. Ilocano. Type of dwarves considered the patrons and shepherds of deer and other wild animals; described as having sparse beards and bushy hair. They are known to change into animals and occasionally play jokes on hunters.

Langgam. Maranaw. Huge, pale creature with large eyes, said to froth at the mouth and sit in bamboo trees located near road intersections to look for victims.

Langitnon. Malitbog. Benevolent spirits said to live in the upper atmosphere, above the clouds.

Lanti. Visayan. Native term to describe the so-called "evil eye."

Lewenri. Romblomanon. Attractive, fair-featured enchanted beings that occasionally appear to people; beneficial to the kind but vengeful to the wicked.

Likit. Waray-waray. Native term for protective talisman, synonymous with the anting-anting.

Limbut. Tiruray. Term to describe a type of love potion.

Li-mum. Bontok. Spirit said to cause "fiendish nightmares" by sitting on a sleeping victim's breast and stomach.

Lisang. Fever or similar ailment derived from extreme fright.

Loos klagan. Bilaan. Mischievous—at times vengeful—spirit said to cause embarrassment to its victims, particularly women.

Lubat. Illness derived from a frightening experience, particularly when coming in contact with the dead.

Luklob. Marinduque. Type of sorcery where the practitioner uses a doll to inflict curses upon its victims.

Lumay. Cebuano. A native form of sorcery that magically induces the affections of a resistant woman. Mixing specific herbs with roots and oil, rubbing this solution on her palms or on her hair and making her inhale its scent under a new or waning moon is said to cause instantaneous affection.

Lupos-na-tilay. Pangasinan. Protective talisman that gives its bearer the ability to breathe underwater; described as the discarded, molted skin of a lizard.

Lutao. Samal. Native term for a ghost.

Mabalian. Bagobo. A native spirit medium.

Maca-amling. Ilocano. Person said to possess malevolent or "evil" eyes, capable of inflicting physical maladies with a glance, particularly to people who are considered vulnerable, like children. The physical discomforts of the victim can only be cured if this afflicting person rubs his own saliva on the sufferer's forehead or feet.

Magbabaya. Nature spirits that dwell in forests, trees, and creeks. Though not necessarily malevolent, they have been known to hurt or kill people who offend them.

Maggalag. Ibanag. Communal healing ritual meant to appease afflicting spirits by inviting people to dance for two days and two nights. Guided by the mengal (tribal sage), the afflicted is then moved to confess the offenses that may have caused the illness.

Magluluop. Type of diviner who specializes in determining illness caused by environmental spirits through a ritual called luop. This method includes the use and manipulation of a shell, leaves and charcoal, salt, as well as tin plate and a pot lid. Though not healers in their own right, practitioners instead defer to the appropriate specialist once the type of affliction has been determined.

Magpapaanak. Term for a midwife, predominantly females who are experts in assisting mothers deliver their babies. Skilled in native massage (hilot), these practitioners have sometimes been attributed with supernatural powers for their proficiency.

Magtitima. Bukidnon. Type of spirit that resides within the balete tree. If not propitiated with chicken sacrifices, it can send sickness, as well as prevent forest trees from being cut.

Maguro. Samal. Type of witch who uses a piece of paper inscribed with Arabic script to cast its curse. Placing the paper near its target is said to cause the victim to become mentally ill, or even die.

Magut-Ayem. Bilaan. Term to describe a type of feared flesh-eating demon.

Mahomanay. Bagobo. So-called "guardian of animals." Enchanted beings said to reside inside balete trees. The male counterpart of the tahamaling, it is said to have a fair complexion.

Maingal. Gadang. Term to describe a type of ghost deity.

Maka-on. Ifugao. Fireballs in the shape of a chicken cage that fly to a victim's house at night, believed to be a sorcerer's familiars.

Maka-usog. Type of witch that casts illness, particularly against children, through the so-called "evil eye."

Makinaadmanon. A layperson whose knowledge and power of mysticism is said to be equal to that of a sorcerer or shaman.

Malakat. Visayan. Type of shape-shifting aswang, described as a person who can turn into a dog or a pig and viciously attacks its victims. In its animal form, its hair is said to reach out and smother its victim's eyes, nose, mouth and ears, rendering him vulnerable to being mauled.

Maldisyon. Cebuano. Derived from Spanish, meaning "curse." Term to describe a native form of sorcery, where an invocation of evil is then followed by the systematic breaking of 13 candles into pieces, from the top to the base. This is said to ensure that the curse works from the head to the feet.

Maligno. A malevolent entity or spirit that is often encountered in the darkness at night.

Malik-mata. To visually confuse or mistake a person, object, or action as something else, or when there's nothing there. This is sometimes used in the context of the supernatural.

Malina. Term for a native nymph. Synonymous with nimpa.

Malulugud. Bilaan. Malevolent spirit whose sole intent is to frighten people; it even assumes the guise of ferocious-looking animals for this purpose.

Mama-o. Ifugao. Method of native divination to determine sorcery, which involves placing unhusked rice in a bowl of water while mentioning the name of the suspected sorcerer's town. If the unhusked rice rises to the surface, then the identity of the sorcerer is confirmed.

Mamalaktol. A practitioner of the sorcerer art of paktol.

Mamaw. A fearsome ghost, monster, or supernatural entity, usually encountered in the dark or in remote places at night.

Mamamaraya. Regional term for a male or female practitioner of witchcraft, this type specializing in making the victim's lips or abdomen swell up as if having devoured something heavy. This is achieved by taking the victim's clothes and placing them inside a pot, along with a piece of paper inscribed with magical phrases, and burying them under the sand on the beach. The victim's stomach will then expand and contract with the ebb of the tide.

Mambabarang (barangan, mamalarang). Cebuano. Type of witch who employs various insects (beetles, grasshoppers, moths, etc.) to attack her victims at night, training them to embed themselves within the body to cause illness, and even death. When not using her pets to attack, the witch keeps the insects inside a bamboo tube.

Mambubuga. Folk healer who specializes in using prayers and saliva, or spittle derived from chewed betel nut to cure wounds and other ailments.

Mambubuno. Zambal. Regional term for a mermaid, described as a beautiful, dark-haired woman from the waist up, but having twin fishtails for a torso or legs. Fishermen who are enthralled by her and follow her to her underwater home do not drown, and a day in her world is said to be a year in human terms.

Mameleu. West Visayan. Enormous serpent that lived in the deep ocean, described as having massive horns and a scaled body that was as thick as a water-buffalo. It had a frightening bellow and spewed green liquid when hungry.

Mammol-lo. Ilocano. Native term for a folk orthopedist who uses prayers, herbs, and massage to diagnose and cure dislocated bones and fractures. He also uses his own saliva as an ointment to determine the details of the injury.

Mamomolong. Maranaw. Folk healer who works together with the pundarpaan in dealing with cases of spirit possession.

Mamumuyag. Visayan. Type of reclusive witch who inflicts sickness on those who offend her. She is avoided by villagers, who do not want to incur her wrath.

Mammuyon. Ilocano. Type of witch who can deduce the identity of a thief simply by ritually analyzing any personal items left behind by the perpetrator. Using various means, it is also capable of predicting if a person is going to die from an illness or not.

Mana-abig. Igorot. Type of native fortune-teller who aids the dadawak by reading the sacrificed entrails of an animal to determine what type of spirit has caused a victim's affliction.

Managilunod. Ilocano. Type of witch capable of cursing the target of its envy simply by wishing misfortune upon them, usually in the form of lighting candles in church and making the request.

Managpalad. Ilocano. Native term for a palm-reader.

Managsapata. Ilocano. Type of witch that curiously curses himself and sacrifices his own well-being if he is discovered to be wrong, untruthful, or unsuccessful.

Managsuma. Pangasinan. A snake-bite specialist, said to be able to cure victims without the use of anti-venom serum.

Managtanem. Ilocano. Type of witch that uses a doll facsimile of the intended victim, pricking it in different areas to inflict pain.

Mananabang. Cebuano. Native term to describe a midwife.

Mananambal. Cebuano. Regional term for a folk healer or shaman who uses various herbs, prayers, and other methods to diagnose and cure illnesses.

Manananem. Pangasinan. Type of witch who practices black magic, known for using a doll to inflict physical ailments against victims that cannot be explained by Western medicine.

Manananggal. Perhaps the most famous and horrific of all the aswangs. A beautiful maiden by day, it then sprouts claws, wings, and fangs at night, detaching its upper body at the torso and flying out to feed. It is notorious for feeding on the livers of its victims, or using its thread-like tongue to eat the fetuses still inside a sleeping mother's womb. It must reconnect its upper torso to its lower trunk prior to dawn, or it will burn and die in the sunlight. Sprinkling salt or ashes upon its exposed trunk will prevent it from re-linking, bringing about certain death.

Mananawal. Tausug. Native term for a male shaman or folk healer.

Manangibanbano. Type of witch that casts illness through the so-called "evil eye," particularly against children.

Manaog. Debabawon. Miniature spirits whose heaven is large as a small leaf. They are known to scare little children.

Mandadawak. Igorot. A practitioner of the art of dawak, a type of shaman with the power to ward-off evil spirits, retrieve stolen souls, as well as heal the spiritually afflicted. He wears an arubo, a type of protective bead talisman, to augment his powers.

Mandurugo. A beautiful woman by day, she transforms into a winged creature at night and drinks blood. She is said to be fond of marrying men, only to secretly drain them of blood over a long period of time until they die. Physically strong at night, this creature loses its strength at dawn.

Mang-aamulit. Regional term for a male or female practitioner of witchcraft, this type specializing in using insects to attack its victim. Retrieving the intended target's clothing, it then allows its familiars to become acquainted with victim's scent, later sending the insects out in the night to inflict sores upon the body.

Mang-alisig. Lubuagan. Native term for a spiritual medium.

Manganito. Type of male or female shaman or folk healer with the power to ward off evil spirits, commune with spirits, and heal the spiritually afflicted.

Mangalos. Visayan. Archaic term for goblins that killed people by eating their bowels.

Mangalok. Type of self-segmenting witch who detaches her upper body from her waist and flies out at night in search of victims' livers or their unborn children. This type is said to sleep in the forest canopy by day, draping her long hair over her face, until nightfall when she awakes to feed. She is also notorious for turning banana trunks into the likeness of corpses.

Mangaluk. Palawan Batak. Type of black forest demon that attacks people who walk through the forest at night. It's described as humanoid, possesses wings, and in place of nails it has talons, which it uses to claw its victims to death. It is also known to eat corpses.

Manggagamod. Type of witch who employs a doll to attack her victims, pricking it under a full moon to inflict pain. She is also known to cause harm by collecting the soil under the victim's footprint, storing and heating it in a clay pot to induce fever. This witch is said to specialize in using poison.

Manggagaway. Term to describe a type of sorcerer. Generally old women, they are as much feared for their powers to cast spells upon victims as they are for their abilities to heal them. There are generally two types of manggagaway: those who use incense and holy candles (palipad-hangin), and those who use a wax or a rag doll (manikaan).

The palipad-hangin waits until dusk to perform her sorcery, taking three candles (each representing various meanings) to an altar, praying, and then lighting the candles in a particular sequence. Blowing the smoke

Manananggal

from the candles in the direction of the victim is said to initiate the curse, causing him to suffer from various physical ailments.

The manikaan uses a wax doll (manikang-kandila) or a rag doll (manikang-basahan). The wax doll is secretly molded from the melted candles in a church, and is ritually used to draw out an infant's soul, causing the baby to die. The rag doll is mystically bonded to the intended victim via prayers and magical words and, once connected, can be pricked with a pin on a spot that corresponds to the victim's body.

Manghihilot. Folk healer who specializes in native massage, or hilot. They are experts in healing sprains, fractures, extreme muscular pain, and bone dislocations by using massage techniques combined with oil and prayers.

Manghuhula. Tagalog. A fortune-teller, a person skilled in personal divination.

Mangisalat. Type of sorcerer capable of preventing a person from being loved.

Mangkukulam. A practitioner of "kulam" or witchcraft; one who casts spells or pricks dolls to attack their victims. Although there are some male practitioners, they are generally solitary old women who live on the outskirts and fringes of a community.

Manglalaga. Cebuano. Practitioner of the deadly art of laga, which involves boiling a representation of the victim in a toxic brew to induce pain.

Manglulumay. Practitioner of the sorcerer art of lumay, which is used to induce affection from a resistant woman. A lock of her hair is retrieved and burned, then secretly mixed into her food. She falls ill, and only her suitor is able to cure her. Another method involves mixing herbs with oil and rubbing it on the woman's palms or hair, again inducing affection.

Mangmang. Bontoc Igorot. Ceremony in which a chicken is beaten to death, then offered to appease an angered ancestor spirit.

Mangmangkik (mangmangkit). Ilocos Norte. Term to describe guardian spirits of the forest, said to live in trees.

Mangubat (mangungubat). Tausug. Native curer, non-denominational in status, who acts as an intermediary between humanity and the spirit world. He conducts private sessions in healing and palmistry, at times even obtaining the aid of lesser spirits to acquire knowledge.

Maniniblot. Zambales. Type of witch who employs a doll to attack her victims.

Manlalabas. A ghost or shadow that likes to appear in front of people to frighten them.

Manlalayog. Woman nefarious for using her long hair to kill her victims. She wrestles with them while snaking her hair through each bodily orifice, ultimately suffocating them.

Mannumang. Ilocano. A snake-bite specialist said to cure victims without the use of anti-venom serum, instead using only oils, various herbs and stones together with rituals and incantations.

Mannumba. Ilocano. A practitioner of the dreaded sumba form of witchcraft, capable of inflicting debilitating hexes upon victims, as well as imprisoning their souls in a bottle.

Manok-manok. Type of supernatural illness, described as temporary blindness experienced after sunset. Only by carrying a hen's nest and beating it repeatedly while walking around the house will the affliction be cured.

Mansalauan. Negros Island. Term for a fearsome, bird-like creature with the head of a lizard and the hands of a monkey. Similar to a large bat in size and wingspan, it has a hairy tail, and feet the size of a human male. It is notorious for inserting its sharp tongue into the stomach of women and feeding.

Mansusupsop. Type of witch said to hover over houses, alighting on the thatch roof and lowering its thread-thin tongue to a sleeping victim's stomach and draining the body of blood.

Mantabungal. Tagbanua. Horrific beast described by natives as being cow-like in appearance, but possessing upper and lower tusks. It is covered in a shaggy coat of hair.

Mantala. Benguet Igorot. Sickness brought about from someone's staring.

Mantianak. Wandering child spirit that waits and attacks unsuspecting victims as they walk along the forest path. It is believed to have originally been a child who died and was buried within its mother's womb. It is also known as a muntianak.

Mantiw. Visayan. Term for a type of ghost or apparition.

Mantiw. A type of giant, said to be as tall as a coconut tree. It is known for playing pranks on people who stay out late at night.

Mantiyu. Malitbog. Benevolent supernatural spirits described as muscular with long hair, and measuring over ten feet tall. Scantily clad, they reside beneath tall trees and sleep while standing up.

Manugtabang. Type of minor witch or sorcerer who only uses his powers to protect his family, friends, and property. Using prayers, paper formulas, and various ingredients, he ritually induces physical sickness in offenders until they return to apologize, upon which he ceases the curse.

Mapparasi. Ibanag. Communal healing ritual meant to appease afflicting spirits by ritually inviting them to a feast, with each attending member symbolically eating meals meant for the spirit.

Marayawan. Mangyan. Native medium, said to be always in touch with benevolent spiritual helpers.

Maria Cacao. Visayas. Female engkanto popular in native folk stories, said to live in a cave on the highest mountain of Argao. Named after the cacao plantation that she owned, she was described as a beautiful woman who brought silverware, utensils, and chinaware back from her travels. She would generously lend them to townspeople for their personal affairs on the condition that they be returned. All they had to do was approach her cave and request the items, and they would then be delivered the following day. However, she stopped lending after some of them failed to bring back the items, disappearing from sight completely.

Mariang Makiling. Luzon. Female engkanto popular in native folk stories, said to live on the summit of Mt. Makiling located in Laguna. Described as a beautiful and ageless, she once stayed among mortals, living alone while helping others by curing their illnesses with her magical herbs, as well as selling fruits she harvested, the profits of which she would later generously distribute to the poor. But her neighbors' greed became too much, prompting her to leave her home on the edge of the forest and ultimately reside on top of the mountain. Like her counterpart Mariang Sinukuan, she was involved in several love affairs.

Mariang Sinukuan. Luzon. Female engkanto popular in native folk stories, said to be one of three daughters of the god Sinukuan, who lived on Mt. Arayat in Pampanga. Described as being beautiful, wealthy, and extremely generous, she lived with twelve maidens and twenty-five Aeta servant women in a palace made of gold. But after villagers murdered some of her servants in order to steal her gold, she cursed the perpetrators and retreated to her palace, never to return. Like her counterpart Mariang Makiling, she was involved in several love affairs.

Mariit. Malitbog. Areas owned by supernatural spirits, used for assembly or play. These include deep pools of water, caves, boulders, and bamboo groves. Anyone foolish enough to reside on that property will suffer great illness and misfortune.

Markupo. West Visayan. Mythological red-crested serpent that lived on the mountaintop. Possessing two tusks, a bristled tongue, and a forked tail, it had breath that was said to be venomous, causing any trees it breathed on to become poisonous as well.

Mediko. Derived from the Spanish "medico," which means medical doctor. Type of folk healer who combines native folk healing with modern medicinal techniques and drugs to cure ailments.

Mga bata ng limbo. Batangas. "The Children of Limbo," said to be the spirits of aborted fetuses who yearn and cry for prayers from the living in order to go to heaven.

Minokawa. Bagobo. Mythical bird said to be as large as an island, with claws and a beak made of steel. It is believed to be the cause of lunar and solar eclipses, flying from the eastern horizon to swallow the moon or the sun. Only shouting or making loud noises will make the creature release the celestial bodies.

Mirida. A premonition of one's own death.

Mnguhul. Bilaan. Harmless class of spirits that befriend people, warn them of danger, and even foretell luck.

Mt. Banahaw. Venerated mountain on the island of Luzon, long considered to be the home of spirits and the retainer of magical properties. Pilgrims from around the world hike its slopes to commune with nature and bathe in its supposedly purifying waters.

Mt. Cristobal. The sinister counterpart of the venerated Mt. Banahaw in Luzon, said to be the home of evil spirits and of negative properties or influences.

Multo. Tagalog term for a ghost or a spirit, derived from the Spanish word "muerto," or dead.

Mumbaki. Ifugao. Term to describe a shaman that performs harvest rituals.

Mumu. A nonspecific term for a frightening spirit or entity, often used to admonish children from going to places they are forbidden to visit.

Mun-amlag. Ifugao. Native term for spirit possession.

Munketema. Ifugao. Term to describe a native spirit medium, responsible for the physical well-being of fellow tribesmen.

Munpa-anap. Ifugao. Method of native divination to determine sorcery, using a sneeze, a burp, or a bristling of the hair.

Mutya. A precious gem or stone, sometimes believed to act like a talisman and grant its wielder extraordinary abilities. It is similar to an anting-anting.

Nangyarihis. Mysterious tree-dwelling spirits who inflict illness upon those that cut down their homes.

Ngata. Ibanag. Malevolent spirit said to be so frightening that seeing it alone would make one sick.

Ngilin. Kalinga. Dwarfish, humanoid spirits believed to consume the spirits of newborn children.

Ngipen-na-aba. Pangasinan. Protective talisman that gives its bearer the ability to repel water from his body; described as a tooth-like object found inside the rolled-up leaf of a cassava plant.

Nimpa. Term for a native nymph. Synonymous with malina.

Numputul. Ifugao. Mythical headless demon from the underworld, known for cavorting about while cramming various centipedes and serpents down its neck with pleasure.

Nun spirits. Ghostly Catholic nuns that reportedly haunt old religious schools and dormitories, continuing to chastise and discipline living students.

Nuno sa punso. Diminutive "old man of the woods." A dwarf-like being said to live under the ground or inside ant mounds that are located along paths or in remote areas. Like the duwende, it too exacts punishment to those who trespass or desecrate its earthen home.

Odom. Bicolano. Native term for protective talisman, a magical herb said to make its bearer invisible to the human eye.

Ogima. Visayan. Demons said to resemble a satyr: a man above the waist, but with the hind legs of an animal.

Omalagar. Term for a snake said to be born alongside an infant, considered a birth twin from the same mother.

Omayan. Bagobo, Mandaya. So-called "spirit of the rice"; dwarf-like entity similar to a duwende and said to reside in rice fields. Farmers would often make offerings to it prior to planting and reaping.

Onglo. East Visayan. Mythological giant that lived in the dark swamps, known for using its formidable knees and elbows to smash open its shellfish food.

Ongo (ungo, unglu). Zamboanga. Type of shape-shifting witch, someone possessed by supernatural influences that cause the person to go out in search of victims in order to devour their livers or drink their blood. This term is sometimes used synonymously with the fearsome aswang.

Orasyon. Latin-sounding prayers or incantations used to empower the person reciting them with extraordinary abilities and protection. When written on a piece of paper, these prayers can sometimes turn the paper itself into a kind of magical talisman.

Oriol. Bicol. Serpent entity said to live beneath the Tiwi hot springs. In order to deliver souls to its father (the evil god Asuang), it takes the form of a beautiful woman and enchants her male victims on moonlit nights into jumping in the boiling water after her. It is also known as irago.

Oro, plata, mata. "Gold, silver, death." Corresponding sequence of threes whose ascribed attributes are applied to the number of steps of a staircase. When counted out, the last step of the stairs must NOT end on "mata," which means death.

Oropok. Visayan. Type of sorcery that causes rats to increase in numbers in another person's field.

Osikan. A practitioner in the sorcerer art of osik, the mystical insertion of inanimate objects (rice, wood, glass, even pins) into a victim's body to cause sickness.

Padugo. The spilling of animal blood (usually a chicken's) upon a property designated for development or construction. This procedure is meant as an offering for the residing spirits of the land itself to grant the occupants permission to settle.

Paghinang-hinang. Tausug. Term for a love charm believed to induce affection from a girl when given to her.

Pagikan. Leyte. Healing ritual held to cure illnesses attributed to supernatural beings. This method involves the community bringing food to the river as an offering to the offended spirits, with the tambalan (medicine man) later setting adrift a miniature boat of offerings meant for the entity to follow and go away.

Paglumisan. Batak. Nature spirits that inhabit small stones.

Pahuot. Cebuano. "To cause to fit tight." Term to describe a native form of witchcraft where the sorcerer causes the body of the intended victim to swell. Procedurally similar to the panghasol form of witchcraft, sea water is added to the pot along with the cut-out representations, and this pot is then thrown into the sea. The victim's stomach in turn swells with the tides.

Paktol (Paktul). Type of sorcery that uses representational objects to attack the intended victim. One form uses a small wooden doll bored with holes that is prepared for witchcraft by hiding it beneath the garments of the attacking sorcerer's first-born as it is being baptized. Pasting a piece of paper with the victim's name on the doll, the witch then recites the Apostle's Creed. As he comes to the passage that recounts the nailing of Jesus to the cross, he inserts nails into the bored holes of the figure, thereby causing pain to the victim. The pain will continue for as long as the nails remain inserted in the doll, and can be varied by shifting them in place or inserting them even deeper.

Another form of paktul involves the sorcerer writing the intended victim's name on a piece of paper, wrapping it in leaves, and then binding it around a skull with a black cloth. The sorcerer then commands the spirit of the skull itself to attack the victim, causing physical distress and ultimately death within a month.

Palakad. Cebuano. Term for a native form of sorcery, where a sorcerer puts a match in oil and baptizes it in the name of the intended victim. The match is then placed in a spot on the ground where the victim frequents. Once the victim steps over it, he collapses.

Palakaran. Type of dangerous sorcerer that specializes in inducing severe stomach pains in his intended victim. Secretly drawing a line to his prey, the practitioner curses the victim with stomach distress when he crosses over this imaginary line. When the victim ultimately goes home, he vomits and dies a day later.

Palalanti. Native term to describe a practitioner or possessor of the so-called "evil eye."

Palasekan. Ilongo. Benevolent enchanted beings that live in trees near villages. They are extremely helpful to people and communicate with them through whistling. They have also been described as dwarves that appear at dawn and at dusk, inflicting minor illnesses on those who inadvertently bother or offend them.

Palata. Cebuano. "To cause to rot." Term to describe a native form of sorcery that involves wrapping a representation of the victim in cloth and then binding it to or inserting it inside a skull. The color of the cloth wrapping (along with the representation's placement on the skull itself) determines the type and severity of the curse. Performed at specified times of the day when sorcery is said to be most effective (noon, 8 PM, midnight, or 3 AM), the ritual begins with burning candles in front of the skull, reciting a curse backwards, and then saying a prayer as if the victim is already deceased. This ritual is repeated daily between nine and thirteen days, until it has taken effect. The victim, however, can successfully repeal the curse if he repents and follows the prescribed rituals for doing so.

Palina. Cebuano. Type of fumigation technique used by mananambals to remove foreign matter or objects inserted by a witch or a sorcerer from a victim's body.

Palinawa. Kalinga. Type of dance meant to revive a deceased relative's spirit. While dancing, a priestess uses a china bowl to collect imaginary hairs (believed to be the spirits of the dead) floating in the air. She then plants these strands on the head of each grieving family member.

Palmanis. Tausug. Type of love potion employed by women to gain the affection of their desired men.

Pamanglo. Mangyan. Type of love-inducing talisman, described as a leather strap worn as an armband and used during courting.

Pamayinan. Type of charm that protects against the attack of wild animals.

Pananggalan (Pananggahan). Jama Mapun. Malevolent supernatural entity that preys on women in labor and newborn infants. It is described simply as a head with its entrails dangling behind it.

Panata. Jama Mapun. The spirit of a person who has escaped its grave to haunt the living. It will continue to terrify people unless a guard is posted at its gravesite.

Panday. Term for a blacksmith or a carpenter.

Pangangata-o. Maranaw. A practitioner of magic capable of countering spells and hexes.

Panghasol. Cebuano. "To cause someone to become disturbed." Term to describe a native form of witchcraft where the sorcerer retrieves a full-body photograph of the intended victim, cuts its outline from the rest of the picture, and uses it as a prototype to create a paper doll representation. He writes the victim's name on the paper facsimile, then wraps this paper around the original cut-out photograph, and in turn wraps the whole bundle in a black cloth that has been secured with thirteen pins. This package is next placed inside a pot whose lid is topped with a banana leaf and secured with yet another black cloth. Thirteen pins are affixed on the leaf in a cross formation. Shaking the pot will make the intended victim ill.

Panghilas. Tausug. Love potion that may be mixed into the food or drink of the intended victim to induce affection.

Pangontra. Object or prayer meant to counter sorcery, bad luck, or spiritual influence.

Panguruskus. Unusual scratching or clawing sounds heard at night, believed to be made by an aswang prowling about the house, or other supernatural entities playing tricks with its inhabitants.

Paniang. Ilocano. Ritual curing of a person afflicted with a supernatural illness, using songs and singing to induce a possessing spirit to leave the victim's body.

Pantak. Tausug, Maranaw. Native form of witchcraft that uses malevolent forces and spirits to induce physical and mental distress that can lead to death. A practitioner is called a pamamantak.

Pantasma. A ghost or spirit.

Pantom. A ghost, spirit, or mysterious shadow.

Paraduno. Camarines. Foul-smelling ghouls that roam the night in search of corpses; fetid in odor like its food. They are known to lie facedown on rooftops and wait for the sick to perish.

Paraghuwas. Visayan. Native term to describe a practitioner who can undo the effects of the so-called "evil eye."

Paragtigo. Type of witch who can determine the true identity of a thief from among a list of suspects. Lighting a candle next to each suspect's name while reciting an incantation, he determines the culprit by observing which flame blows out first next to its corresponding name.

Parahinmalad. Visayan. Term for a palm-reader.

Paraya. Marinduque. Type of sorcery where the practitioner uses a doll to inflict curses upon victims.

Paririmar. Maranaw. Witch who can deduce the identity of a thief simply by ritually analyzing any personal items left behind by the perpetrator. This type uses a book called a rimaran that contains a calendar of days, months, and years to aid in its determination.

Pasu simud. Tausug. "Hot breath." Type of illness generated literally by spoken word, utterance, or by breath. It is usually incurred with the complimenting of someone.

Pausok. Ritual purification with the use of smoke, meant to cleanse a house or property of evil spirits or influences.

Pilay. Isneg. Male and female rice spirits that reside in granaries and kitchens and guard them.

Pimpinading. Tinguian. Type of ritual to cure the supernaturally afflicted, using a miniature house called a bawbaw-i positioned at the village entrance to attract and communicate with spirits.

Pina'ching. Gaddang. Term for ghost deities.

Pinading. Sagada. Spirits that dwell in sacred trees, invoked for various fertility rites, whether human, animal, or crop.

Pinteg. Bontoc Igorot. The spirit of a person who died from being beheaded. This type is favored for aiding in sorcery, due particularly to its vengefulness toward its enemies and protectiveness toward its tribe.

Psychic surgery. Extremely controversial form of folk healing, wherein practitioners claim to cure the afflicted simply by inserting their hands inside the victim without a scalpel and removing the objects or foreign matter they believe is causing the illness. Upon completion of the procedure, no entry or exit wound can be found on the patient. But skeptics insist that this procedure is a sham, and that the objects were retrieved by simple sleight-of-hand techniques.

Pual. Ifugao. Ritual performed by a mumbaki or shaman after the death of a grandmother or grandfather, invoking the spirits of ancestors and of the dead. Raw meat is then distributed after the ceremony.

Pugot. "Beheaded." Term for a headless man, sometimes described as tall, dark, and hairy. It is known for frightening its victims, as well as courting village women. It lives in large trees and has the ability to change into various animals.

Pundarpaan. Maranaw. Spirit medium who works together with the mamomolong, dealing with cases of spirit possession.

Ragit-ragit. Romblomanon. Miniature enchanted beings that can only be seen by infants. Fair in complexion and unable to blink their eyes, they are known to make babies that are left outside sick.

Ramut. Tiruray. Type of protective charm said to cause sickness or death in intended victims; described as consisting of bones, grasses, and stones wrapped and sewn into a cloth bag.

Ranggas. Ilocano. Type of ailment said to be caused by supernatural beings.

Sagay. Surigao. Dwarf-like entity similar to a duwende, said to reside and protect goldmines. They are known to exchange their gold for the blood of children, whom they steal from families in the dead of night.

Sa-i-ro. Ilocano. Native term for demons.

Sakabat. Tiruray. Type of protective charm that warns its bearer of anyone wishing to do him harm.

Sakit. Maranaw. Supernatural entity said to be the cause of illnesses and afflictions.

Salak. Cebuano. Term to describe a native form of sorcery that makes the intended victim physically tired. This is done by mixing fifty specific ingredients and wrapping the concoction in a black cloth. Secreting the juices on any part of the victim's body will cause him to tire, particularly when the attacker confronts him.

Sali-maong. Dog-like creature similar to a sigbin. With its hind legs longer than its front, it walks backwards and can kill with its bite. It can be ridden and commanded to attack its enemies.

Salimbawong. Mythological creature described as a dragon or a giant eel, said to live in marshes and swampy areas in Lanao and Cotabato.

Salimbo-ag. Leyte. Literally "farewell, spirits." Healing ritual held to cure illnesses attributed to supernatural beings.

Salindagao. Maranaw. Type of saitan.

Sampal. Type of sorcery that involves the use of a jellyfish (bahagbahag) to curse a victim. Procuring a representation of the target and wrapping it in a leaf, the sorcerer inserts the small figure inside the jellyfish and secures it with the hairs from a dead woman at noon on Friday. The sea-creature is then returned to the sea, and fastened to a rock. As the jellyfish's body expands and contracts with the ebbing and rising tides, so too does the victim's body, eventually causing him to burst.

Samsam. Cebuano. Term to describe a native form of witchcraft where the sorcerer causes his victim to turn blue and collapse simply by speaking words in his direction. Finding a cluster of seven coconuts, the sorcerer picks one fruit each week on consecutive Fridays, carving a hole into each coconut and plugging it with the piece of a specific tree. Burying the entire cluster once the seven weeks have elapsed, he then retrieves each coconut one week at a time on consecutive Fridays. The plugs are soaked in oil made from a coconut that has blossomed singularly on a tree. The magician in turn rubs this oil on his teeth, and this solution gives him verbal powers.

Sangachil. Bontok. "Death chair." Chair made of pine boughs, used to display the body of the dead for viewing during funeral ceremonies. A pig is sacrificed to the deceased's spirit prior to the body being sat in place.

Sangasang. Type of village guardian spirit that resides at its entrance (podayan). If not properly propitiated or respected, it will retaliate with misfortune or illness.

Sangasang. Ilocano. Ritual curing of a person afflicted with a supernatural illness, involving burning dried guava leaves and blowing the smoke over the affected area. This remedy is also accompanied by prayers.

Sangud. Type of charm that gives its bearer a fortunate chance of procuring monetary success, or great powers.

Santilmo. Ball of light or fire, believed to be the wandering, lost souls of the deceased with unfinished business. Though known to mislead people who follow them in the dark, they occasionally reveal the location of buried treasure.

Sappaw. Apayo. Mythological giant known for its great size and strength.

Sarangay. Ibanag. Tall, dark giant with wooden earrings and long coarse hair, known for possessing a magic jewel that glows in the dark. Whoever steals his jewel is said to gain the strength of ten men.

Sareno. So-called "evil air," undercurrents of air controlled by engkantos or enchanted spirits of the forest, believed to cause illness and misfortune.

Sarut. So-called supernatural "tempters," unusual-looking animals that intentionally position themselves to be injured by people. Though harmless when left alone, they inflict illness on those that harm them.

Satanas. The Christian Satan, the ruler of hell and ultimate source of evil.

Saytan. Maranaw, Tausug. Evil spirits of the Muslim world, believed to reside within banyan trees and large rocks. They are notorious for possessing people and animals who encroach upon their domain.

Segben (sigbin). Dog-like creature with raised hindquarters and huge flapping ears, said to have been created from vine roots encased in a bottle of oil. Its head is constantly positioned between its legs, always looking backwards, and is capable of moving forward and backward with equal ease. It is invisible to everyone except its master, who can command it to do his bidding. If not fed its diet of blood, it will go out and kill children, pregnant women, and even devour corpses. If it bites the shadow of the sickly, it will hasten the victim's demise.

Semanget (sumangat). Jama Mapun. Native term for the spirit or vitality of life present throughout nature.

Sibbarayungan. Apayao, Isneg. Mythological female giant who once concealed a lost traveler from her husband to spare his life. Concealing the man in a chest until her suspicious husband went away, she then fed him and showed him the way to go home.

Sigbinan. Person who could transform himself into a snake or a crocodile and kill people.

Silagan. Catanduanes. A flightless, liver-eating aswang, said to tear out and devour the livers of anyone dressed in white.

Silew-silew. Pangasinan. Term for a ball of light or fire that leads those that follow it astray. Found in isolated swamps and fields, it comes in different colors and doesn't burn its immediate surroundings.

Siling. Bilaan. Term to describe a type of feared flesh-eating demon.

Siloit. Gaddang. Type of dwarf-like entity, said to be a manifestation of the kalanget.

Sinan baboy. Supernatural creature described as resembling a pig. Said to be found under mango trees, the diminutive creature is notorious for passing between the legs of people before suddenly growing to enormous size and then trampling them.

Sinakayan. Tagalog. Spirit possession; the occupying of a person's body by an evil spirit.

Sinsinnucat. Tinguian. Type of ritual exorcism meant specifically for schools occupied by spirits.

Siocoy. Tagalog. Term for a merman, described as a diminutive human male from the waist up, but with a fish's tail for a torso or legs. Depending on the account, they are either benevolent to children (bringing them to their underwater kingdom), or they drown victims in the sea. In movies, siocoys are often portrayed as more fish-like than human, men with bulging fish eyes, gills, and webbed feet and hands. Also known as ugkoy in Waray.

Siquijor Island. Mysterious island located in the Central Philippines, said to be the home of native sorcery and witchcraft.

Sirena. Indigenous mermaid, described as a woman with long, dark hair from the waist up, but with a fish's tail in place of legs. Living in the ocean as well as the river, they occasionally bring people into their underwater domain. However, they are also sometimes blamed for unexplained deaths along bodies of water.

Sir'ing. A hideous, curly haired man said to live in the forest trees. Possessing long nails, he targets victims who wander the forest alone, assuming the form of the person's relative in order to deceive and later abduct him. He is repulsed by bees' wax, as well as the burning of peppers and lemons.

Siring. Dwarf-like entities said to live inside fig trees. They are believed to take care of the souls of deceased children whose bodies are placed inside this tree.

Soblay (somang). Kalinga. Type of charm used to determine if a food about to be eaten has been poisoned or not. Made from a mixture of roots and coconut oil, it is carried in a small bottle and, if placed next to food that has been poisoned, the oil itself oozes out of its container.

Sukdan. Mamamua. Native term for a medium, an intermediary with the spirit world.

Sulingbungain. Batak. Nature spirits that inhabit large rocks ("taraw").

Sumpa. A mystical curse, hex, or vow bestowed upon a victim. It can also take the form of a protective object.

Suna. Visayan. The art of curing snake bites.

Sunahan. Visayan. A practitioner in the art of curing snake bites.

Supok. Bontoc Igorot. "To blow." Form of healing in which the curer blows on the patient to drive away the spirit of illness.

Ta-awi. Maranao. Hideous giant known for approaching villages with the sound of thunder and spiriting victims off through the air, bringing them to its mountain home. However, it is unable to digest human eyeballs after devouring the person, and it only imprisons beautiful women.

Tabi po. Tagalog. Phrase that means, "Excuse me." When encountering earthen mounds along a path, it is widely believed that one must first ask permission to pass before proceeding. Such mounds are said to be the home of duwendes (dwarves), and failure to show respect might incur their wrath. Desecrating the mounds will certainly lead to even harsher retribution.

Tac-taco. Ilocano. Ritual curing of a person afflicted with a supernatural illness that involves putting rice inside a coconut shell and placing it on the skin of the injured. This remedy is also accompanied by prayers.

Sirena

Tagalilung. Type of orasyon or incantation said to be derived from the devil and procured from a cemetery, enabling the user to become invisible to human eyes.

Tagamaling. Mansaka. Type of benevolent spirit that resides within the balete tree. They are said to interact with humans, at times even marrying the attractive ones. They are also credited with introducing different art forms to the tribe, as well as the concept of trade. Some accounts describe them as ogres who are benevolent one month and then dangerous the next.

Tagarlum. Visayan. A so-called "charmed herb" that causes its bearer to become invisible.

Tagi-amo (taga-amo). Ilocano. A type of love potion.

Tagi-ruot. Ilocano. A type of love potion.

Tagibulag. Type of protective amulet said to make its bearer invisible to his enemies.

Taglugar. Nature spirits or entities that are said to dwell specifically within a particular area or territory. The name literally translates as, "of the place."

Tagosilangan. Visayan. Person who possesses a charm that enables him to see things that are hidden.

Tagtaguilinged. Type of talisman or anting-anting that gives its bearer the power of invisibility. It is procured from the body of an exhumed black cat, which is killed through a specific ritual of time and prayers. The bearer must defeat various supernatural entities prior to obtaining it.

Taguisirang. Malitbog. Spirit said to live in the atmosphere ("between the clouds and the sky") and control the weather. This type resides where the sun rises.

Tahamaling. Bagobo. So-called "keeper of animals." Enchanted beings said to reside inside balete trees. The female counterpart of the mahomanay, it is said to have a red complexion.

Taitih. Tausug. All Saints' Day, the month of Shaaban in the Muslim calendar. People can visit the graves of their deceased on any day of the month to clean and offer prayers.

Taiyaban. Ifugao. Predatory deity known for snatching souls and mating with, devouring, or enslaving them.

Talahiang. Zamboanga. Dark-skinned, muscular giant that towers over four meters tall, living in trees and getting travelers lost. Capable of changing into animals, it is said to be afraid of loud noises.

Tama. Manobo. Malevolent giant that lives in a balete tree in the deep jungle. It lures travelers off their paths and devours them. Natives claim to have even seen their footprints.

Tamawo. Visayan. Enchanted, capricious beings said to live inside luxurious homes that appear to the ordinary human eye as unusual rock or tree formations.

Tambalan. Visayan. Regional term for a folk healer or shaman who uses various herbs, prayers, and other methods to diagnose and cure illnesses.

Tamban-a-kau-a. Manobo. Giant tarantula said to be the cause of lunar and solar eclipses, engulfing the moon or the sun with its body. Only shouting, making loud noises, or shooting arrows in its direction will cause the creature to release the celestial bodies.

Taming. Visayan. Type of witch whose specialty is undoing cast spells.

Tao sa sulup. So-called "men of the woods," spirits that live within tree trunks and who can intervene in human affairs.

Tarabusao. Maranao, Maguindanao. Term for a giant ogre that lived in Mt. Matutum.

Tawas. The diagnosing of an illness and its cure simply by observing the pattern and shape of melting candle wax that has been dripped onto the water's surface.

Tayhup. Method of folk healing in which the practitioner blows on the crown of the head where the sign of the cross has been made.

Tigaalis ng tibo. Folk healer who specializes in removing fish bones lodged in the throat of a person.

Tigagamot ng sakit sa ngipin. Folk healer who specializes in folk dentistry, using prayers to cure pain and remove teeth without the use of dental apparatus.

Tigagamot ng taga. Folk healer who specializes in stopping profuse bleeding or hemorrhaging from deep cuts.

Tigbanua (Tagbanua). Bagobo, Manobo. Diverse class of nature spirits that dwells in the vast hills, forests, mountains and valleys. Ruling over different areas, these spirits and their territories must be revered and respected. Some accounts describe them as ogres that live in trees.

Tikbalang. Folkloric creature described as a dark, extremely long-legged man, but with a horse's head. It is known to intentionally lead travelers astray along their way, and turns people into its own kind by having them unsuspectingly consume bread that it created. If the sun is out while it is raining, Tikbalangs are believed to be getting married.

Tiktik. Malevolent bird named after the sound that it makes. Its appearance signifies the presence of an aswang prowling about nearby. It is sometimes referred to synonymously with the manananggal, using its thread-thin tongue to feed on unborn fetuses.

Tilik. Men said to have devilish or supernatural eyes. One look into their reddish eyeballs is believed to cause sickness or even death.

Tindok. Type of talisman or anting-anting that gives its bearer the power of invisibility. It is said to come from gold that emerges from the blossom of a banana plant. This gold is mixed with water, and the liquid is then injected into the body. The gold itself is inserted into the skin.

Tingawok. Leyte. Healing ritual held to cure illnesses attributed to supernatural beings. This method involves the afflicted squatting on a mat while the tambalan (medicine man) shakes and throws betelnuts on the floor. He then interprets the nuts' positioning to determine if the possessing or afflicting spirit intends to stay or leave the body.

Tirtiris. Ilocano. Miniature enchanted people said to live in bagbagotot bushes. Fair in complexion and wearing clothes of fine silk embroidered with gold, they possess gold teeth and are often seen dancing on people's yards in the early evening. They are known to add rice to the granary bins of people they favor.

Tiw-tiw. Visayan. Type of charm used to draw fish to a fisherman. Consisting of several types of roots that were gathered from inside a cave during dry season, it is placed inside a bottle of coconut oil and poured slowly into the water. This induces the fish to come to the fisherman for easy gathering.

It has also been described as a type of spell that induces animals to follow their respective predators, making wild boars follow a hunter out of the forest, or fish follow a fisherman to shore.

Tikbalang

Tiyanak. Nefarious creature disguised as a weeping infant that is often encountered in open grassy fields or in the remote woods. When picked up and coddled by a concerned person, the child then turns into a hideous monster and proceeds to scratch or kill its unsuspecting victim. It is called patianak in some regions.

Tiyu-an. Type of non-flying aswang that can transform into a pig. This type is said to keep puppies around that never age, which are actually the creature's masters.

Todos Los Santos. "All Saints' Day." National Catholic holiday held annually on November 1. It is an occasion where relatives visit local cemeteries and clean-up the gravesites of deceased family members, often spending the entire day there while praying and eating meals. It is then followed by Todos Los Difuntos, or All Souls' Day, on November 2.

Tonong. Maranaw. Type of spirit that belongs to the so-called apo, or "tornado" spirits. Those possessed by this entity are known as pitonongan. Farmers usually offer newly harvested rice to this spirit prior to consumption.

Tubangkit. Jama Mapun. The spirit of a sinful person who has returned to haunt the living.

Tubignon. Visayan. Resident spirits that exist within a specific body or area of water.

Tulung (tuwung). Pinatubo. Horse-like creature similar to a tikbalang, described as having long hair, clawed feet, and extremely large testicles.

Tuman-on. Visayan. Dwarf-like entity said to live in mounds. It makes itself invisible with the use of a talisman.

Tunguquibul. Term for so-called "death guards," Muslim family members who take turns watching over the grave of a deceased loved one for several days.

Tuthu. Method of folk healing in which the practitioner chews and spits out medicine over the afflicted area while saying a prayer.

Tuub. Native remedy for fright, in which the victim places his head over a pot of boiling water filled with herbs (or a representation of what frightened him), and then inhales the steam while under a blanket.

Tuyaw. Type of supernatural punishment for those that ridicule the rituals or ceremonies of a baylan or native priestess. It can cause madness and even death.

Tuyob. Cebuano. Term to describe a native form of witchcraft where the sorcerer curses the intended victim by making his urination painful. Locating a spot where the victim has previously relieved himself, the magician declares offense and retribution while exclaiming the person's name. He then recites the Christian Credo and later stabs the spot with the tail of a stingray when he comes across the passage that describes Jesus' nailing on the cross.

Tuyup. Ifugao. Heavy winds that shake a house, believed to be an attack of sorcery. The origin of the wind's direction is believed to be the location of the sorcerer's domicile.

Udtohanon. Malitbog. Benevolent spirits said to live at the apex of the atmosphere, where the creator and the angels reside.

Ugaw. Pangasinan. Elusive enchanted beings that live behind rice containers and granaries. Miniature in size, they are known for secretly stealing rice that has spilled or that isn't adequately protected.

Ukoy (ugkoy). Term for a small man who lives in the sea, known for drowning his victims. It is sometimes synonymous with a merman.

Umagad. Manobo. Spiritual companions; a person's invisible counterpart without whom one could not exist. Although a bit diminutive in size, it resembles its corporeal version and mimics its movements. This spirit is considered a guardian angel.

Umalagad. Visayan. Term for ancestor spirits, revered as personal guardians.

Umayum. Mandaya. The spirit or soul of rice.

Ungà-ungà. Type of self-segmenting witch who detaches her upper body from her waist and flies out at night in search of victims. With her intestines dangling behind her, she must return to her lower half before sunrise to become whole again. But if anyone were to sprinkle ashes or sand over her carefully hidden stump, she cannot reconnect and will therefore die in the sunlight. She is said to be afraid of bamboo grooves, fearful of snagging her entrails among the branches. Most likely synonymous with the manananggal.

Ungit. Tiruray. Type of charm said to increase the ferocity in dogs. Extracted from the sap of a particular tree, it is then burned and given to dogs to smell. This is turn causes them to be even more feral.

Usik. Cebuano. "To waste or spend extravagantly." Term to describe a native form of sorcery that is similar to the barang, but the chants employed are different and the insects introduced to the victim's body are much smaller.

Usikan. Cebuano. Type of witch whose name is used synonymously with the Buyagan witch. This practitioner is said to possess the so-called "evil tongue," or buyag, sorcery derived from envy, in which the exponent (intentionally or inadvertently) curses a prosperous victim with a verbal compliment, reversing the good fortune and resulting in financial or even physical decline.

The title is similar to the witchcraft "usik," but the usikan inherited its skills, whereas the former learned the magical procedures to implement it.

Usog (usug). Term to describe an affliction attributed to the so-called "evil eye," in which the victim (usually a child) falls ill from a glance or a greeting from someone possessing that power. The cure involves the afflicting witch rubbing its saliva on the feet or on the forehead of the victim.

Vampira. A blood-drinking creature of the night, a general term to describe male and female Western vampires.

Vicera sucker. Term to describe a class of self-segmenting witches, women who have the ability to detach their upper body from their waist and feed at night. Alighting on the rooftops of pregnant women, they lower their thread-thin tongues through the thatch fronds and devour the child while it is still inside the womb.

Viga. Bisayan. Charm that protects its bearer from becoming wet while swimming.

Vongig. Ifugao. Term to describe the supernatural ability to use one's own envy to make other people's crops and animals die.

Wakwak. Visayan. Type of bird named after its call, said to come out at night and hover over houses to indicate the presence of a nearby aswang. In some accounts, however, it is synonymous with the dreaded manananggal.

White Lady. Extremely popular supernatural entity commonly seen throughout the country. Described as a beautiful woman dressed in flowing white garments, she is often encountered by the roadside procuring a ride from passersby, only to disappear when arriving at her destination. She is also seen walking in remote areas and in old buildings or structures. Linked specifically to a street called Balete Drive in Quezon City, this spirit is believed to originally be a woman who was raped by Japanese soldiers during World War II.

Wirwir. Apayao. Type of flesh-eating ghoul, known for devouring bodies and stealing valuables from their graves.

Witawit. Obscure term for a native tree-dwelling spirit.

Wiwit. Term for a ghost.

Yawa. Visayan. A non-Christian pagan, but originally referencing a devil or demon.

The Pacific Islands, Including Hawai'i, Tahiti, New Zealand, and Papua New Guinea

Adaro. Solomon Islands. San Cristobal. Type of sea sprite described as a hybrid of human and fish in appearance. Traveling in waterspouts and rainbows, they stun men unconscious with flying fish, then require an offering in exchange for a cure. Their chief is called Ngorieru.

Agiba. Papuan Gulf. Kerewa. Skull rack. Ornate rack that displays the skulls of enemies; carved to represent a stylized human ancestor spirit.

Ahi-matiti. Maori. Type of makutu (witchcraft) that causes a victim to become mentally deranged.

Ahi-whakaene. Maori. Type of makutu that centers around a sacred fire created by a tohunga makuta (wizard-priest). He will then recite a spell against his adversary, killing him or persuading him to change his ways.

'Aiaru. Tahitian. Malevolent tupapa'u (ghost) that causes illness and death to families and villagers. This spirit can be dealt with by turning its exhumed body face-down in the grave, burning the corpse, and then slitting its throat.

'Aito. Tahitian. Spirits of ancient heroes that protect their descendants and sacred temples.

Aitu. Samoan. Term for a wandering ghost, originally referring to a personal animal sacred to natives, but later denounced by missionaries as pagan.

Akaku. Hawaiian. Unexpected vision or epiphany that one receives, usually as a form of warning.

Akua. Hawaiian. God or goddess; reference to the various deities of the native pantheon.

Akua hele loa. Hawaiian. So-called "great travelers"; term to describe playful ghosts fond of pranks and mischief. They have been known to swarm old byways in troops, playing and dancing and feasting on imaginary food.

Akua noho. Hawaiian. The possession of a person by an akua or deity.

Akuaku. Rapanui (Easter Island). Term for a ghost.

Akualele. Hawaiian. Fireballs, often referred to as flying gods or spirits, used in ho'ounauna to destroy enemies. They have also been viewed as omens.

Amalau. Nukuoro. Term to describe a community spirit house, which is rectangular with three open sides. This structure is used to house figures that represent spirits.

'Ana 'ana. Hawaiian. Native term for sorcery, the use of magic to bring about sickness and death.

Ao kuewa. Hawaiian. The homeless spirit of a person who had no property or friends when alive.

Atua. Marquesan. General term for a god, although it can also refer to a deified ancestor.

'Aumakua. Hawaiian. Deified ancestor spirits or ghosts specific to an immediate family or familial structure; worshipped and invoked in times of need. As with other native deities, 'aumakua can assume many different forms, particularly animals and plants. They have also been described as guardian angels, spirits who didn't enter the underworld upon dying, instead hovering around their families.

Baloma. Papua New Guinea. Trobriand Islands. Native term for spirit.

Bis poles. Papua New Guinea. Asmat. Ornate twenty-foot pole carvings believed to contain the spirits of clan warriors slain by the enemy. Only when the poles are anointed by the blood of a retaliatory victim from the offending clan (which involves killing, beheading, and eating him) can the spirits be released to go to the land of the ancestors. These beautiful poles could stand in a village for weeks or even years until their inhabiting spirits are properly released.

Bulubwalata. Papua New Guinea. Trobriand Islands. Umbrella term for the many forms of evil magic or sorcery.

Bwaga'u. Papua New Guinea. Trobriand Islands. Male sorcerer who practices black magic; capable of inflicting disease and death on his victims.

Cargo cults. Papua New Guinea. Religious beliefs and movements created by New Guinea and Melanesian islanders as a response to the influx of Western artifacts. Transposing the native belief of cause and effect as applied to acquiring material wealth, native cult leaders rationalized that, by ritually imitating European behavior and recreating the cargo artifacts from native resources, the supernatural forces that produced them would bring about the same blessings to the islanders as to the Europeans. Cargo cults were first documented in 1867, and appeared sporadically throughout and shortly after World War II.

Dogai. New Ireland. Malignant changeling spirit fond of impersonating a man's wife to seduce him. Its gender varies from region to region. In its natural state, it is described as a hideous being with large ears. It also has destructive powers, such as killing fish, influencing the tides, and plaguing coconut trees.

'E'epa. Hawaiian. Umbrella term for mysterious and incomprehensible spirits that live in remote areas. They have also been described as gnome-like beings, said to be suffering from various physical deformities and weaknesses. In native lore, they have sometimes been relegated to spiritual caretakers of children.

Fa'atosaga. Samoan. Term for traditional midwife.

Faceless woman. Hawaiian. Dreaded modern ghost often encountered while alone in public bathrooms. First reported in 1959. Frightened witnesses have described the apparition as a woman combing her long black hair. When the witnesses turned to glance at the woman's face, they saw that she didn't have eyes, a nose, or a mouth. The ghost also didn't have any legs and possessed only an upper torso.

Folklorists have compared the faceless woman to a Japanese ghost called mujina, a faceless spirit first described by Japanophile Lafcadio Hearn in his famous ghost story anthology Kwaidan.

Falealupo Peninsula. Samoan (Savai'i). Picturesque area that natives believe is actually the gateway to the underworld of ghosts (aitu), located where the sun sets into the ocean. Ghosts who roam the night must return there by daybreak or face the punishing sunlight.

Fehuluni. Tongan. Popular ghost said to appear as a woman to men and conversely as a man to women. It is more commonly known as a woman who removes her head from her shoulders and combs her hair.

Figonas. Solomon Islands. Diverse class of spirits associated with specific locations where one feels a certain sense of awe.

Fehuluni

Firewalking. Native Fijian. The practice of ritually walking across hot stones, based on a legend in which the warrior Tui-na-vinggalita was given immunity against fire by a god whose life he spared after ensnaring it while fishing.

Firewalking. Fiji East Indian. A coincidental transplant from mainland southern India, the ritual practice of walking across hot embers, meant mostly for purification or as symbolic gratitude to the god Kali (Durga).

Fofo. Samoan. Native healer who practices traditional massage.

Fofogau. Samoan. Traditional healer capable of setting broken bones.

Fumeripits. Papua New Guinea. Asmat. The mythical creator of the Asmat (tree) people, who were carved from wood and then drummed into life.

Gas. New Ireland. The so-called "spirit double" of a human being. This duplicate dies along with its corporeal counterpart.

Gesges. New Ireland. The spirits of unborn children whose mothers died during pregnancy.

Haast's eagle (Harpagornis moorei). Maori. The largest known eagle ever to have existed, possessing massive claws and a wingspan of ten feet. Known as pouakai or hokioi to the Maori, this extinct bird was believed to have hunted the giant flightless moa birds, and even people, carrying them off from villages.

Hailona. Hawaiian. The art of native divination, predicting the future and the outcome of events by reading leaves, flowers, stones, and even the movements of animals.

Haka. Hawaiian. Spirit medium through whom spirits and akua speak.

Hau. Maori. One of three souls the human body is believed to contain. This soul is the life-essence of a person, and is considered the spirit's intellectual aspect.

Haus tambaran. Papua New Guinea. So-called "spirit houses" meant to contain the spirits (Tambaran), or the carvings that represent them.

Varying in size from region to region, these structures can only be entered by initiated men.

Hei-tiki. Maori. "Ancestor pendant." Term to describe an heirloom ceremonial ornament made of greenstone. It is associated with ancestors and is passed on from generation to generation. It is addressed by its own personal name, and is worn or exchanged in formal and significant occasions such as weddings, funerals, and treaty ratifications.

Heheve. Papua New Guinea. Papuan Gulf. Elema. Female sea spirits that are depicted as towering masks worn by dancers and appearing at the conclusion of various cyclical rituals that take several years to complete. Throughout the month after their grand unveiling, the dancers perform with other participants on the beach, before being symbolically killed at the end of the celebration.

Heiau. Hawaiian. Shrine or temple in which offerings and ceremonies are made to the gods.

Hōʻailona. Hawaiian. Term for omens; the art of reading occurrences, movements, and patterns within nature to carefully predict the future.

Hoʻokalakupua. Hawaiian. Native term for magic.

Hoʻounauna. Hawaiian. The so-called practice of "sending spirits," wherein a kahuna sends forth spirits of the deceased to convey a warning, or sends akualele to destroy his enemies.

Hore. Maori. Term to describe mythical giant reptiles said to live underground, creating massive chambers or tunnels and even uprooting trees as they travel beneath the earth. It is sometimes considered a type of the mythical taniwha.

I-culanibokola. Native Fijian. Cannibal fork. Ornate wooden fork used by natives in the past for consuming cannibal victims, as using one's fingers to eat human flesh was considered improper.

ʻIke pāpālua. Hawaiian. Term used to describe the innate sensitivity and awareness of a psychic.

Ipu ʻōlelo. Hawaiian. The so-called "speaking gourd," used to read signs during divination.

Jipae. Papua New Guinea. Irian Jaya. Asmat. Term to describe masked, costumed dancers that represent spirits of the deceased. They emerge from the forest and visit living relatives to tell them of their happiness and readiness to depart for the afterlife. Villagers also stage a mock battle to reassure these representational spirits that they are no longer welcome in the village.

Ka huakaʻi o ka pō. Hawaiian. The infamous "night marchers," a ghostly, torch-lit procession of dead chiefs, priests, warriors, and attendants that, unless proper care is taken, strikes dead anyone unfortunate enough to witness the parade. Believed to occur on certain nights of the month (usually on the original paths used by the spirits when alive), these processions are still sighted and greatly feared.

Kahoaka. Hawaiian. The soul of a living person, said to be visible to particular classes of priests.

Kahu. Hawaiian. The caretaker, keeper, or guardian of a specific knowledge, structure, or deity. It originally meant the guardian or nurse of a child.

Kahuna. Hawaiian. Generic term to describe an expert, priest, or a specialist in a particular art, profession, or trade. Most associated in modern times with malevolent sorcery.

Kahuna ʻana ʻana. Hawaiian. An expert in malevolent magic and sorcery.

Kahuna kuni. Hawaiian. A sort of counter-magician to the kahuna ʻana ʻana; someone who could seek revenge upon an attacking sorcerer by ritually assaulting him in return.

Kaiaimunu. Papua New Guinea. Namau. Large wicker-work monster used in ceremonial rites of passage for young men. Over ten feet long, they are often filled with objects for different functions.

Kakamora. Solomon Islands. San Cristobal. Class of diminutive spirits (ranging from six inches to three feet in height by different accounts) that are fond of singing and dancing. Naked, with straight, long hair that comes down to their knees, these physically strong entities are, in temperament, enigmatic at best.

Kākāola. Hawaiian. The soul of a living person.

Ka-mahunu. Maori. Type of spell that induces an evildoer to feel guilty for his transgressions and mend his ways for a better life.

Kāne o ka pō. Hawaiian. Literally, "man of the night," a mysterious spirit lover who comes to a woman's bed at night and makes love to her, at times getting her pregnant.

Kapu. Hawaiian. Base word for the term "taboo." Any of the various civil, social, or religious prohibitions that applied to different segments of native society. Also known regionally as tapu.

Karkarau (karau). Papua New Guinea. Irian Jaya. Humboldt Bay. Term to describe protective wooden carvings, usually depicting a man squatting beneath a bird with its wings outstretched, found on the finial caps of native buildings. The term "kararau" also means "frog."

Kāula. Hawaiian. Prophet.

Kaupe. Hawaiian. Mythological weredog creature said to reside in L huʻe on Oʻahu.

Kava. Pan-Pacific Islander. A numbing, non-alcoholic drink that comes from the dried root of the kava plant, Piper methysticum. Its consumption is an important component of various Islander rituals, ceremonies, and events.

Kilo. Hawaiian. Term for prophet.

Kilokilo ʻuhane. Hawaiian. Ancient ritual sorcery used to raise the dead.

Kini akua. Hawaiian. Little elves said to inhabit the woods.

Kino wai lua. Hawaiian. A spirit who has temporarily left its living host body, only to return sometime later. This ghost can be persuaded to return to life by other ghosts, or through the use of ritual offerings. It has also been described as a composite being made up of two ghosts, an 'uhane and an 'unihipili.

Koʻa. Hawaiian. Term to describe several types of fishing shrines meant for the gods, placed near bodies of water to ensure bountiful catches.

Kolohe spirits. Hawaiian. So-called "rascal" spirits who cause mischief to unsuspecting victims.

Korambo. Papua New Guinea. Abelam. A type of ceremonial house.

Korwar. Papua New Guinea. Irian Jaya. Geelvink Bay. Wooden ancestral figures created by native Mon shamans to communicate with the deceased. These shamans would entice the spirits to reside inside the figure itself, asking for advice on daily and important matters. Sometimes containing a piece of the deceased's skull, the sculpture's head is thought to be its seat of power.

Kula ring. Papua New Guinea. A complex system of ritual exchange among several Island communities within the Milne Bay Province. Centering around an invisible ring that spans the Trobriand Islands and its neighbors, traders participate in the exchange of ceremonial gifts based on its direction in relation to the ring: red shell necklaces (bagi or soulava) if clockwise, or white shell armlets (mwali) if counter-clockwise. With traders having specific Kula partners in each direction, the rituals performed are believed to uphold clan-based hierarchies and reinforce the status and authority of hereditary chiefs. The traded objects must be passed on to others within a given time, and it can take years for the items to return to their place of origin.

Kulap. New Ireland. Term to describe small, mortuary chalk figures that were believed to temporarily house the spirit of the deceased.

Kuni. Hawaiian. The ritual burning of an offending sorcerer's own belongings or clippings, assaulting and destroying him in return.

Kupua. Hawaiian. Spirits and entities that were more than human, yet less than a god. Often described as the demigod offspring of humans and akua, they were able to communicate with humans by occupying the bodies of people and animals.

Kuru. Papua New Guinea. "Laughing disease." Mysterious ailment that attacks the body's central nervous system, leaving victims with smiles on their faces. Specific only to women and children in the Fore area, it was later found to originate from the ritual cannibalization of brain tissue of dead clan members.

Kwita. Papua New Guinea. Trobriand Islands. Giant octopus said to be so large its body could encompass an entire village. Its arms were the size of palm trees.

Lapu. Hawaiian. Term used to describe a wandering or restless spirit.

Leina a ka ʻuhane. Hawaiian. The so-called "leaping place" of spirits, a jump-off point for the dead to literally leap into P , the native underworld.

Long pig. Informal term for a cannibal victim.

Lua ʻuhane. Hawaiian. So-called "spirit hole," a point on the inner eye where the soul is believed to exit the body when it wanders about. It then re-enters the body through the same location.

Luve-ni-wai. Native Fijian. Friendly water spirits adept at conjuring and who were believed to teach devotees songs and dances.

Maʻi tapiri. Tahitian. Type of illness caused directly by ghosts or spirits.

Ma-heheve. Papua New Guinea. Papuan Gulf. Elema. The mother of the heheve, female sea spirits that appear at the celebratory conclusion of native cyclical rituals. Her arrival with her two daughters at the men's house is said to initiate the creation of the representational heheve masks, which are then worn by dancers and later introduced to the villagers at the appointed time.

Makemake. Rapanui (Easter Island). Chief deity of the so-called "Bird Man cult," around whom various rituals were centered, particularly a contest of skill and endurance in which the cult followers journeyed to neighboring islands to procure the first egg of a tern. The winner and his village were given status, glory, and the gods' favor for one year.

Makutu. Maori. Generic term for native forms witchcraft as practiced by the tohunga makutas or wizard-priests.

Malae (marae, me'ae). Maori. Native ceremonial center or ground.

Maliu. Hawaiian. Term for a deified dead chief.

Mana. Pan-Pacific Islander. Hawaiian. Spiritual power, prestige, or divine energy derived from the native deities, found in various forms and quantities throughout the natural world. Often used in magic, the possession of mana can be either acquired or inherited.

Manaia. Maori. Spirit figures that are depicted in profile view. Human in shape, they are sometimes portrayed as having bird or animal features.

Mane kisu. Melanesian. Type of shaman who specializes in curing illnesses as well as other forms of divination.

Marakihau. Maori. Mythical sea spirit said to resemble a person, but who posesses an extended proboscis tongue called a ngongo that it uses to devour men or their canoes.

Marsalai. New Guinea. Arapesh. Powerful spirits believed to have established the existing customs of clans. Living in mystically charged pools, slopes, and rocks, they are considered guardians of their own hunting grounds, and are fiercely territorial. They can cause floods, landslides, and earthquakes, and may cause stillbirths and miscarriages. They sometimes manifest themselves as striped or two-headed reptiles.

Masalais. Papua New Guinea. Malangan term for the spirits of the bush and water.

Masengi (maasenge). Papua New Guinea. Madang Province. Moam River. Mischievous and potentially dangerous water spirits known for irksome pranks and for creating whirlpools that drag people and their canoes down underwater. They are described as being small and chubby, part human and part animal. Masks of cultural heroes are carved to protect villagers from these pesky creatures.

Masi. Solomon Islands. San Cristobal. Class of spirits that were physically strong, but gullible and easily tricked. Their descendants became artisans and craftsmen of stone and canoes.

Matakai. Maori. Incantation used to kill a victim while the person is in the act of eating.

Mauri. Maori. One of three souls the human body is believed to contain. This soul is the so-called "spark" or "breath" of life within a person, and is considered the spirit's physical aspect.

Mbalolo (palolo). Term for segmented sea worms that swarm to the surface by the millions to propagate, appearing twice a year like clockwork and getting harvested as a delicacy by Islanders in Fiji and Samoa.

Mehameha. Tahitian. The experience of having odd or mysterious feelings, particularly as they pertain to the supernatural.

Mejenkwaad. Marshall Islands. Malevolent demon infamous for possessing women who are pregnant or who have just given birth. Women who die during childbirth are also believed to turn into this creature.

    The afflicted are described as having insane-looking eyes and bleeding between the teeth, and having a nape that appears to breathe. If the

Mejenkwaad

victim isn't treated immediately, a mouth appears on the nape, making the transformation permanent.

Known for devouring villagers (particularly husbands), it has the ability to stretch its neck or upper body for miles to another island, particularly when in pursuit.

Menehune. Hawaiian. Legendary dwarf-like beings believed to have been the first inhabitants of Hawai'i. Described as diminutive in size, they were expert stone craftsmen and were credited for building the ancient fishponds, irrigation ditches, and temples found throughout the islands. Working only at night and living in forests and caves, these squat, large-eared beings are more commonly seen today as caricatures on construction site billboards.

Milamala. Papua New Guinea. Trobriand Islands. Big feast held for spirits, who return to their own villages annually to receive offerings.

Mo'o. Hawaiian. An 'aumakua described as black gecko- or dragon-like reptiles of immense size that live in fishponds and lakes. They are

Menehune

considered fierce guardians of the families that worship them. The term has also been used to describe different types of large sea creatures.

Moai. Rapanui (Easter Island). Term for the towering statues found throughout the island. Carved from volcanic stone, they vary in size and form, from two to twenty meters high, with pronounced geometric facial features and capped with a topknot.

Moai kavakava. Rapanui (Easter Island). Term for carved, wooden figures that represent spirits or ancestors. Said to have been created by cultural hero Tuu-ko-ihu after seeing the spirits Hitirau and Nuku-te-mango sleeping on a crater, they are described as having elongated bodies, skull-like heads, and prominent ribcages. The figures are predominantly male, and are sometimes depicted combined with lizards and birds.

Moe 'uhane. Hawaiian. Dreams, regarded as an important form of communication between humans and the divine. Interpreted properly, they often provide solutions to problems, remedies for illnesses, and warnings against imminent danger.

Moehau. Maori. Unclassified hairy hominid said to live in the Coromandel-Moehau ranges of the country's North Island, considered the native counterpart of the North American Bigfoot.

Mokonui. Maori. Term to describe large or enormous reptiles, used synonymously in the past to describe the mythical taniwhas.

Mon. Papua New Guinea. Irian Jaya. Geelvink Bay. Term for native shamans, who could create korwar ancestral figures to communicate with the dead.

Mud Men. Papua New Guinea. Asaro. According to popular belief, they were originally villagers who placed second in a tribal contest and later decided, in their revenge raid, to wear mud masks and cover their bodies in gray mud. They are now a popular tourist attraction.

Mulukwausi. Papua New Guinea. Trobriand Islands. Dreaded flying witch who is the byproduct of the Yoyova. She flies out from her host body at night and searches for corpses or shipwrecked sailors to eat. Aside from directly attacking her prey and feeding on the innards, the Mulukwausi is also known to steal organs and save them in a secret hiding place, leaving the victim in a near-death state. Retrieving the missing organs makes it possible to save the victim's life.

Mwasila. Papua New Guinea. Trobriand Islands. Kula magic. System of spells and rituals meant to influence one's Kula partner into giving gifts. See Kula Ring.

Nalik. New Ireland. Mandak. Term to describe ornate and hermaphroditic wooden figures that were believed to contain and embody the deceased's spiritual energy. They were used in ritual ceremonies and kept inside houses to provide aid to the village.

Nduduwine. Papua New Guinea. Abelam. "Grandfather man." Term to describe ancestral, clan-specific spirits that are personified as ornate, anthropomorphic figures displayed inside a korambo, or native ceremonial house. Along with other visual symbols, elders use these figures as teaching tools to initiate people to the mysterious afterlife.

Ngārara. Maori. Taniwhas that resemble giant reptiles. They are also known by the less familiar term, kumi.

Ngwalndu. Papua New Guinea. Abelam. "Grandfather man." Ancestral, clan-specific spirits that are personified as ornate, anthropomorphic figures displayed inside a korambo, or native ceremonial house. Along with other visual symbols, elders use these figures as teaching tools to initiate people to the mysterious afterlife.

Ngwalngwal. Papua New Guinea. Abelam. "Grandfather man." Term to describe ancestral, clan-specific spirits that are personified as ornate, anthropomorphic figures displayed inside a korambo, or native ceremonial house. Along with other visual symbols, elders use these figures as teaching tools to initiate people to the mysterious afterlife.

Noho. Hawaiian. Term used to describe spirit possession.

Nuwakekepaki. Papua New Guinea. Trobriand Islands. Malevolent living stones said to pursue canoes, leaping out of the water to smash them. This type can be found in the Dobuan seas.

Origoruso. Kiwaian. Humanoid creature said to have ears the size of large pandan leaves. He uses one ear to wrap himself with; the other he uses to recline on. It is known as Siho i Salo in Ulawa in the Solomon Islands.

'Oromatua. Tahitian. Term to describe spirits of the dead, the incorporeal souls of famous warriors, and rulers of the country.

'Oromatua-'ai-aru. Tahitian. A disembodied evil spirit. It can spiritually possess small effigies called ti'i, images that are used in native witchcraft.

Paikea. Maori. Mythical whale that native mariners prayed to in times of danger.

Palaoa. Hawaiian. Term for a carved ivory talisman worn by chiefs around their necks.

Patupaiarehe. Maori. Fairy-like entities said to inhabit the deep forests and the mist-covered hills and mountaintops, described as having very fair skin and red hair. Their size varying with different accounts (from short-statured to the size of an adult human), they fear sunlight and exist only on raw foods. They are also known for abducting humans—particularly beautiful women—luring them with the sounds of their flutes. They are repulsed by the smell of cooked food, and are afraid of fire.

Pe'a fanua. Samoan. Type of flying fox that natives believe is the guardian of the forest.

Pe'a vao. Samoan. Type of flying fox that natives believe is the guardian of the forest.

Pele. Hawaiian. The goddess of fire. Known affectionately as "Madame Pele," this Island deity is as much revered for her beauty as she is feared for her anger, which manifests itself as volcanic quakes and eruptions. The daughter of deities Haumea and Kane-hoa-lani, she is said to live in K lauea Crater on the island of Hawai'i, and her life and exploits are well-known within local folklore. She is also fond of walking among mortals, appearing in guises that include vanishing hitchhikers, beautiful maidens, and even old women. She often appears unexpectedly in photographs taken all over the islands.

Her anger is so respected that locals will often admonish tourists to refrain from bringing volcanic rocks off the islands. Doing so will incur her wrath, and unless the rocks are returned, their holders will have catastrophic bad luck. Even though the late park ranger Narou Tovley of Hawaiʻi Volcanoes National Park claimed to have made up the story to preserve the natural environment, locals still adhere to the ages-old warning. Lava rocks to this day are still shipped back to the Islands from tourists who claimed to have suffered from Madame Pele's curse.

Pī kai. Hawaiian. The use of salt water for the ritual purification of locations, objects, and people.

Pōhaku. Hawaiian. Native term for stones, highly revered in olden times for their possession of mana. Used extensively in material culture, their magical properties played significant roles in healing, birthing, and religious rites.

Ponaturi. Maori. Fairy-like entities said to inhabit the coastal sea, described as having very fair skin, red hair, and long, menacing claws. Afraid of sunlight and fire, they only rise from their underwater world to walk on land at night.

Pwemwa. New Caledonia. A type of water spirit whose motif is carved in masks.

Rabaramb. Vanuatu Islands. Term to describe a native mortuary figure.

Raku-nene. Gilbert Islands. A malevolent, possessing spirit, originally a man who, upon his death, became an accomplice spirit invoked by men who were rejected by women they were courting. This spirit's specialty was avenging the men's rejection. Once invoked through ritual (retrieving the woman's hair and then burning it in leaves), this spirit would visit the intended victim in a dream and cause her to go insane over a period of six days. She would grow bloated, then tear at her own flesh while moaning and chanting "raku-nene." The victim would ultimately become rigid and die.

Rambaramp. Vanuatu. Malekula. Ornate painted statues created to preserve the skulls of important deceased men.

Shark-calling. Papua New Guinea. New Ireland. Native method of summoning sharks by splashing a rattle made of coconut shells in the water. Using spells and incantations, the caller then ensnares the shark inside a noose and bludgeons it to death.

Shark worship. Pan-Pacific Islander. The veneration of sharks is common in many Pacific cultures. In Hawai'i, for example, they were considered akua or 'aumakua (gods or deified ancestors). Ancestral shark gods (man kumupa'a) were protective guardians, humans deified after death, and were helpful against the many dangers of the sea. The most important of these gods were Ka-moho-ali'i, Ku-hai-moana, Kane-huna-moku, Kahu-huhu and Kane-i-kokala.

Sinamatanoginogi. Papua New Guinea. Trobriand Islands. Localized torrential rain that comes from above and breaks up canoes.

Star mounds. Samoan. Mysterious stone and earthen mounds found throughout the Samoan Islands, described as resembling a star in layout, with rays branching out from a central point. Their function has been an issue of debate, ranging from pigeon hunting to higher ritual purposes.

Suruhana. Guamanian (Chamorro). Spanish term to describe a female traditional healer.

Suruhano. Guamanian (Chamorro). Spanish term to describe a male traditional healer.

Swan maiden motif. Pan-Asian and Pacific Islander. Recurring story theme in which a maiden from either the sky world or the ocean visits the earth and loses her ability to return, usually after a human suitor hides her wings or fins. She eventually rediscovers her means and, with a few variations, leaves the family she has made behind.

Taho'o. Tahitian. Term to describe a curse.

Tahu'a. Tahitian. An expert or specialist in magic; a healing spirit doctor.

Tahu'a pifa'o. Tahitian. A malevolent tahu'a; an evil specialist in magic.

Tamate. Banks Islands. Generic term for a ghost.

Tambua. Native Fijian. The polished tooth of a sperm whale, ritually presented, particularly to guests of honor, during important ceremonies and functions as a sign of respect.

Taniwha. Maori. Diverse class of fabulous beasts and monsters said to inhabit lakes, rivers, and the ocean, and devour people. While some taniwhas have been described as giant reptiles, others take the form of whales, sharks, octopus, and even magical logs. Some types are also considered protectors of tribes and clans.

Taotaomona. Guamanian (Chamorro). Diverse class of supernatural entities believed to be the ancient spirits of native Islanders. They live in the jungle and among ancient caves and ruins, especially among the winding roots of massive Banyan trees. They appear in many forms (from so-called "white ladies" and dwarves to unusually strong and big men), and are greatly respected out of fear. They are notorious for pinching trespassers and noise makers and for leaving unusual marks on the skin.

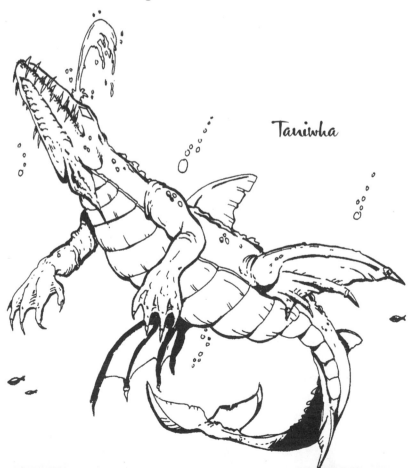

Taniwha

Tatanu. Papua New Guinea. Malangan term for the soul, most associated with carved figures used in mortuary rituals. These rites must be performed if the deceased's spirit is to enter to their ancestors' world. Also known as tanuato.

Taulaitu. Samoan. Term for a spirit medium who exorcises ghosts.

Taulasea. Samoan. Term for a native healer, an herbalist who uses the plants and the resources of the rainforest to cure diseases.

Tauva'u. Papua New Guinea. Trobriand Islands. Invisible spirits that cause epidemic disease. They are known to march through villages and strike their victims down with their sword-clubs, causing them to fall ill and die. They can also turn into animals at will, and have even been reported to have intercourse with women, who in turn become dangerous witches.

Tevolo. Samoan. Term to describe a devil spirit.

Tiki (ti'i). Society Islands, Tahiti. Term to describe the image or likeness of a deified ancestor.

Tindalo. Melanesian. Solomon Islands. Florida. The spirit of a deceased man who, when living, was believed to possess great power. Possessing such mana was thought to partially carry over to his afterlife, allowing him to enter effigies made in his honor, as well as animals.

Tino. Nukuoro. Sculpted female ancestral figures, varying in size and generally associated with the island's community spirit house, or amalau.

Tipua (tupua). Maori. Generic term for ghost or spirit, sometimes referencing any person, object, or animal associated with the supernatural or having supernatural attributes.

Tohunga. Maori. Native priests expertly trained in various cultural arts, including healing, warfare, and agriculture. They also act as mediums between the gods and human beings.

Tokway. Papua New Guinea. Trobriand Islands. Wood sprite. Mischievous spirit that lives in trees and coral rocks, occasionally stealing food, frightening people at night, and inflicting minor ailments on victims. When building canoes, villagers must exorcise these spirits from the wood for structural safety.

Tufuga. Samoan. Traditional tattoo artist.

Tuoro. Maori. Term to describe mythical giant reptiles said to live underground, creating massive chambers or tunnels and even uprooting trees as they traveled beneath the earth. It is sometimes considered a type of the mythical taniwha.

Tupapaʻu. Tahitian. Term to describe the wandering ghost of the formerly living, the so-called "post existence" of the varua or soul. It was originally in reference to a corpse.

ʻUhane. Hawaiian. The soul or spirit of a person, known to wander about at night when the host is asleep. It is sometimes used synonymously with ghost (lapu).

Ulu o lei walo. Hawaiian. Breadfruit tree said to be located at the gateway of the leina or "leaping place" of souls. The tree had two branches that pointed east and west, one for leaping into the underworld, while the other was a meeting place for spirits.

ʻUnihipili. Hawaiian. A familiar used by kahuna to do their bidding, usually the enslaved spirit of a dead relative or friend whose service has been retained by carefully preserving its bones. It is a non-ancestral ghost.

Urar. Solomon Islands. Term to describe an ancestor spirit.

Uruuru whenua. Maori. Native ritual of appeasing spirits or deities by leaving offerings, usually vegetation, at specific locations.

Vahine-hae. Marquesas Islands. Man-eating sea siren described as having a tongue that could flicker to the ground, and eyes that could protrude from their sockets.

Varua. Tahitian. The soul of a person when alive; also a generic term for a ghost

Varua ʻino. Tahitian. A malevolent spirit, a type of soul eater that devours the tupapaʻu, spitting out its blood and destroying the spirit in the process. It is also known to spiritually possess small effigies called tiʻi, images that are used in native witchcraft.

Veli. Native Fijian. Gnome-like spirits found in Vuniwaivutuka, described as having small, pale bodies with large wooly heads, and wearing native tapa clothing. Though friendly to their human neighbors in the forest, they are known to steal iron for use in their tools. They are also quite protective of their tree house dwellings, particularly against people foolish enough to chop them down.

Vineylida. Papua New Guinea. Trobriand Islands. Malevolent living stones said to pursue canoes, leaping out of the water to smash them. This type is believed to be inhabited by witches.

Wagen. Papua New Guinea. Iatmul. A type of spirit that aids a community. It is personified in an orator's anthropomorphic stool or chair carving. No one actually sits on this sculpture, but it can temporarily house the spirit itself inside its prominent head.

Wahine o ka pō. Hawaiian. Literally "woman of the night," a mysterious spirit lover who comes to a man's bed at night and makes love to him.

Wairua. Maori. One of three souls the human body is believed to contain. The astral version of the physical body, it can leave and travel to other planes.

Waitoreke. Maori. Mythical creature described as being otter-like in appearance, possibly an actual creature that has gone extinct.

Waiwaia. Papua New Guinea. Trobriand Islands. Term for a spirit child created from the discarded skin of a spirit who has bathed in Tuma, the island of the dead. Unable to remain in that realm, the child must return to the land of the living via spells, dreams, or bathing in the ocean, entering a woman of the same matrilineal lineage as the spirit that it was created from.

Wero-ugereugere. Maori. Incantation that causes a type of leprosy (ugereugere) against an intended victim.

Yalulawei. Caroline Islands. Term to describe water spirits that mariners and navigators appeal to when requesting protection. Through the use of small, anthropomorphic weather charms, practitioners can also ask the beings to divert storms, direct magic toward enemies, and perform divination.

Yipwon. Papua New Guinea. Southern Sepik. Upper Karawari. So-called "hook-style" abstract figures that represent spirits, and believed to aid men with hunting. Kept inside men's houses, they are described as figures standing on one leg, with extended, protruding ribs hooking around a central heart. They range in size from large sculptures to small charms. Through ritual, spirits can be induced to occupy these objects. The larger figures are inherited and can be centuries old.

Yoyova. Papua New Guinea. Trobriand Islands. Malevolent witch whose powers are derived from sorcery and magic. She can become invisible at will (or send an invisible double in her place), and can take the form of a flying fox or bird. She also develops a small coconut-shaped artifact or substance within her body that flies out at night and becomes the dreaded Mulukwausi. These witches are groomed in sorcery from an early age, usually by mothers who are also Yoyova.

—

Australia

Ancestral beings. Original beings that arose from the mythical Dreamtime period of history; entities that laid the archetypal foundation for culture, cosmology, and ancestral lineage.

Arumburinga. Aranda. Term to describe a spirit double.

Bone pointing. Type of sorcery in which a shaman uses the femur bone of a kangaroo or another shaman to induce sickness in a victim. This is done by mystically drawing the victim's soul through the bone, then burying and later burning the implement. As the bone burns and disintegrates, the victim progressively gets sicker and eventually dies.

Budabuda. Melville and Bathhurst islands. The spirits of children who, after existing as a mobadidi (see entry), become a budabuda by reentering their former mothers to be born again.

Bull-roarer. Oval-shaped piece of wood attached to a string and spun repeatedly around in a circle. Used in many sacred ceremonies, it produces a sound that is believed to be the voice of ancestors presiding over the rituals.

Bunyip. Mythological amphibious creatures capable of devouring animals and people and said to dwell in waterholes. Varying by region in appearance and size, they have been described as possible descendants of dinosaurs, a reference to Australia's relative geologic isolation and prehistoric past.

Burrawungal. Malevolent female water sprites who live in pools and wait for male victims to wade into the water before dragging them under and drowning them.

Djang. The mythological energies contained within a sacred place or object.

Doolagarl. Mysterious hairy men believed to exist in the Cockwhy and Polawombera mountains. Described as stocky with long arms and no neck, they are said to weaken their victims, spirit them off from their camps, and then feed on them.

Doowan. Mysterious tribal avengers and executioners capable of flying through the air and pursuing those who violate tribal law.

Dreamtime. Term used to describe time immemorial, a mythical period of native Creation from which all ancestral beings, creatures, and mystical energies arose. It also connects all native cultures to the same history, lineage, and cosmology.

Giant dogs. Story motif of enormous, predatory canines that recur in numerous native mythologies.

Giro giro. Mythical beings known from rock drawings, described as dwarves in some accounts and ghosts in others.

Guneena. Magical stones charged with malice and used by natives for ritual purposes.

Gooin. Type of malignant spirit.

Gudjull. Type of malignant spirit.

Hollow log coffin. Ornately painted upright coffin used by various Aboriginal tribes to contain the bones of their dead. It plays a significant role in different funerary customs.

Kadimakara. Mythological creatures known primarily from bones; most likely fossils from Australia's prehistoric past. Believed to have lived in a sky-world canopy of trees and branches, they were forced to live on the earth in marshes when the so-called pillars of the earth came falling down.

Kutji spirits. Malevolent, illness-causing spirits said to live in holes and in the shade of bushes. Shape-shifting into different birds and even clouds and mirages, they can only be contained by a shaman, whose communion with these entities gives them their supernatural powers.

Mamu. Bidjandjara. Malignant spirits said to live in their own camps and caves and kidnap victims (particularly children) to devour them. Generally human in appearance (although they can shape-shift into animals), they are described as heavily built and tall, with long teeth and claws, and hair that grows to a peak. The males carry massive clubs. These beings are believed to have existed since the Dreamtime.

Mimi. Western Arnhem Land. "The little ones." Stick-like spirits believed to live within the rocks; they are so thin that they are afraid to venture out in the wind from fear of having their necks broken. They are also known to be excellent hunters and artists, painting their portraits and activities on the rocks. Some are friendly, but they cannot be depended on. They are antagonistic to humans and will try to capture them when they can. They can eat human meat, but their staple food is a kind of yam.

Mirrioola. Mythological creature said to resemble a bunyip; also lives in rivers and waterholes.

Mobadidi. Melville and Bathhurst islands. Term to describe the spirits of the dead who return to where they were born and live in communities as if still alive.

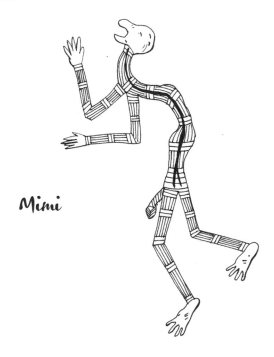

Mimi

Mopaditis. Tiwi, Melville, and Bathurst islands. Spirits of the dead who live around sacred places. Although similar to human beings, they are invisible during the daytime but appear as white during the evening. Upon a person's death, his or her mopaditi often remains and ritually participates in the funerary process, until it can be reinitiated spiritually or reincarnated.

Muramura. Various totemic entities from the Dreamtime that wandered about the country and instituted ritual.

Murinbungo. So-called "water lubras," or Daughters of the Rainbow Serpent. They are described as tempting sirens that live in waterholes, lagoons, and rivers and assume disguises to lure men to their deaths.

Papinjuwaris. Tiwi, Melville Island. Mythical race of one-eyed giants said to feed on the blood of the sick and the bodies of the dead. Stalking the skies and living where the earth meets the sky, they detect their prey by scent and then secretly draw blood through the victim's arm without leaving a mark. As the victim gets progressively weaker, it then shrinks in size and enters the mouth to drink the remaining blood.

Pungalunga men. Giant cannibals said to hunt people for food during the Dreamtime. All but one was destroyed in the mythical battle of Uluru.

Quinkin (kwinkin). Spirits that are the manifestation of lust, depicted in rock paintings as entities with extremely large and misshapen male organs.

Rainbow Snake. Mythical serpent deity whose body is said to arch across the sky as a rainbow. Known by various names across the Aboriginal continent, this totemic ancestor resides in waterholes and rock pools that contain his life-giving rain. He is most associated with human fertility and nature, particularly the regeneration of life. It is this distinction that makes it the most significant Aboriginal deity, and great care must be taken to treat its resources respectfully and to avoid its wrath.

Spirit children. Child spirits believed to dwell in particular waterholes and so-called "strong" places waiting for suitable women whose wombs they may be born in. Women seeking to bear a child often visit the spirits' dwelling in the hopes of being entered by them, eventually learning they

Rainbow Snake

are pregnant through a dream. The nature of the dream and the site at which the child was "conceived" determine its totemic affiliation.

Totemism. Broad term used to describe the worldview of all Aboriginal tribes, binding them together in a unified and unbroken relationship with their history, ancestry, and cosmology, leading to associations and affiliations with all things sacred (objects, animals, and natural phenomena).

Tjuringa. Type of amulet displayed during various sacred ceremonies. Described as being made of wood or stone and inscribed with arcs and concentric circles, it embodies the creator beings, as well as the totemic spirits of its bearer.

Uree women. Term to describe mysterious spirit women.

Wee-un. Term to describe individuals who possessed supernatural abilities.

Yahoo. A towering ape-like creature with draping arms and covered with long hair. It predates the use of the word "Yowie," which scholars now see as a possibly more modern reference to the same ape-like creature sighted in Australia.

Yowie. Native version of the North American sasquatch, described as a towering ape-like creature with draping arms and covered with long hair. Their fur coloration varying with each account, Yowies have been known to approach people in curiosity before disappearing back into the wilderness.

Islamic

Afreet (Afrit). Middle East, Pan-Muslim Asia. Malevolent demon believed to be the revengeful spirit of a murdered man. It is said to rise from the spilled blood of the victim himself. Only by driving a nail into the blood-soiled ground can this spirit be prevented from rising. It is also considered a snatcher of women.

Al-Basti. Central, Northern Asia. "The Red Mother." An Islamic female spirit that attacks women in childbirth and gives them a type of fever. She

Bouraq

is also known to ride horses during the night, only to abandon them in a heavy sweat in the morning.

Bouraq. Fabulous creature said to have carried the prophet Mohammad on the Night Journey, traveling to Jerusalem and the seven spheres of Heaven. It is described as a winged horse with a peacock's tail and a woman's head.

Caliph. Arabic term used to describe a political or spiritual Islamic leader, a successor of the Prophet Muhammad.

Chidkur. Mongolian. The soul of a deceased person that brings ill fortune to the living.

Dhabi'. Arabic term to describe a malevolent hyena who mesmerizes its traveler victims, then lures them back to its lair.

Div (deev). Middle East, Pan-Muslim Asia. Type of malevolent spirit in Persian lore, capable of assuming different forms.

Ghoul. Middle East, Pan-Muslim Asia. Malevolent, flesh-eating desert monster, known for lying in wait for its unwary traveler victims.

Ghoul

Hortlak. Central, Northern Asia. Spirit said to dig up corpses at night and feed upon their flesh. Also identified in Persian as jadi.

Iblis. Middle East, Pan-Muslim Asia. Type of djinn, and king of the shaitans.

Kara-kura. Central, Northern Asia. Islamic term describing a malevolent female goat that jumps on its male victims and suffocates them.

Mantriki. A Muslim exorcist.

Shaitan (sheitan, saytan, shethanth). Middle East, Pan-Muslim Asia. Derived from "Satan." Generic term for a class of malevolent spirits in Islamic belief, capable of possessing victims, particularly women, and assuming many different forms. Like djinns, they are said to have been made from smokeless fire, and their sole purpose is to lead humanity into temptation. Their king is named Iblis.

Sheikh. "One who is old," or an elder. Arabic term used to describe a patriarch.

Sufi. Term for a Muslim devotee who follows a mystical law or doctrine. This doctrine promises to liberate the soul from earthly concerns.

Sultan. Arabic term used to describe a king or an absolute ruler.

Yek. Central, Northern Asia. Term derived from yemek, meaning "to eat." Arabic creature described as a type of cannibal or devourer of men.

Guardians of the
Four Directions

Lokapalas. Pan-Hindu, Buddhist Asia. Sanskrit for "Four Heavenly Kings." Divine entities who guard the four celestial directions of the world. These immensely powerful brothers protect men of faith and their temples, ever ready and vigilant to dispose of the wickedness and vice that threaten the righteous. They consist of Vaisravana (the Guardian of the North), Virudhaka (the Guardian of the South), Dhrtarastra (the Guardian of the East), and Virupaksha (the Guardian of the West). Also known as the Diamond Kings, Heavenly Guardians, Dikapalas or Chaturmaharajas.

In Hinduism, there are eight directional guardians: Indra (East), Agni (Southeast), Yama (South), Surya (or Nirritti, Southwest), Varuna (West), Vayu (Northwest), Kuvera (North), and Soma (or Prithivi or Shiva, Northeast).

Dhrtarastra. Pan-Buddhist Asia. Sanskrit for "The Land-Bearer." The eldest of the famed Four Heavenly Kings, divine guardians of the four celestial directions. He is the Guardian of the East, described as having a white, bearded face and wielding a spear and a jade ring.

Vaisravana. Pan-Buddhist Asia. Sanskrit for "The Well-Famed." One of the famed Four Heavenly Kings, divine guardians of the four celestial directions. He is the Guardian of the North, described as having a black face and wielding a panther-skin bag and two whips.

Virudhaka. Pan-Buddhist Asia. Sanskrit for "The Lord of Growth." One of the famed Four Heavenly Kings, divine guardians of the four celestial directions. He is the Guardian of the South, described as having a red face and wielding a mystical umbrella made of pearls that can affect the atmosphere when raised or opened.

Virupaksha. Pan-Buddhist Asia. Sanskrit for "The Far-Gazer." One of the famed Four Heavenly Kings, divine guardians of the four celestial directions. He is the Guardian of the West, described as having a blue face and carrying a four-stringed guitar.

Names in Other Cultures

Sanskrit
North: Vaisravana
South: Virudhaka
East: Dhrtarastra
West: Virupaksha

Chinese
North: Mo-li Shou
South: Mo-li Hung
East: Mo-li Ch'ing
West: Mo-li Hai

Japanese
North: Bishamonten
South: Zochoten
East: Jikokuten
West: Komokuten

Korean
North: Tamun ch'onwang
South: Chungjang ch'onwang
East: Chiguk ch'onwang
West: Kwangmok ch'onwang

Cambodian
North: Kovero or Peysrap
South: Virulak
East: Tossarot
West: Virulappak

Epilogue
Reflections After the Research

From the onset of this project, I had given myself specific parameters on what I wanted to list as "supernatural." But in tackling such a deep and diverse subject that included virtually all Asian cultures, I quickly realized that my parameters had become limitations, and that they needed to be adjusted. What began as a list of ghosts and demons needed to be expanded in order to give view to the entire scope of the Asian supernatural landscape. As a result, more entries that were borderline supernatural were also included because, for lack of a better term, they became the legs to the table.

As with all things in Asia, art, religion, and mythology are woven into a seamless tapestry, and are very hard to extricate without any surrounding context. Nowhere is this more evident than in the case of religion, where Hindu and Buddhist entities permeate virtually all of Asian culture. Since religion explains the cosmology of a culture, it also explains and details its ghosts and demons. Hence, relevant deities needed to be included in this volume.

The term "supernatural" itself, in a Western sense, can be misleading. When applied to Eastern and Pacific cultures, it goes beyond just referencing ghosts and demons; it encompasses religion, history, cultural celebrations and holidays, superstition, folklore, medicinal belief systems, and general societal norms. It is not something considered separate from everyday life, but rather something taken for granted to be a part of it.

I also learned that, despite the surface similarities and overwhelming differences among Asian cultures, there are definite parallels in supernatural entities. The respect for nature, appeasing the ancestors, the fear of vengeful female spirits (particularly pregnant ones), pressing ghosts, underwater phantoms, fireballs, and shape-shifting demons are quite universal. Magically charged charms, amulets, and inscribed mantras spanned all the cultures, and the power and importance of the shaman as priest, physician, and exorcist was quite significant. The frequent use of carved poles among more tribal cultures was also surprising.

The supernatural traditions of Tibet, China, and Thailand are quite astounding, and only recently has the Philippines been recognized for its exhaustive paranormal heritage. Japan's immense bestiary of characters is a direct reflection of its efforts to systematically catalogue its beings and utilize them in all forms of art and literature.

Despite the amount of information I have gathered and catalogued, the most glaring lesson at the end of the project was how much information had yet to be researched. Beyond the hundreds of books, folk narratives, and mythological sources I have read through, there was always that obscure tome, bestiary, or magazine article cited in a bibliography somewhere that contained more information that needed to be collected.

In short, no one book can possibly contain all the data related to the Asian supernatural.

That said, I hope that this work is a step in the right direction, prompting readers to take what has been collected and research it on their own. Better yet, it may hopefully inspire them to create visual or literary art. Many of the entries in this book are just a single word that pertains to the supernatural, but in my opinion, that's all it takes to pique someone's curiosity enough for them to explore it further. When researching this subject (and this is a personal bias I won't hesitate to share), don't take material you find on the Internet at face value. I love reading through old, turn-of-the-century anthropology books and finding ghost beliefs there, because they're more honest and closer to the source material.

Ultimately, it is not important if these beings can be proven to exist or not, because, as with all things in the Asian/Pacific cultural sphere, belief lies in faith and in intuition. They are extensions of the human mind, expressions of fears and longings that have guided our culture since time immemorial. What is important is that people believe they exist. From the most organized religions, to the most "primitive" tribal superstitions, these souls and places will continue to be just beyond our reach, but always ready to appear just when we think they won't.

Appendices
Asian Investigative Groups

Science and Rationalists' Association of India *(Bharatiya Bigyan O Yuktibadi Samiti)*
hppt://www.srai.org/

Singapore Paranormal Investigators
http://www.spi.com.sg/

Spirit Questors (Philippines)
http://www.spiritquestors.org.uk/

Cross-Cultural Index

Generic term for a ghost:

Aitu. Samoan.
Dab. Hmong.
Hantu. Malay, Indonesian.
Khmoch. Cambodian.
Kuei (guei, gui, kuai). Chinese.
Kwisin. Korean.
Lapu. Hawaiian.
Ma. Vietnamese.
Multo. Filipino.
Phii. Thai.
Tipua. Maori (New Zealand).
Yurei. Japanese.

Amulets:

Agimat. Filipino.
Anting-anting. Filipino.
Bull-roarer. Australian Aborigine.
Gau. Tibetan Buddhism.
Datloun. Myanmar (Burmese).
Djimat. Javanese.
Gzi stone. Tibetan Buddhism.
Hu Hsin Ching. Chinese.
In. Myanmar (Burmese).
Khawng-khlang. Thai.
Khuruang-rang. Thai.
Lehpwe. Myanmar (Burmese).
Mala. Tibetan Buddhism.
Mamuli. Indonesian.
Ofuda. Japanese.

Omamori. Japanese.
Pai chia so. Chinese.
Phra-khruang. Thai.
Pluk-sek. Thai.
Pujok. Korean.
San chiao fu. Chinese.
Shao hui t'un fu. Chinese.
Tjuringa. Australian Aborigine.
Tsha-tsha. Tibetan Buddhism.
Tumbal. Balinese.
Wan ya. Thai.
Wudu. Chinese.

Architectural Guardians:

Bhoma. Balinese.
Bilu. Myanmar (Burmese).
Changsung. Korean.
Chintha. Myanmar (Burmese).
Dharmapalas. Tibetan Buddhism.
Dvarapala. Sanskrit.
Haet'ae. Korean.
Kala. Sanskrit.
Kirtimukha. Indian.
Kumgang shinjang. Korean.
Makara. Hindu, Pan-Buddhist
   Asia.
Manok-thi-ha. Myanmar
   (Burmese).
Menshen. Chinese.
Ni-o Guardians. Japanese.

Rahu. Sanskrit.
Shisa. Okinawan.
Tantima. Thai.
Thepchumnum. Thai.
Yakshas (Yaksas). Pan-India,
    Southeast Asia.

Children spirits:
Budabuda. Australian Aborigine.
Infant spirits. Korean.
Karako. Japanese.
Konaki jiji. Japanese.
Kumanthanung (Kumantong).
    Thai.
Luuk Krawk. Thai.
Mantianak. Filipino.
Mentèk. Malay, Indonesian.
Muntianak. Filipino.
Patianak. Filipino.
Spirit children. Australian
    Aborigine.
Tiyanak. Filipino.
Tuyul. Malay, Indonesian.
Zashiki Warashi. Japanese.

Devas and angels:
Apsaras. Sanksrit.
Dakini. Indian. Hindu, Buddhist.
Deva (dewa). Malay, Indonesian.
Devaputtas. Pan Hindu/Buddhist
    Asia.
Devata. Sanskrit.
Devi (dewi). Malay, Indonesian.
Diwata. Filipino.
Kiten. Japanese.
Shen. Chinese.
Tennin. Japanese.
Thep. Thai.

Thephanom. Thai.
Thewada. Thai.
Tien. Vietnamese.
Widiadara, Widiadari. Balinese.

Disease spirits:
Arak. Cambodian.
Kwe-yuk tasin. Korean.
Mamo. Hindu, Tibetan Buddhist.
Phii Ha. Thai.
Shitala. Indian.
Tauva'u. Papua New Guinea.
    Trobriand Islands.
Tou Shen. Chinese.

Dwarves and gnomes:
Duwende. Filipino.
Ebu gogo. Indonesian. Flores
    Island.
Gana. Indian. Hindu.
Homo floresiensis. Indonesian.
Kakamora. Pacific Islander. San
    Cristoval.
Kini akua. Hawaiian.
Masengi. Papua New Guinea.
Menehune. Hawaiian.
Nuno sa punso. Filipino.
Veli. Native Fijian.

Fairies and Sprites:
Acheri. Indian.
Ada. Filipino.
Adaro. Solomon Islands. San
    Cristobal.
Burrawungal. Australian
    Aborigine.
Hsi Wang Mu. Chinese.

Iauguay. Chinese.
Iaujing. Chinese.
Matriya. Indian.
Nat-thamee. Myanmar
  (Burmese).
Patupaiarehe. Maori (New
  Zealand).
Peri. Malay, Indonesian.
Ponaturi. Maori (New Zealand).
Shen. Chinese.
Tokway. Papua New Guinea.
  Trobriand Islands.
Xian nu. Chinese.

Fireballs:
Akualele. Hawaiian.
Kitsune-bi. Japanese.
Oni-bi. Japanese.
Phii Khamot. Thai.
Santilmo. Filipino.

Fox spirits:
Huli jing. Chinese.
Kitsune. Japanese.
Kumiho. Korean.

Geomantic placement system:
Feng-shui. Chinese.
Fusui. Japanese.
P'ungsu. Korean.
Vastu. Indian.

Ghostly parades:
Hyakki yako. Japanese.
Ka huaka'i o ka po. Hawaiian.

Giant reptiles:
Bedawang Nala. Indonesian.
  Balinese.
Bunyip. Australian Aborigine.
Hore. Maori (New Zealand).
Kadimakara. Australian
  Aborigine.
Mirrioola. Australian Aborigine.
Mo'o. Hawaiian.
Ng rara. Maori (New Zealand).
Taniwha. Maori (New Zealand).
Tuoro. Maori (New Zealand).

Giant serpents and dragons:
Bakunawa. Filipino.
Kushii. Japanese.
Lung (Long). Chinese.
Mameleu. Filipino.
Markupo. Filipino.
Nabau. Indonesian. Borneo.
Nak. Thai.
Naga. Indian. Pan-Hindu,
  Buddhist Asia.
Naga Anantaboga. Indian,
  Balinese.
Naga Banda. Indian, Balinese.
Naga Basuki. Indian, Balinese.
Orochi. Japanese.
Phya Nahk (Payanak). Thai.
Rainbow Snake. Australian
  Aborigine.
Ryu. Japanese.
Shesha. Indian. Hindu.
Taksaka. Hindu.
Tatsu. Japanese.
Thuong-luong. Vietnamese.
Vritra. Indian.

Giants:

Asura. Indian.
Daityas. Indian. Hindu.
Danavas. Indian. Hindu.
Gergasi. Malay, Indonesian.
Kapre. Filipino.
Papinjuwaris. Australian
  Aborigine.
Pungalunga Men. Australian
  Aborigine.
Raksasa. Malay, Indonesian.
Raksasi. Balinese.
Rakshasa. Indian.

Mermaids and Mermen:

Ikan duyong. Malay, Indonesian.
Kataw. Filipino.
Ngyak. Thai, Pan-Southeast Asia.
Nyi Loro Kidul. Indonesian.
  Javanese.
Ri. Indonesian. Papua New
  Guinea. New Ireland.
Sirena. Filipino.
Siocoy. Filipino.

Mysterious ape-men:

Almas. Mongolian.
Batutut. Malaysian.
Beruang rambai. Indonesian.
Doolagarl. Australian Aborigine.
Hantu Jarang Gigi. Malaysian.
Khaki besar. Malaysian.
Mande Burung. Indian.
Moehau. Maori (New Zealand).
Nguoi Rung. Vietnamese.
Nittaewo. Indian. Sri Lanka.
Orang Mawas. Malaysian.
Orang Pendek. Indonesian.

Sedapa. Indonesian.
Tua yeua. Thai.
Uyan. Malaysian.
Vanamaushas. Indian.
Yahoo. Australian Aborigine.
Yeren. Chinese.
Yeti. Tibetan.
Yowie. Australian Aborigine.

Mystical energy terms:

Baaramii. Thai.
Djang. Australian Aborigine.
Kiwa (Left). Balinese.
Lha. Tibetan Buddhism.
Mana. Hawaiian.
Penengen. Balinese.
Prana. Indian.
Sakti. Balinese.
Semangat. Malaysian.
Tengen (Right). Balinese.

Nature spirits:

Anito. Filipino.
Kami. Japanese.
Lamang-lupa. Filipino.
Nat. Myanmar (Burmese).
Neak-ta. Cambodian.
San sin. Korean.

Ogres:

Bilu. Myanmar (Burmese).
Busaw. Filipino.
Hariti. Sanskrit.
Oni. Japanese.
Tokkaebi. Korean.
Yakshas (Yaksas). Pan-India,
  Southeast Asia.

Pregnancy, childbirth-related spirits:

Al-Basti. Central, Northern Asian.
Anak kerak. Malay, Indonesian.
Churel. Indian.
Gesges. Pacific Islander. New Ireland.
Khmoch pray. Cambodian.
Langsuir. Malay, Indonesian.
Manananggal. Filipino.
Phii Prai. Thai.
Phii Tai Thang Klom. Thai.
Pinam notune. Indonesian. Seram. Nuaulu. Somori.
Pontianak. Malay, Indonesian.
Thabe. Myanmar (Burmese).
Thou-tzu kuei. Chinese.
Ubume. Japanese.
Wéwé. Malay, Indonesian.
Mga bata ng limbo. Filipino.

Pressing Ghosts:

Bangungot. Filipino.
Batibat. Filipino.
Bei guai chaak. Chinese.
Bei guai jui. Chinese.
Dab. Hmong.
Kanashibari. Japanese.
Kara-Kura. Central, Northern Asian.
Phii Mae Mai. Thai.
Polo dhuki. Indonesian. Flores Island. Nage.
Zashiki Warashi. Japanese.

Pretas:

Gaki. Japanese.

Phii Pret. Thai.
Preta (Pret). Pan-Asian.
Tasei (thaye). Myanmar (Burmese).

Rice goddesses:

Bounmagyi. Myanmar (Burmese).
Dewi Sri. Balinese.
Mae posop. Thai.

Self-segmenting witches (Southeast Asia):

Arei ap. Cambodian.
Manananggal. Filipino
Penanggalan. Malaysia, Indonesia
Phii Krasue. Thailand
Soang. Burmese.

Shamans, witches, and sorcerers:

Arhat (Arahat). Buddhist.
Aswang. Filipino.
Athtelan hsaya. Myanmar (Burmese).
Aulan hsaya. Myanmar (Burmese).
Babaylan. Filipino.
Bodhisattva. Buddhist.
Bomoh. Malaysian.
Chomjangi. Korean.
Dalai Lama. Tibetan Buddhism.
Dukun. Indonesian. Javanese.
Fakir. Indian.
Fang-Shih. Chinese.
Itako. Japanese.
Kahuna. Hawaiian.
Kaminchu. Okinawan.
Kumari. Nepalese.

Leyak. Balinese.
Lohan. Chinese.
Mambabarang. Filipino.
Mananambal. Filipino.
Manggagamod. Filipino.
Manggagaway. Filipino.
Mangkukulam. Filipino.
Mau Phii. Thai.
Miko. Japanese.
Moo. Thai.
Mudang. Korean.
Mumbaki. Filipino.
Myongdu. Korean.
Odaisan. Japanese.
Ong Thay Phap. Vietnamese.
Paksu (pansu). Korean.
Pawang. Malaysian.
Pemangku. Balinese.
Rinpoche. Tibetan Buddhism.
Rishi. Indian. Hindu.
Saddhu. Indian.
Sanjinso. Okinawan.
Shaman. Siberian. Tungus.
Simbang. Korean.
Soun. Myanmar (Burmese).
Suruhana, suruhano. Guamanian
   (Chamorro).
Swami. Indian.
Tahu'a. Tahitian.
Tan'gol. Korean.
Taulaitu. Samoan.
Tohunga. Maori (New Zealand).
Trulku. Tibetan.
Txiv neeb. Hmong.
Weikza. Myanmar (Burmese).
Wu. Chinese.
Wundwin soun. Myanmar
   (Burmese).
Yamabushi. Japanese.
Yogi. Indian.

Yuta. Okinawan.
You-you soun. Myanmar
   (Burmese).
Zawgyi. Myanmar (Burmese).

Spirit doubles:
Arumburinga. Australian
   Aborigine. Aranda.
Gas. Pacific Islander. New
   Ireland.
Ikiryo. Japanese.
Rikombyo. Japanese.

Spirits encountered in the forest:
Engkanto. Filipino.
Orang bunian. Malay, Indonesian.
Taotaomona. Guamanian.

Spiritual Festivals:
Fangshuideng. Chinese.
Gui jie. Chinese.
Loy Krathong. Thai.
Ngan Duan Sib. Thai.
Obon. Japanese.
Qingming jie. Chinese.
Taungbyon Festival. Myanmar
   (Burmese).
Todos Los Santos, Todos Los
   Difuntos. Filipino.

Supernatural Games:
Hyaki monogatari. Japanese.
Jelangkung. Indonesian.
Kokkuri. Japanese.

Vengeful women ghosts:
Chordewa. Indian.
Faceless Woman. Hawaiian.
Fehuluni. Tongan.
Futakuchi Onna. Japanese.
Hanthia. Indian.
Hone Onna. Japanese.
Jigarkhwar. Indian. Sind Region.
Kuchisake Onna. Japanese.
Langsuir. Malay, Indonesian.
Mae Naak. Thai.
Mejenkwaad. Marshall Islands.
Mongdal kwisin. Korean.
Mulukwausi. Papua New Guinea.
  Trobriand Islands.
Nure Onna. Japanese.
Nyai Blorong. Malay, Indonesian.
Oiwa. Japanese.
Onibaba. Japanese.
Oopra. Indian.
Pontianak. Malay, Indonesian.
Shiryo. Japanese.
Suangi. Indonesian. Irian Jaya.
Sundel bolong. Malay,
  Indonesian.
White Lady. Filipino.
Yoyova. Papua New Guinea.
  Trobriand Islands.
Yuki-Onna. Japanese.

Water goddesses:
Ba Thuy. Vietnamese.
Mae Kong Ka. Thai.
Mazu. Chinese.
Paesonang. Korean.

Weird feelings:
Ike Papalua. Hawaiian.
Kutob. Filipino.
Mehameha. Tahitian.

Ying-yang:
Um-yang. Korean.
Yab-yum. Tibetan Buddhism.
Yin and Yang. Chinese.

Recommended Reading

Albanese, Marilia. *Angkor, Splendors of the Khmer Civilization*. White Star Publishers, 2002.

Anima, Nid. *Witchcraft Filipino-Style*. Omar Publications, 1978.

Baird, Merrily. *Symbols of Japan: Thematic Motifs in Art and Design*. Rizzoli International Publications, Inc. 2001.

Beckwith, Martha. *Hawaiian Mythology*. University of Hawai'i Press, 1971.

Beer, Robert. *The Encyclopedia of Tibetan Symbols and Motifs*. Shambhala Publications, Inc., 1999.

Berndt, Ronald and Catherine H. *The World of the First Australians*. Angus and Robertson Ltd., 1964.

Berreman, Gerald D. *Hindus of the Himalayas: Ethnography & Change*. University of California Press, 1972.

Blair, Lawrence with Lorne. *Ring of Fire, An Indonesian Odyssey*. Park Street Press, 1991.

Bonnefoy, Yves. *Asian Mythologies*. The University of Chicago Press, 1993.

Braziller, George. *Japanese Ghosts & Demons: Art of the Supernatural*. George Braziller, Inc., 1985.

Bushnaq, Inea. *Arab Folktales*. Pantheon Books, 1986.

Cadiere, L. *Croyances et Pratiques Religieuses des Vietnamiens.* Paris, Ecole Francaise d'Extreme Orient, 1957.

Chaturachinda, Gwyneth. *Dictionary of South & Southeast Asian Art.* Silkworm Books, 2004.

Christie, Anthony. *Chinese Mythology.* The Hamlyn Publishing Group Limited, 1973.

Covarrubias, Miguel. *Island of Bali.* Periplus, 2008.

Cunningham, Scott. *Hawaiian Religion & Magic.* Llewellyn Publications, 1995.

D'Alleva, Anne. *Arts of the Pacific Islands.* Harry N. Abrams, Incorporated, 1998.

David-Neel, Alexandra. *Magic and Mystery in Tibet.* Dover Publications, Inc., 1971.

Demetrio, Fr. Francisco. *Encyclopedia of Philippine Folk Beliefs and Customs, Vol. 1 & 2.* Xavier University, 1991.

Demetrio, Fr. Francisco. *Myths and Symbols Philippines.* National Book Store, Inc. 1990.

Eberhard, Wolfram. *A Dictionary of Chinese Symbols: Hidden Symbols in Chinese Life and Thought.* Routledge & Kegan Paul Ltd, 2000.

Eiseman, Jr., Fred B. *Bali, Sekala and Niskala, Volume II: Essays on Society, Tradition, and Craft.* Periplus Editions (HK) Ltd., 1990.

Eliade, Mircea. *Shamanism (Archaic Techniques of Ecstasy).* Princeton University Press, 1964.

Eliot, Joshua. *Myanmar (Burma) Handbook.* Footprint Handbooks, 1997.

Ellis, Jean A. *From the Dreamtime, Australian Aboriginal Legends.* Collins Dove, 1991.

Emmons, Charles F. *Chinese Ghosts and ESP: A Study of Paranormal Beliefs and Experiences.* The Scarecrow Press, Inc. 1982

Eugenio, Damiana L. *Philippine Folk Literature: The Legends.* University of the Philippines, 1996.

Evans-Wentz, W. Y. *Tibetan Book of the Dead, An Illustrated Edition of the Sacred Text on Death and Rebirth.* Metro Books, 2008.

Fadiman, Anne. *The Spirit Catches You And You Fall Down.* The Noonday Press, 1997.

Fischer, Joseph. *Story Cloths of Bali.* Ten Speed Press, 2004.

Foster, Michael Dylan. *Pandemonium and Parade, Japanese Monsters and the Culture of Yokai.* University of California Press, 2009.

Freed, Ruth S. and Stanley A. *Ghosts: Life and Death in North India.* American Museum of Natural History, Anthropological Papers, Number 72. 1993.

Ganesha Society. *Aspects of Indonesian Culture: Java – Sumatra.* Cahaya Printing Co., 1979.

Geertz, Clifford. *The Religion of Java.* The University of Chicago Press, 1976.

Grant, Glen. *Obake Files: Ghostly Encounters in Supernatural Hawai'i.* Mutual Publishing, 1996.

Guelden, Marlane. *Thailand, Into the Spirit World.* Times Editions Pte Ltd, 1995.

Han, Suzanne Crowder. *Korean Folk & Fairy Tales.* Hollym International Corp., 1991.

Han, Suzanne Crowder. *Notes on Things Korean.* Hollym International Corp., 1995.

Hearn, Lafcadio. *In Ghostly Japan.* Charles E. Tuttle Co., Inc., 1971.

Hearn, Lafcadio. *Kwaidan, Stories and Studies of Strange Things.* Charles E. Tuttle Co., Inc., 1971.

Hickey, Gerald Cannon. *Village in Vietnam.* New Haven and London, Yale University Press, 1967.

Hitchcock, Jayne A. *The Ghosts of Okinawa.* Shiba Hill, 1996.

Hurwood, Bernhardt J. *Supernatural Wonders From Around the World.* Barnes & Noble, Inc., 1993.

In-sob, Zong. *Folk Tales from Korea.* Grove Press, Inc., 1979.

Iwasaka, Michiko and Toelken, Barre. *Ghosts and the Japanese (Cultural Experience in Japanese Death Legends).* Utah State University Press, 1994.

Jansen, Eva Rudy. *The Book of Hindu Imagery (The Gods and their Symbols).* Binkey Kok Publications BV, 2003.

Kao, Karl S. Y. *Classical Chinese Tales of the Supernatural and the Fantastic (Selections from the Third to the Tenth Century).* Indiana University Press, 1985.

Kawai, Hayao. *The Japanese Psyche (Major Motifs in the Fairy Tales of Japan).* Spring Publications, 1996.

Kerlogue, Fiona. *Arts of Southeast Asia.* Thames and Hudson Ltd., 2004.

Keyes, Charles F. *The Golden Peninsula: Culture and Adaptation in Mainland Southeast Asia.* University of Hawai'i Press, 1995.

Kiej'e, Nikolas. *Japanese Grotesqueries.* Charles E. Tuttle Company, Inc., 1973.

Kil-song, Ch'oe. *The Anthropology of Korea, East Asian Perspectives* (Senri Ethnological Studies no. 49), *Belief in Malevolent Spirits,* pp. 95-109. National Museum of Ethnology, Osaka. 1998.

Knappert, Jan. *Indian Mythology, An Encyclopedia of Myth and Legend.* Diamond Books, 1995.

Knappert, Jan. *Pacific Mythology, An Encyclopedia of Myth and Legend.* Diamond Books, 1992.

Leeming, David. *A Dictionary of Asian Mythology.* Oxford University Press, 2001.

Lehmann, Arthur C. and Myers, James E. *Magic, Witchcraft, and Religion (an Anthropological Study of the Supernatural).* Mayfield Publishing Company, 1993.

Levy, Robert I. *Tahitians, Mind and Experience in the Society Islands.* University of Chicago Press, 1973.

Licauco, Jaime T. *The Truth Behind Faith Healing in the Philippines.* National Book Store, Inc., 1982.

Licauco, Jaime T. *True Encounters with the Unknown (The Psychic, the Mystical & the Strange).* National Book Store, Inc., 1986.

Lieban, Richard W. *Cebuano Sorcery, Malign Magic in the Philippines.* University of California Press, 1977.

Long, Max Freedom. *Recovering the Ancient Magic.* Huna Press, 1978.

Mac, Carol k. and Dinah. *A Field Guide to Demons, Fairies, Fallen Angels, and Other Subversive Spirits.* Henry Hold and Company, LLC, 1998.

Malinowski, Bronislaw. *Argonauts of the Western Pacific.* Waveland Press, Inc., 1984.

McArthur, Meher. *Reading Buddhist Art (An Illustrated Guide to Buddhist Signs & Symbols).* Thames & Hudson, 2002.

McNeely, Jeffrey A. and Wachtel, Paul Spencer. *Soul of the Tiger, Searching for Nature's Answers in Exotic Southeast Asia.* Doubleday, 1988.

Meyer, Anthony JP. *Oceanic Art.* Konemann, 1995.

Miller, Judith. *Tribal Art, The Essential World Guide.* DK Publishing, Inc., 2006.

Monigold, Glenn W. *Folk Tales from Vietnam.* Mount Vernon, New York, The Peter Pauper Press, 1964.

Morrill, Sibley S. *The Kahunas, The Black and White Magicians of Hawaii.* Branden Press, 1969.

Mudrooroo. *Aboriginal Mythology.* Thorsons (an Imprint of Harper CollinsPublishers), 1994.

Panganiban, J.V. *Diksyunaryo-Tesauro Pilipino-Ingles.* Manlapaz Publishing Co., 1972.

Poignant, Rosalyn. *Oceanic Mythology.* The Hamlyn Publishing Group Limited, 1967.

Pucci, Idanna. *Bhima Swarga, The Balinese Journey of the Soul.* Bulfinch Press, 1992.

Rajadhon, Phya Anuman. *Essay on Thai Folklore.* Editions Duang Kamol, 1968.

Ramos, Maximo D. *The Creatures of Philippine Lower Mythology.* Phoenix Publishing House, 1990.

Robinson, Roland. *Aboriginal Myths and Legends.* Sun Books, 1966.

Ross, Catrien. *Supernatural and Mysterious Japan (Spirits, Hauntings, and Paranormal Phenomena).* YenBooks, 1996.

Sakya, Jnan Bahadur. *Short Description of Gods, Goddesses and Ritual Objects of Buddhism and Hinduism in Nepal.* Handicraft Association of Nepal, 2000.

Scott, William Henry. *Barangay (Sixteenth-Century Philippine Culture and Society).* Ateneo de Manila University Press, 1994.

Scott, William Henry. *PreHispanic Source Materials for the Study of Philippine History (Revised Edition)*. New Day Publishers, 1984.

Segaller, Denis. *Thai Ways*. Post Books, 2001.

Slattum, Judy and Schraub, Paul. *Balinese Masks, Spirits of an Ancient Drama*. Periplus Editions (HK) Ltd., 2003.

Spiro, Melford E. *Myanmar (Burmese) Supernaturalism*. Prentice Hall, Inc., 1967.

Stepanchuk, Carol and Wong, Charles. *Mooncakes and Hungry Ghosts: Festivals of China*. China Books and Periodicals, 1991.

Storm, Rachel. *Illustrated Encyclopedia, Eastern Mythology*. Lorenz Books, 2001.

Tan, Michael L. Tan. *Usug, Kulam, Pasma (Traditional Concepts of Health and Illness in the Philippines*. AKAP, 1987.

True Philippine Ghost Stories series. Psicom Publishing Inc., 2004.

Walters, Derek. *Chinese Mythology: An Encyclopedia of Myth and Legend*. Aquarian/Thorsons, 1992.

Watson, C.W., and Ellen, Roy. *Understanding Witchcraft and Sorcery in Southeast Asia*. University of Hawai'i Press, 1993.

Westervelt, William D. *Hawaiian Legends of Ghosts and Ghost Gods*. Mutual Publishing, 2003.

Williams, C.A.S. *Outlines of Chinese Symbolism & Art Motives*. Dover Publications, Inc. 1976.

Yoda, Hiroko, and Alt, Matt. *Yokai Attack! The Japanese Monster Survival Guide*. Kodansha International Ltd., 2008.

Yu, Chai-shin and Guisso, R. (editors). *Shamanism, the Spirit World of Korea*. Asian Humanities Press, 1988.

About the Author

Alex G. Paman is a professional illustrator and freelance journalist based in Northern California. A graduate of Sacramento State University, he is an avid researcher of Asian culture and is currently a contributing writer to *Filipinas Magazine*.